What Others Are Saying About This Book

"This enjoyable biography of Dr. Roger Nicole flows along in a novel-like way, which makes it more than simply a documentation of facts, dates, and events. Truly, this book is a page-turner, and one that, to my pleasant surprise, led me to many smiles and chuckles along the way. Surprisingly, this book is also a theology text. For although the author does not set out to simply list the theological propositions of his subject, the reader finds himself being theologically taught (or at least challenged) by Dr. Nicole as he takes, as it were, a long, leisurely stroll with him. Along with some well-stated tautologies that made me laugh out loud ("Among Protestants it ought not to be a terrible thing to be protesting"), this book was inspirational as well as educational. This is perhaps the most enlightening biography I have ever read and certainly one of the most entertaining. In a genre that this reader has not seen before, Dr. Bailey writes in such a way that one wonders at times where Dr. Bailey stops narrating and Dr. Nicole muses on certain fascinating events in his own life. This blending is seamless as we journey through *The Life and Legacy of Roger Nicole*, a man who indeed spoke and is still speaking the truth in love." – **Dr. Rick Walston**

"Have you seen the movie, *Forrest Gump*, where Forrest ends up being present at all (or many) of the important events of the mid-twentieth century? In the real life of Roger Nicole, it seems that he was there at all of the important events in 20th century Evangelicalism and knew everybody. This is as much a theological summary of Nicole's thought as it is a biography. Much of the book is verbatim reports of personal interviews with Roger. Whether you know him personally or not, anyone interested in theology and biblical studies will find this semi-autobiography to be a fascinating study of this unusual man. Thanks to David Bailey, we will not forget." – **Dr. Russ Bush**

" Though Roger Nicole is not as well known as some other Evangelical leaders of the last sixty years, he has played a key role in the formation of what we know as Evangelicalism and rightly deserves to be remembered in the biographical study you are holding in your hands. A Christian with wide reading interests and detailed acquaintance with the broad sweep of Evangelical theology and history, he has given the Evangelical movement ballast, something so needed in recent days. Read this book and praise God for this extraordinary servant of the Lord Jesus." – **Dr. Michael Haykin**

" This is a fascinating overview of the life and labors of one of America's most gifted evangelical theologians. Drawing deeply from the wells of Reformation theology in the tradition of Calvin, Bunyan, Owen, Edwards, and Bavinck, Roger Nicole has set forth a compelling vision of theology as a discipline in the service of the church. And he has done so with grace, wit, insight, passion, and the kind of wisdom evangelicals need more of today. Though I never took a class with Roger Nicole, I am certainly one of his students and I commend this telling of his story to all who care about the Bible's God, the church's faith, and the world's need for the gospel of grace." — **Dr. Timothy George**

"Here is a review of one of the most interesting Reformed theologians of the last seventy years. Roger Nicole's life has been spent in training ministers. Most of his students have known him only behind a lectern or in a brief meeting; here is much more of the story from WWI Germany to pre-War Paris, to Canada and beyond. Read and be encouraged to give your all in service to Christ." – **Pastor Mark Dever**

"This is a moving tribute to one who has been valiant for the truthfulness of God's Word throughout his whole life. Not only is the measure of the man included, but the amazing story here is the way Dr. Nicole's life has intersected with almost all the major events of the evangelical world in the past three-quarters of a century. It is a vivid reminder of the faithfulness of God and the bold necessity of ever speaking the truth in love both to those who are part of the household of faith and those who are not." – **Dr. Walter C. Kaiser, Jr.**

"The biography, based as it is on lengthy personal interviews with Dr. Nicole, has been both thoroughly researched and is well written. Between his Preface and Conclusion Bailey takes us in the eight intervening chapters from Dr. Nicole's paternal grandfather's professorship in Greek language and literature at the University of Geneva and his father's pastoral ministry in Germany and Switzerland through his childhood and education and his teaching and pastoral ministry both in Europe and America up to the present. More, much more, could be written about this biography of Dr. Nicole's life and legacy but space constraints will not allow it. So I will close by stating unequivocally that anyone who takes the time and makes the effort to read it will be richly rewarded. He will be moved many times, as I was, both by Dr. Nicole's encyclopedic knowledge of the entire theological terrain and by his deep personal Christian humility. I can only hope and pray that through this biography more people will come to know and appreciate what a choice gift God has given to his church in the person of Roger Nicole." – **Dr. Robert Reymond**

"David W. Bailey has collected all the available material on Roger Nicole to write this biography in which he reveals to the reader a person of intellectual superiority who has been blessed with a photographic memory, a joyful disposition, and a pleasing sense of gentle humor. Bailey exposes the legacy of a man whose aim in life has been to teach and defend the inerrancy of the Holy Scriptures. We are indebted to Bailey for sharing with us the influence of a man who as a master theologian in the Reformed persuasion has done more than many other theologians to promote sound biblical research." – **Dr. Simon Kistemaker**

"Awesome for brain power, learning and wisdom, endlessly patient and courteous in his gentle geniality, and beloved by a multitude as pastor, mentor and friend, veteran Reformed theologian Roger Nicole comes beautifully to life in this warm-hearted biographical tribute. Thank you, David Bailey." – **Dr. James I. Packer**

"I am thankful to see this interesting and detailed biography of Roger Nicole appear in print. I think everyone who has known Roger over his many years of ministry has been so thankful for his genuine love for God and for the Bible as the Word of God, as well as for his immense knowledge that has been put to use for great benefit to the kingdom of God, and for the kindness with which he holds his convictions even when interacting with those with whom he differs. I am thankful for his long life and excellent, God-honoring ministry." – **Dr. Wayne Grudem**

"Although Roger Nicole is not a widely known Reformed Baptist theologian, his life and prodigious work deserve to be entered into the annals of the history of Reformed theology. Those of us who both studied under Nicole and were teaching colleagues with him can only be delighted that Bailey has produced this fascinating biography along with its appendices. I learned so much from Nicole; my most abiding lessons are captured in this book's title: *Speaking the Truth in Love.*" – **Dr. David Scholer**

"Roger Nicole was and remains a major force within the Evangelical world. At 90, he is still producing thoughtful analysis of key issues facing Evangelicalism. His success as a theologian is due not only to his theological acumen but to his great big gracious heart. I have rarely met a man who is so beloved by so many. I heartily commend David Bailey's biography: *Speaking the Truth in Love: The Life and Legacy of Roger Nicole.* Please do read this book—it will stimulate your mind and bless your soul." – **Dr. Frank James**

SPEAKING THE TRUTH IN LOVE

For Dawn,
without whom I would not be completely me

and

For Charissa, Claire-Elise, Catherine and Ethan,
my gifts of love to the Kingdom

SPEAKING THE TRUTH IN LOVE
The Life and Legacy of Roger Nicole

By David W. Bailey, Ph.D.

SOLID GROUND CHRISTIAN BOOKS
BIRMINGHAM, ALABAMA USA

Solid Ground Christian Books
715 Oak Grove Road
Birmingham, AL 35209
205-443-0311
sgcb@charter.net
http://solid-ground-books.com

SPEAKING THE TRUTH IN LOVE
The Life and Legacy of Roger Nicole

Dr. David W. Bailey

First edition November 2006

Cover work by Borgo Design, Tuscaloosa, AL
Contact them at nelbrown@comcast.net

1-59925-093-4

Acknowledgements

Christian biography is, essentially, the telling of a person's life story. What makes it ultimately "Christian" is the recognition throughout that the "footprints of God" accompany the entire journey. This is true, not only for the subject, but also for the biographer! God has sent special people into my life to make my work on this project much easier. I wish to acknowledge my deep indebtedness to the following in the preparation of *Speaking the Truth in Love* –

To Michael Gaydosh, my publisher, whose enthusiasm and encouragement in the publication of this work has been the Lord's means to see a dream come true.

To Freeman Barton, Librarian at Gordon-Conwell Theological Seminary, whose early support and loan of materials was invaluable (especially the transcripts by George Harper); to Ric Walston, President of Columbia Evangelical Seminary, for his meticulous editing in the midst of a busy schedule—I owe you a steak; and to Daniel Wright, whose personal insights from his close friendship with Roger Nicole were particularly helpful.

To Reformation Baptist Church of Eustis, Florida, my beloved flock and fellow pilgrims, whose patience and generosity constantly humble me. Thank you, John Nichol, for being a faithful co-laborer and for taking on the preaching responsibilities so I could complete the manuscript!

To Ray Rhodes, who has kept before me the vision of this biography and its potential for glorifying our great Lord and Savior, Jesus Christ. Thanks for pushing me over the finish line.

To my dear family-by-marriage: Delene Hill, John Hill, Christopher and Dana Brenyo, and Savannah, Jacob, Caleb, Abigail, Jameson and Elijah Brenyo—thank you for providing joyful pauses in the midst of this long work. Christopher, your excellent preaching during my absences from the RBC pulpit allowed me to complete the book (and greatly blessed our people).

To my parents, Owen and Fran Bailey, to my brother, Brian Bailey, and to my grandmother, Laura Tomberlin: you have taught me and given me so much in terms of life, love and joy. My own 'biography' is marked on every page by your influence. From the kind providence of God that brought me to your home as an infant, to the present counsel that I seek in nearly every area of life, you are a constant reminder to me that "every good gift and every perfect gift is from above, and comes down from the Father of lights, with whom there is no variation or shadow of turning" (James 1:17).

To my beautiful, precious, witty and very intelligent wife, Dawn, and to my children, Charissa, Claire-Elise, Catherine and Ethan. As you know, I do not like amusement park thrill rides. Recently, when someone tried to get me to ride one, I replied, "I am thrilled enough by everyday life; I do not require artificial thrills." This is a true statement because of you. You make every moment a perpetual adventure. God's sweet kindness is expressed to me everyday by the constant hugs and kisses of you, my dear children. And thank you, Dawn, for making sure your acknowledgement was phrased just the way you wanted it! You five make me the richest man in the universe.

To Roger and Annette Nicole, whose friendship, hospitality, godliness and assistance in this project have been incalculable. Never has a biographer had such cooperation from the principal. Working with you has been one of the great privileges of my life. My family and I love and appreciate you both more than you could know this side of heaven.

To my great God and Savior Jesus Christ, thank You for saving me and calling me to Your service. You alone are worthy.

Table of Contents

List of Illustrations
(appearing between pp. 110,111)

* Roger & Annette are teetotalers, and they did not drink the champagne they are holding up in this picture.

INTRODUCTION

It is a great privilege, and an equally great delight, to introduce David Bailey's excellent biography of my dear friend Roger Nicole to the Christian public.

It was, I think, George Bernard Shaw, Irish journalist and playwright, who used to speak of 'the Chesterbelloc,' meaning the partnership of G.K. Chesterton and Hilaire Belloc in their advocacy of a social policy called Distributism. As advocates they appeared to him to be like a doubles team on the tennis court, each actively supporting the other; hence his name for them in their joint effort. Ever since I came to know them, I have thought of Roger and Annette Nicole in the same way, as 'the Rogerannette,' for though they are quite different they form a partnership to which anyone might point to illustrate the egalitarianism of men and women together that Roger so implacably defends. One of my cherished memories is of the day, nearly half a century ago, when they lunched in our home and Annette laid into me with passion for being an Anglican and not a Baptist while Roger, beaming all over his face (and how that man can beam!) sat silent enjoying the fun. They are two of the most warm-hearted, free-spirited, and altogether delightful believers that it has been my privilege to know. So the first thing I want to say about Roger is that he is the front end of a twosome, 'the Rogerannette,' and it remains beautiful to see them together.

The second thing I must say is that for a man of such power of mind, clarity of thought, range of knowledge and strength in argument, Roger's patience and courtesy toward the less well favored is a marvel that has become a legend. He was said when first I knew him to have learned to greet people in something like fifty different languages so that he could always welcome overseas students and make them feel at home.   Such sweet pastoral care in the conventional coolness of academia is also the stuff of legend, and deservedly so.   No one could ever accuse Roger of throwing his weight about; very much a Swiss gentlemen in style, he is also a gentle man and a great encourager, overflowing with goodwill at all times.   He has been a model for me in this, as in so much more.

Roger stands at the head of my private list of persons worth celebrating, and I am sure I am not the only one who would say that.   I guess there are thousands who would affirm the same, and I expect the sales of this volume to reflect the fact.   Salutation, Roger!   We love you in the Lord, and rejoice to see this biographical tribute appear.   You deserve every word of it.   God bless you, and Annette too.

Dr. J.I.Packer

Author's Preface: Do You Know Roger Nicole?

Do you know Roger Nicole? If you are a Reformed Baptist you might, though probably not. Southern Baptists, whose latter twentieth century denominational record was one of intense struggle over the nature of Scripture, owe a debt to Roger Nicole that most would not recognize. If you have ever read from the NIV Bible, you have encountered him, for he was an assistant translator for that version. He was a founding member of both the International Council on Biblical Inerrancy and the Evangelical Theological Society (of which he is a past president). His family history, academic career, and Christian statesmanship are the stuff of legend. Perhaps most lists of influential twentieth-century theologians would overlook this remarkable "man of God," a title conferred by no less an evangelical commentator than David F. Wells (he dedicated his 1985 release *Reformed Theology in America* simply "to Roger Nicole, a man of God"). If this oversight should occur, I am convinced it would be the result of a regrettable unawareness of the man and of his impact on Christian theology. I ask the reader to permit me a personal observation before I proceed.

A strange thing happens when I read William F. Buckley, Jr. Since I am a political conservative, he is one of my favorite authors. But Buckley has this paradoxical effect on me: when I encounter his thoughts in print, I feel both more intelligent and less intelligent at the same time. His mind is massive, a fact that does not escape Buckley himself (John Leonard, in his introduction to a collection of Buckley essays, recalled the following exchange when the political analyst appeared on the television show *Laugh-In*: "Mr. Buckley I notice that on your own program you're always sitting down. Is this because you can't think on your feet?" Buckley paused for a moment, then replied, "It is hard . . . to stand up . . . under the weight . . . of all that I know." [*Happy Days Were Here Again*, xix]) One just *feels* smarter after reading Buckley. In fact, during the week prior to my oral comprehensive exam at the completion of my doctoral studies, I read Buckley to steel myself for the coming intellectual challenge. Encountering such a mind stretches one's own. But at the same time, there is a sense of humiliation when I read Buckley, for I realize that my own mental prowess is paltry by comparison. And what cerebral acumen I *do* possess I have not improved as I should.

This smarter/dumber paradox faced me whenever I was with Roger Nicole. His mind, like Buckley's, is legendary (though Nicole's own Christian humility would demur at the description). Pastor and author John Piper once quoted Nicole's affirmation of John Owen as the greatest theologian who has ever written in the English language. Piper recalled that Nicole paused in the midst of his presentation and said that Owen was 'even greater than the great Jonathan Edwards.' "That really caught my attention," said Piper, "because I am sure Nicole has read more of those two greats than most theologians and pastors have." Nicole always assumed I knew more about whatever subject we discussed than was actually the case. I am not sure if my T.Q. (theological quotient) ever advanced more than a point or two, but I felt like a world-class scholar for having been in his presence. Simultaneously, as names, facts, figures, dates, and personages rolled effortlessly off Nicole's tongue, I was sure that no Ph.D., pastor, and sometime professor was as utterly ignorant as I!

Who is Roger Nicole? Why should one read his biography? These are valid questions. Until the summer of 1997, I, too, was unfamiliar with the nonagenarian Swiss theologian, mathematics devotee, world-class bibliophile (his personal library contains, among other gems, a copy of the first edition of Heinrich Bullinger's *Decades*, published in 1552), and acknowledged expert in the thought of Reformation leader John Calvin. Nicole was for decades an avid philatelist, with an encyclopedic knowledge of the hobby and a personal collection of approximately one million stamps. He enjoys reading detective novels. He was named to *Who's Who,* and served as Associate Editor for the *New Geneva Study* Bible and Corresponding Editor for *Christianity Today.* Nicole holds two earned doctorates (a Doctor of Theology from Gordon Divinity School and a Doctor of Philosophy from Harvard University). He helped draft the

Chicago Statement on Biblical Inerrancy and he is a biblical egalitarian. Nicole defies classification. Though you may not recognize the name, you have likely encountered him, indirectly if not directly. He has contributed articles to reference works that are probably on your library shelves or in your computer hard drive. The more I got to know Roger Nicole, the more I learned as a theological student and pastor. And the more I got to know the man, the more I knew his story must be told.

Nicole is an amiable man. His genuine love for persons is immediately evident. He converses as effortlessly with a five-year old child as with an academic colleague. This derives, in part, from his mature Christian humility. Speaking of several great theologians, Nicole quipped, "God works with big shots and with little shots, like me; He is not an elitist. God makes His people elite, but He does not demand elitism as a precondition for working with persons." When I approached him about the prospect of a biography, his response was typical: "I don't know if I am important enough, but if a biography were done, I would want it to glorify God rather than me." The author's prayer is the same: that the God Who molded and fitted and gifted Roger Nicole for kingdom service might be praised for His goodness. For, indeed, God was good to His church when He gave her this "mind in love with God."

This is the story of a life, a Christian life, a Christian theologian's life. It traces the "footprints of God" throughout the lifetime of Roger Nicole, those providential connections in a life that form the basis of a valid Christian biography. The title, chosen by Nicole, is instructive, for it encapsulates the man and his ministry: speaking the truth in love. Fittingly, it is a *biblical* quotation (Ephesians 4:15), extracted from a context concerning Christian maturity. Nicole's existence has been marked by commitment to Scripture, progress in sanctification, and instruction of the church in the same. The title is also striking because it reveals the *balance* that is so characteristic of Roger Nicole. Truth is always expected of evangelical, Reformed theologians; love, sadly, is often neither found in nor required of them. In Nicole, the church and the academy have a happy mixture of both truth and love.

Dr. David Bailey

Subject's Preface: A Biography, Not a Eulogy

In perusing and reading this biography, prepared in a very conscientious way by Dr. David Bailey after scores of meetings with me and with others, the dominant effect I find is that of surprise. This sounds like a eulogy, such as are given at funerals. A funeral is a time when people who are present desire to honor the deceased and to express gratitude for the good points of their lives, and it would be grossly inappropriate to make more than purely passing remarks with respect to defects and faults that everybody knows. One could well say something about the fact that a believer is saved by grace through faith that covers all our sins, but it would be very inept to proceed to enumerate single defects and individual cases of disobedience in the deceased's life.

But this is a biography, not a eulogy. I am a Christian, which means that more than eighty years ago and ever since, I have confessed with tears that I am a miserable sinner "born in iniquity, inclined unto evil, incapable by myself of any good thing, and who transgresses every day in several ways God's holy commandments." This is what I was saying every Sunday and a very realistic summary of the biblical doctrine of sin. I know myself as a disobedient sinner, proud, selfish, unbelieving, deceptive, lustful, lazy, insensitive, a "lover of pleasure rather than lover of God" (II Tim 3:2). I have even now not yet begun to plumb the abyss of wickedness from which I desperately needed salvation—how is it that none of these things is very apparent in this biography? How can I be presented as a mountaineer who never slipped on the slope, never fell in a crevasse, never gave up because the climb was too rough for me, almost always succeeded where others had failed? There are no such mountaineers except in books!! And there is no Christian who is fully on the level of his/her biography!

The biography was written to emphasize the footsteps of God Himself in the path of my life. It deals with God's faithfulness, with His loving and forgiving kindness toward one who is unworthy of the least of His blessing. It does not deal with *my* achievements, but with His mercy (I Cor 15:10; II Cor 4:5, 7).

Another matter that modifies the story, beside the unilateral emphasis on good events and commendable attitudes, is the fact that it so greatly concentrates on one person: Roger Nicole. I have filled a whole page with the names of those who have exercised an immense influence on me over the years: my family (parents and siblings), my teachers (in infancy, in secondary school, in Bible Institutes and university, at Gordon Divinity School and at Harvard University), my colleagues (in seminaries, in churches, in broader connections, in preparing the NIV translation of Scripture), my pastors (throughout the churches where I was a member), my students (in my various places of teaching, and especially my assistants called "Byington" fellows at Gordon and who are listed in Appendix E), my friends who bestowed a special affection on me when no official relationship required it (Dr. Dimitri Andropov, George Aubert, Georges-Ali Maire, Philippe Blocher, Irving Howard, Burton Goddard, Lloyd Kalland, Luder Whitlock, Simon Kistemaker) and their wives, my children (who have adopted us as "Papa and Mama," and who are listed on page 162, and supremely, forgivingly, supportively and with amazing honesty and faithfulness, my dearly beloved wife, Annette Nicole whom God placed at my side for more than sixty years, and to whom I dedicated my book that promised the widest circulation, *Our Sovereign Saviour* (2002):

> *In grateful recognition of my beloved wife*
> *ANNETTE CYR NICOLE*
> *who for more than fifty years*
> *has been a loyal supporter*
> *and an active participant*
> *in all ministries God entrusted to us*
> *I dedicate this book to her*
> Roger Nicole

An almost identical text is found on a plaque on one of the benches at Reformed Theological Seminary in Oviedo, Florida.

Finally, I want to thank my friend David Bailey who took the initiative for this book, and then carried it indefatigably through interviews and adjustments so as to glorify God.

Dr. Roger Nicole

CHAPTER 1

1915-1920
Family

To understand Roger Nicole the *theologian*, it is necessary to go back at least two generations, to his paternal grandfather, for a glimpse of the fortunate combination of genetics and familial instruction that produced Roger Nicole the *man*. "God's footsteps in the path of a man's life" – that is Nicole's own vision for this biography. Divine intervention is clearly evident in his ancestry and in his own experience.

Jules Louis Adolphe Nicole was born in Geneva, Switzerland on November 20, 1842. Here the reader begins to see a pattern of God's marvelous bestowal of intellectual and spiritual gifts upon a family. Jules Nicole distinguished himself as a papyrologue, an expert in the study of ancient documents written on papyri. He was known as "the father of papyrology in Switzerland." After completing his baccalaureate, he resided in Madrid for two years, then lived for six years in St. Petersburg, Russia. During the time in Russia, he "absorbed just about the whole of ancient Greek literature." He took an M.A. from the Sorbonne in Paris and was immediately retained there as a professor. In 1874 Jules moved back to Geneva where he served as Professor of Greek Language and Literature at Geneva University.

Jules was awarded two honorary doctorates. The first, a Doctor of Letters, was bestowed by the University of Basel in 1901. This was followed in 1912 by a Doctor of Laws from the University of Athens, granted for his discovery of an ancient legal papyrus. Jules received both degrees because of his erudition in Greek. He also found in the university library at Geneva an obscure, heavily annotated manuscript of Homer's *The Iliad*. The existence of the manuscript was known in academe, but its location was a mystery. Jules published the manuscript in three volumes as *The Genevan Scholia on The Iliad*, adding to his already prodigious scholarly endeavors.

Always abreast of papyrological discoveries, Jules anticipated that recent findings in Egypt would open new vistas on Greek literature lost for centuries. He made two trips to Egypt to buy papyri (assisted by the labor and affluence of an Egyptologist colleague, Ernest Naville), organized and deciphered many of the lacunae (fragmentary papyri, like the pieces of a puzzle), and was able to analyze quickly the reconstructed texts because of his encyclopedic knowledge of ancient Greek literature. The collection of Greek papyri in Geneva rivaled that of Oxford, Berlin, and Paris thanks to the efforts of Jules Louis Adolphe Nicole. His scholarship was well known in Switzerland, earning him a citation with photograph in the French encyclopedia *Larousse du 20ème Siècle*. The University of Geneva also produced a Festschrift for him entitled *Mélanges Nicole* with contributions by major scholars in classical studies, particularly papyrology.

A devout Christian, Jules joined an independent Presbyterian church (although Switzerland has an official state church). This was to the great delight of leaders in the Swiss Free Church movement, for Jules was a university professor. His academic stature was a "feather in their cap" enhancing the intellectual respectability of the Free Church. Because they could claim him among their ranks, the Free Church could not justly be considered provincial and faddish. Thus, not only in scholarship but also in churchmanship did Jules distinguish himself.

Jules was married on June 8, 1872 to Marie Benoist, the daughter of a mathematics professor at the University of Caen, Normandy. Her father had a driving ambition, however, to be a professor at the University of Paris; ironically, on the day he received an invitation to teach there, he was overcome with joy and died on the spot! Her background was shrouded in mystery, Roger recalled, and he knew little about her because the family did not broach the subject. What he did know was that she was a person of devout prayer and "really an admirable Christian of very fine spiritual stature." Marie grew up in a Roman Catholic home, but she joined her husband in affiliation with the Free Church. Evangelicals of the day considered her a "prayer helper" for her faithful ministry of intercession. Marie had the same housemaid for fifty years, enabling her to engage actively in ministry; on his deathbed, Jules asked the housekeeper to stay with Marie for the remainder of his beloved's life. Roger noted that his grandfather worked too hard which led to bouts of depression later in life. Jules died April 14, 1921. Throughout her married life, Marie always signed her name "Marie *Jules* Nicole" because she was so proud of her husband.

Marie (1845-1946) bore two sons and one daughter that did not survive beyond infancy. Each of the boys died at the age of three; the girl was stillborn. God blessed Jules and Marie with two more sons who did live to adulthood. Roger Nicole's father, Albert Nicole, was born on April 7, 1873, in Paris, France. Georges Nicole was born on February 22, 1880. Both Roger's father and his uncle impacted his life greatly, and both further evidenced the remarkable intellectual and spiritual blessings of God upon the Nicole family.

Albert studied in Geneva at an independent seminary founded in the 1840s by Merle D'Aubigné and Louis Gaussen. Upon graduation, he was awarded three fellowships for further study in Scotland. Concentrating his graduate research on Old Testament studies, he was for a time French tutor to the children of Alexander Whyte and had opportunity to attend classes with S. R. Driver at Oxford. He was ordained on April 24, 1898. His New Testament professor, Edouard Barde, preached on Luke 14:15-24. The title of the ordination sermon was "Get Out." Some years later, on a Wednesday night, there was a terrible rainstorm. Albert, thinking that the prayer meeting would be unattended, was inclined to stay at home and study his favorite subject: Hebrew. His scholastic bliss was interrupted by continual thoughts of that long-ago ordination sermon entitled "Get Out." Albert donned his raincoat, grasped Bible and umbrella, and headed for the Free Church of Puyoo (where he served as pastor until early 1900). God was pleased to send revival that night to the congregation.

Albert was a gifted pastor. In addition to his expositional skills (enhanced, surely, by his love for the Hebrew Old Testament), Albert was also a compassionate pastoral counselor. His congregants could depend upon their shepherd for a sympathetic ear and biblical guidance for the challenges of life. His consideration for others led him to mentor other ministers in need of encouragement and theological instruction. He was also a Christian statesman, being denominated by liberal leaders one of "seven dangerous men" for his unswerving devotion to evangelical truth and for his opposition to liberalism and to the dictates of the state church.

When his ministry was completed at Puyoo, Albert moved to Frankfurt, Germany, to serve as associate pastor of the Huguenot church. It was there that he met his future wife, Bertha de Neufville. From 1905 until 1914, Albert was the pastor of another Huguenot church in Berlin (of the six pastors serving together at the church, Albert was the only one ministering in French). As such, he belonged to that general Protestant faith known as *Evangelisch* in German, though the term did not carry any connotations of theological conservatism or evangelicalism. The official documents of the congregation stipulated that French services were to be held. These Huguenot believers were loyal German citizens ("ferociously Germanophile"). During a public service, Albert once forgot to pray for the emperor. Since this was considered a breach of patriotism, a formal complaint was lodged with the royal consistory. Fortunately, he had an influential friend at the consistory that persuaded the officials that this was an unintentional oversight (being pastor of a state church, Albert was obligated to pray for the emperor). When the hostilities of World War I commenced, the German government cancelled church services in French.

Albert became chaplain for French Protestant prisoners of war. In this capacity he ministered among thirty-eight different prisoner camps between 1914 and 1919. The French government decorated him with the *Legion of Honor* for his work among French prisoners of war. Albert thus bore the title *Chevalier de la Légion d'Honneur*. As an official state employee, Albert was entitled to a salary that the German government could only cancel in the case of moral turpitude or doctrinal heresy. An illness afflicting his eyes (which began early in the Berlin pastorate) rendered him practically blind for life. This made his chaplaincy during the war even more extraordinary: with his very poor eyesight, he traveled—alone—by train, making multiple connections throughout Germany. One of the more painful consequences of the blindness was the discontinuation of special studies in his beloved Semitic languages. His concentration shifted to pastoral ministry and New Testament (Greek) scholarship, which providentially led to the ultimate publication of a commentary on First John entitled *Walk in Obedience and Love* ("probably Dad's best work"). In addition to a variety of pamphlets, he also published three books: *Before, During and After Preaching* (dealing with the way in which the public worship service could be exploited to the maximum for the blessing of the hearers); *True Life* (a book of twelve sermons); and *Words of Comfort and Encouragement* (a volume of his addresses to the French prisoners of war).

After the war, Albert was pastor of the Free Church in Saint-Imier, Switzerland from 1920 until 1928. After a conflict at the church contributed to his poor health, he heeded his doctor's recommendation and moved to the more salutary climate of Lausanne. For one year (1928-1929) he was a professor at the Emmaus Bible Institute near Lausanne, Switzerland; he resigned, however, when some of the students complained that his teaching was not sufficiently practical. The Nicoles had sought and taken a three-month lease for their lodgings; this ultimately became a thirty-eight year stay. Albert's later ministry involved service as an itinerant minister, preacher, and instructor in numerous places throughout Switzerland, France, Belgium, and Czechoslovakia. Albert Nicole died in 1966.

Georges Nicole, Roger's uncle, was born February 22, 1880, and died August 5, 1937. He was awarded the Doctor of Letters from the University of Geneva. An active archeologist, Georges directed excavations in Rome, produced a famous catalogue of painted vases housed at the Museum of Athens, and taught archeology as an assistant at the University of Geneva from 1904 to 1907. He married Isabelle Cabane, the daughter of famous painter Edouard Cabane, on October 8, 1914. They had one son who taught college-level French at Geneva. Though denied a permanent chair at Geneva, Georges remained a very gifted scholar who was in constant contact with researchers at the University of Paris concerning a variety of projects. He served as director of Librairie Honoré Champion, a publisher of classical work.

Roger Nicole's mother, Bertha de Neufville, was born August 8, 1876, and died April 6, 1976. She was the daughter of Julius de Neufville, the director of a major bank in Frankfurt, and Elisabeth

Passavant. A committed French Huguenot, de Neufville and his wife
Elisabeth produced three offspring, two boys and one girl. Bertha
was the youngest. Both boys, Gustave and Robert, followed their
father into the world of finance. Bertha's influence was to be
domestic, but no less dramatic. On August 6, 1903, Albert Nicole
married Bertha de Neufville in Frankfurt. From their marriage until
his death, Bertha was an enthusiastic supporter of Albert in his
ministry. She was especially helpful to him in his blindness, as was
Roger: Bertha learned the Greek alphabet so she could read the
Greek New Testament to her husband; Roger learned the Hebrew
alphabet at the age of fifteen so he could read Hebrew to his father.

Albert and Bertha Nicole had 3 children. The eldest, Jules
Marcel, was born June 8, 1907 and died in December 1997. His
influence on Roger, as well as Roger's admiration for his brother,
was unceasing. The Nicole family tradition of scholarship and
service to God was not broken with Jules Marcel. He lived with his
parents until 1925 when he took a baccalaureate at La Chaux-de-
Fonds. He next received the M.A. in Classical Languages from the
Sorbonne in 1927. The following year, he was awarded a diploma
from the Bible Institute of Nogent-Marne. This was a school that
was founded primarily to train ministers called to God's service later
in life. The Institute claims approximately one thousand alumni, is
the oldest of its kind in Europe, and is still in operation.

Jules Marcel taught French at another Bible Institute near
Lausanne, Switzerland (1928-1929). He pursued further training at
Gordon Divinity School, a school founded in 1889 by A. J. Gordon
to train Baptist missionaries for ministry in the Congo. His rationale
for choosing Gordon was simple: "I wanted to study in a school of
faith rather than a school of doubt." The fact that he was engaged to
teach French at the school also influenced his decision to attend
Gordon rather than Dallas Theological Seminary. Upon his arrival,
however, the position of French instructor was not offered as
promised. Jules Marcel desired to teach French while studying
theology; instead, he sang bass in a Baptist quartet. He took the B.D.
from Gordon in 1930 and the S.T.M. with honors in 1931.

During his studies at Gordon, Jules Marcel was the pastor of the
French Baptist Church in Woonsocket, Rhode Island (1930-1931).
After completing the S.T.M. degree in 1931, he was approached by

six different institutions, both academic and ecclesiastical, which wanted him to continue his studies and teaching in the United States. Three assemblies from Canada sought him as well. Instead, he returned to Europe, having no definite offers of employment but sensing strongly the call of God to France. When he disembarked, Jules Marcel was met by the director of the Bible Institute of Nogent-Marne with an offer of a professorship. He held the teaching post from 1931 until 1995. Teaching was never to bring him great wealth; in fact, his stipend from the French government for having two children was greater than his salary at the Bible Institute.

Jules Marcel taught as a visiting professor at Aix during the 1940s and during the 1960s through 1980s at the French Evangelical Seminary of Vaux. His areas of teaching included Greek, church history, history of religions, history of denominations, systematic theology, individual Bible books, homiletics, and Hebrew (he taught advanced Hebrew at the seminary in Vaux). He wrote within the same disciplines, producing works in New Testament Greek grammar, church history, theology, homiletics, and ethics, as well as various Bible studies (most significantly a two-volume commentary on Job) and printed addresses. He considered Ruben Saillens, founder of the Bible Institute at Nogent-Marne, to be his mentor. Roger would later affirm the godliness and evangelical statesmanship of Saillens, remarking that "it was a privilege just to be in contact with him." The scholarship of Jules Marcel was not merely academic—for fifty years (1945-1995) he annually read the entire Bible in the original languages. Roger said of his brother, "He was definitely my major teacher in Christian studies." Surely *Roger* must have been his major student! He taught Roger much, taking time to explain in detail the answers to his brother's questions (they sometimes took four-hour walks on Sundays), whereas Albert simply gave summary responses.

Jules Marcel served as a key committee member for the revision of the French Bible (*Nouvelle Version Segond Revisée*), a task that lasted twenty years. He was the only member of the committee involved from inception to completion. This was a monumental work, being the first Bible for the French with such notes and scholarly material (allowing the common person to get close to the original text). He had admired the work of the American

Standard Version (1901) and wanted to reproduce the quality of translation and notes for a French Bible.

During his sixty-five years of ministry, Jules Marcel probably trained more than 1500 pastors, missionaries, evangelists, and other Christian workers. His teaching effectiveness was enhanced by readings in the classroom of relevant primary sources. Through his writings, Bible translation, and pastoral ministry he impacted countless others. He was unbiased in his judgments, even with regard to the cults—he asked broad questions and sought to be very fair with opponents (a characteristic shared by Roger). Jules Marcel was married to Aimée Paget on December 1, 1943. Gordon-Conwell Theological Seminary awarded him the D.D. in 1981.

God's enabling grace seemed to flow into every branch of the Nicole line. Jules Marcel presented Roger with two nephews, each remarkable in his own right. One of Roger's nephews, Jacques, serves as a missionary in Togo. The other, Emile, is dean of the seminary in Vaux (and contributed an article to the Festschrift for Roger published in 2004). Nicole's enthusiasm for his family is manifest,

> I wrote to Emile after the publication of the Festschrift. I told him, "When you wrote your doctoral thesis in Strasbourg, on Exodus 30 and the doctrine of the covenant, which the critical people say is a late development in Jewish thought, you went like a Daniel into the lions' den. And now you have made an encore. By taking a passage from Exodus as being part of the Mosaic revelation—radically opposite to the critical outlook—you again went into the lions' den, and in both cases you came out of it without a scratch."

Concerning the roles of men and women in church and society, Roger and Jules Marcel shared the egalitarian view.[1] Their grandfather Jules Louis Adolphe was a complementarian, as was their father Albert. Egalitarians teach that God intends men and women to share authority equally. Complementarians, on the other hand, insist that God distinguishes between men and women, with leadership being predominantly a male prerogative. Jules Marcel

---

[1] For a discussion of Roger's view of egalitarianism, see Roger Nicole, "Biblical Egalitarianism and the Inerrancy of Scripture," *Priscilla Papers* Vol. 20, No. 2 (Spring 2006): 4-9.

believed that women might even be permitted to serve in the military. This egalitarianism was not a major component of his teaching, but Jules Marcel derived it from a careful consideration of how God treats women in Scripture. When he first began to embrace egalitarianism, his opinions were considered "unusual" in Switzerland and France.

Roger's sister, Desirée Mariella, was born near Berlin on January 24, 1912. Because of the ravages of war, she suffered from food deprivation during late infancy and early childhood. This led to fragile health into her teens, and has left her physically challenged for life. Also, her education was inconsistent during childhood. A remarkable woman, Mariella served as an elder at a Presbyterian church near Lausanne. Her ministry included counseling the discouraged by telephone. She was a trained practical nurse and a graduate of the Bible Institute at Nogent-Marne (1933) where she studied Christian doctrine. Until 1940, she worked with a Baptist church in Paris, visiting the infirm and doing personal counseling. She was part of the desperate flight of the French from official German oppression in 1940.

Mariella struggled not only with physical challenges; she underestimated her gifts living in the shadow of her brothers' successes. She spent a year at Bern, where she learned Switzerdeutsch, a Swiss dialect of German (she learned it "like nobody's business," according to Roger). She was very capable intellectually, despite the early disadvantages of nutritional and educational depredation. After 1940, she was repatriated from France to Switzerland through the assistance of the Red Cross. She cared for her parents, Albert and Bertha, for more than thirty years until their deaths. She remained a patriotic Swiss and a staunch supporter of the Presbyterian (Reformed) church in Switzerland. Mariella "fell asleep in Jesus" in April 2004.

Roger Robert Georges Nicole (Roger Robert Nicole is on the birth certificate; Roger was given the name Georges for his uncle but, as he explains, "in Europe you don't take these other names for your signature, so I always sign Roger") was born on December 10, 1915, in a hospital in Charlottenburg, Germany, a West Berlin suburb populated by about 300,000 inhabitants. Charlottenburg is dominated architecturally by a castle. Technically, it is the town containing the hospital in which Roger was delivered. But because of Switzerland's citizenship laws, Roger Nicole is considered a native-born Swiss, not German.

Another early influence on Roger, in addition to his parents, was Bertha Perrinjaquet, his godmother ("Potite" to the family). She cared for the children while his parents were away ministering. Bertha lived in the Nicole home from the arrival of Jules Marcel. Roger was especially dependent upon her care during his later teens. Bertha helped to orient the lives of the Nicole children to God's service: Jules Marcel in the area of teaching; Mariella in personal witness; and Roger in theology/Christian statesmanship. Roger's wife, Annette, viewed Bertha Perrinjaquet as a remarkable Christian woman.

At the age of one, while still nursing, Roger learned to talk. Like his sister, Roger was deprived of good nutrition in early childhood because of the exigencies of the war. Even as a teenager, his health was challenged. Thankfully, neither Roger nor Mariella suffered any adverse effects on their mental development as a result. The family did have a sort of sylvan retreat in the woods at Lichtenrade where they could supplement the meager wartime rations with mushrooms (Roger recalled that his brother maintained an encyclopedic knowledge of mushrooms for life). Two of his earliest memories, though vague, persisted in his mind. Roger remembered a sort of bell system that could be rung from various rooms. Part of the contraption (called a *payoupe* by the Nicoles) was made of glass, and Roger broke it playing with a ball. The owner of the house (the *wirt*) came to punish little Roger, who hid in fright under the bed. He also remembered something about a nebulous set of notepapers that he was unable to take with him when they moved.

CHAPTER 2

1920-1928
Jura Bernois

When Roger was 4 ½ years old, the Nicole family moved to Sonvilier, in a French-speaking region in the northwestern part of the state of Berne. His father Albert was to serve as pastor of two Free churches (*Eglise Libre*): one in Sonvilier, a watch-making community with a population of two thousand; the other in St.-Imier, a larger village of seven thousand situated near the ruins of an old castle. Interestingly, a watchmaker in St.-Imier told Albert that Roger's brother, the future scholar of renown, should be a watchmaker, and thus needed no secondary education! The churches were both Presbyterian in doctrine (though Baptists were admitted and respected, receiving baptism by aspersion in the pastor's study), and the entire district had experienced a religious revival during the mid-nineteenth century. Albert enjoyed an eight-year ministry there, during which the churches prospered in every particular. The first book in Roger Nicole's personal library of thirty thousand volumes was a gift from his father. It was a conflation of the four gospels and his father wrote: "To my dear little Roger in memory of page 103 which he read for me on April 7, 1923 – A. Nicole." So Roger's early childhood development occurred in the context of familiar language (French had been spoken in the Nicole home since Roger's infancy) and spiritual vitality. There was also a sense of "specialness of class" that he had to unlearn from his parents, a sort of superior self-estimation that was detrimental to one in ministry.

God providentially provided for the family's financial needs through pensions, as well as through teaching and pastoral salaries.

Roger observed his parents as they lived a life of trust. Albert received a check from the German government, and his salary continued after his French services were cancelled until his retirement when he began receiving a pension. This legacy of living by faith was passed on to Roger, whose salary as a world-class theological professor was generally lower than that of public school kindergarten teachers. But God proved a most generous provider to His faithful servant. Roger related the following example of God's financial care in later years,

> Throughout my time at Gordon, the salary that I received was not commensurate with my academic preparation. I received a great deal less, but it did not bother me because this was the Lord's work, and so I was happy in doing the work that God had given to me. Annette was doing well in exercising financial discipline in the home so that we "were doing fine." However, at one point, the trustees realized that the salaries of the professors were inadequate as compared with other institutions. They decided to give to those professors who had been there for a period of some years an acre of ground. The school could readily afford this, for more than one thousand acres had been acquired, and it was never thought that the college or the divinity school, or both combined, would need to have access to that much land. We were given the land free of charge so that we could build a home there near the school. The acre of land that I received was at the time assessed at $500.00. The treasurer (of both the college and the divinity school) mentioned that there should not be any kind of limitation on the gift, since a lien on the land would be unfair because of the $500.00 assessment. He was opposed to having a binding clause, so that if the professor should leave, the land would have to return to the school, or if sold, a certain percentage had to go back to the school. It was an outright gift and we could do with it as we wished. Annette and I did build on that lot in 1954, and our house cost us less than $20,000.00. Though not visible from the house because of foliage, our acre lot was situated on a lovely lake and was very desirable.
>
> Well, when we left in 1989, that same land was valued in the town's assessment at $200,000, and we were paying taxes on that basis. Add to that the value of the home, which was assessed at $69,000, and we were paying on an assessment of $269,000. When we sold the property, we were able to gather about

$250,000. This is the money that allowed us to buy our home in Apopka ($160,000) and we had nearly $100,000 above that. I viewed this as being money from the Lord, and we put it in annuities, which was important because it meant the increase by virtue of interest was not taxable unless we used it in our lifetime. That money has more than quadrupled since 1989. The 1990s were a good period for interest, so that the advice we received from the Presbyterian Ministers' Fund representative was very good. By the time we die, there will be a substantial sum that will be used for scholarships at seminaries that we wish to support. That money has grown marvelously well. I still view it in a sense as the Lord's money, so I would not feel free to use a good deal of it just for my living.

If you take $200,000 and remove $500 for the initial gift of the land, you have $199,500. If you divide that figure by the number of years that I taught, which is 41, then you get close to $5000 per year—like an annual bonus of $5000 per year. Of course, that would have been very considerable at the beginning of my career. My salary at first was $1800 per year, and for that I was teaching and also serving as dormitory director. Prior to that I was not getting a regular salary, but was instead paid by the course. But now I was in the school, and I was teaching French and German, and also I was teaching one course in the divinity school (the year was 1945). For that I received $1800, plus $300 for the course at the divinity school. When I got married in 1946, they gave me a raise of $900, so that I was getting $2700. But my colleagues, who were not teaching more than I did, and without my doctorate and the M.A. from the Sorbonne, were getting $3000. My salary increased over time, but it was a slow increase. I was not unhappy about it, and I did not feel I was being neglected, because I felt I was doing the Lord's work.

I am not attempting to compare what I actually received with what I might have received if I were involved for the sake of money. My thinking is that the pastor is not really in ministry for the money; he is in for the service, and the money is intended to free him from some of the concerns and problems that may arise simply because of money. The employer is really God, not just the church. I do not like the word "hire" for securing a pastor; a pastor receives a call. It is a call of God, forwarded by the church, in connection with their situation. I really was not fretting about my financial situation, and then I got $200,000 from the Lord just like that! Gordon will get something back when I die; in fact, one-third of our estate goes to Gordon Divinity School for scholarships. In some way, we have a chance to continue the work that we were doing in the three major places of our activity: Gordon Divinity School, Reformed Theological Seminary, and the Baptist work in Canada. For twenty-five years I was going there once or twice annually. I am eager to support that French Canadian work, especially since the churches I pastored were comprised of French Canadian people. I am very eager to see the Lord's blessing there.

Roger had many hobbies and interests outside of theology. First, he was a mystery reader. His father had some Sherlock Holmes books but Roger, in his mid to late teens, could not read English. When he was eventually able to read them, he devoured the Sherlock Holmes stories, Ellery Queen mysteries, and his favorite, Earle Stanley Gardner. He possessed a complete collection of *Ellery Queen* magazines from the inaugural issue. Roger liked the analytical aspects, the resolution and optimism that characterize the genre. In this way, his enthusiasm for mystery reading paralleled his love of mathematics. "Mystery novels provide a confirmation of the principle of divine justice," he observed, and sharpen the observational skills essential to sound biblical interpretation and theology. David Wells, J. I. Packer, and J. Gresham Machen were other theologians of note who also liked mystery stories. For Roger, the best mystery stories demonstrate "the triumph of the intellect *committed* to truth over the appearance of intellect *opposed* to the truth."

Roger enjoyed tennis and mountaineering (described below), though by his own assessment he was "not a sports figure." His other avocations included statistics (from his early childhood he enjoyed almanacs and other reference works containing data about the countries of the world). He did some work in physics with the principles of attraction in small tubes that he enjoyed (capillarity). However, his parents limited his natural love for chemistry as a boy. Mathematics was a subject of which he was particularly fond; in fact, Roger once noted, "mathematics was the sacrifice I made for a career in theology." He also loved bibliography, collecting books and employing them in research. In all of this, there was the common thread of what he called "the collector's instinct."

The two athletic events of which Roger was most fond were tennis and mountain climbing. He described his zeal for tennis as follows:

First I played against the door of the garage at our home; only later did I move on to the tennis court. I was playing with a proper racquet from 1928 to 1935. Prior to that, I had a little wooden racquet that somebody had made for me. Then the landlady saw that I was playing against the door, and she had racquets that were not used, so she gave them to me and then I started playing with regular tennis racquets. So before leaving the home in 1935, I had played tennis for several years. I appreciated the sport because it not only gave me strength in my biceps, but I was actually playing fairly well. I was very good in smash hits particularly—not putting it on the net, but beyond the reach of the other player, putting it on the line. So that was a source of considerable enjoyment.

But my father had misgivings about it because my uncle who played tennis had, on account of a tennis match, overlooked a note that he had made of something that later came up on his doctoral examination. And so he had something that he could have incorporated in his thesis, but didn't, because when he came back from the court, he overlooked it. And my father felt that as a result he was not as brilliant on his doctoral thesis as he could have been. He thought tennis was, at least academically, a dangerous pastime, and he particularly was eager that I should not play tennis while the written exams took place. The written exams were, I recall, in the afternoon and I wanted to play tennis every morning as a relaxation before those written exams. And so I told my father that this was what I planned to do (with his permission of course) but that I was willing to put this kind of gambit on it: if my marks on the written tests were less desirable than my normal achievement, then I would acknowledge his point and give up tennis. Now, this was not to say if I happened to fall below the level of my fellow students—that would not have been very impressive to him—but if I fell below my *own* level. As it turned out, I performed even better in the exams than I did during the term.

In any case, after that I didn't have as much opportunity to play because I was in the Bible Institute and there was no tennis court there. And when I came to the United States, I had very little time or opportunity to play tennis, maybe one or two hours per week. I finally gave my racquet to one of my colleagues who had three very young children, I think in 1993. Until then, I was still thinking of playing occasionally. But the end of my tennis playing occurred when my colleague, Glenn Barker (with whom I played tennis quite a bit while I was teaching) actually died on the tennis court while provost at Fuller Seminary. After that my wife said "You are finished for tennis." And that was good, because I liked to play very hard—not just flirting with the ball—and tennis could have become a real distraction.

Roger was very fond of mountaineering. He climbed on three 4,000-meter mountains in Switzerland, with his highest peak being 4,330 meters (about the height of Mount Evans). This was climbing on foot from the road at the very bottom to the summit. He also ascended Mount Hood during a series of lectures he presented at Western Conservative Baptist Seminary in Portland, Oregon. He scaled that mountain with a group called the Mazamas, an organization of mountain climbers in the western United States. Nicole wanted to climb on Mount Rainier during this same trip, but he could find no climbing companions at the time. He also ascended Mount Katahdin and Mount Washington (the latter mountain, the highest in the United States east of the Mississippi River and north of the Mason-Dixon, he climbed by half a dozen routes). Roger enjoyed the view from the heights: if there was a mountain, a skyscraper, or a tower, he wanted to ascend it to revel in the outlook thus afforded. He recalled,

> Mountaineering is something that has been a source of great pleasure for me physically, yet never in a way to expose my life unnecessarily. I wasn't doing anything that was really dangerous, but I had a great desire to climb and to experience this new challenge. In Costa Rica, near San Jose, I climbed about ten thousand feet—the air was delicious! Even in circumstances where I couldn't climb, I was doing it by proxy, so to speak, in reading mountaineering adventures. I still have about two shelves of mountaineering books right here in my bedroom and I've read many, many books on the subject. I have been interested where there are mountains anyplace in the world. If

someone were to ask me about the Himalayas, I could tell them about the fourteen tallest mountains in the world because I *know* them through reading about them. So that is something that has been significant for my life and in a certain sense the mountain view is something I find especially attractive.

Roger used illustrations from his hobbies in his sermon work. The pastimes tended to put his "feet on the ground" in the sense of providing connection with his hearers instead of just theory from the academic lectern. If one is on an airplane, Roger noted, there is a view of earth that resembles the vantage of "our Father who is in heaven." Thus, hobbies may serve as a spiritual illustration in pastoral or academic ministry. He also enjoyed working cryptograms and word scrambles for fun, but also to develop his vocabulary. He readily admitted that his background in Latin, French, and German helped his English communicative skills immeasurably.

Another pursuit that occupied Roger's free time (and free shelf space) was philately. At its height, his stamp collection numbered approximately one million specimens ("an unmanageable quantity"). For some countries, such as Germany, his compilation was exhaustive. He possessed a copy of the very first postage stamp, from Great Britain in the year 1840. Nicole's half-century interest in philately developed some time after his arrival in the United States. His wife, Annette, had an operation that the couple hoped might enable her to bear children. The surgery was rather critical, necessitating a lengthy and quiet recovery. At that point, she began to be interested in stamps from an artistic point of view. Roger had brought some stamps to America in order to give them to other people (both his father and his brother had plenty to spare from their own collections). From the miscellaneous samples Roger gave to her, Annette began collecting stamps into quite impressive albums. Being a novice, she had no idea how to recognize the values of stamps or how to go about collecting systematically. So Roger's interest in stamps developed with that of his wife; his enthusiasm for all things statistical and quantitative merged with her love for the beauty of stamps. He noted,

> Annette might take an interest in animals, and so she would have stamps of different countries with cats on them. She was

collecting topically. And in my family, my father and my brother were very avid collectors, and so at times, when I was still at home, we were involved helping them sort things or removing stamps from the paper and so on. The family was engaged in the hobby at times, even though they were not collecting stamps. I made a little collection of Swiss stamps at the time, out of the duplicates that my father had, so I knew something about philately. And so I sought to give advice to my wife; I went with her to stamp shows that she wanted to attend and so on. She enjoyed stamp collecting for a while. And in that process, I began to develop a taste for it myself, and so my stamp collecting started in earnest, let's say, in 1950 and then it ended this year (2004).

Roger's memory of his conversion was vivid. The churches pastored by Albert Nicole did not have mid-week services; rather, the congregation gathered for Sunday morning worship only. This pattern was broken, however, with the coming of an evangelist by the name of Bernard de Perrot. He conducted a series of evangelistic meetings that included more lively singing than the psalms and hymns to which Roger had become accustomed. The evangelist really "reached the people" with his sermons, especially young Roger, who was just a week short of his eighth birthday. At the conclusion of one of the services, Roger responded to the evangelist's appeal to trust Jesus Christ as Lord and Savior. He remembered feeling a deep sense of sin ("I was shaking the bench in conviction"), recognizing the redemptive work of Jesus on his behalf, and committing himself freely to the Lord; in that moment he was converted. Roger kept the church card recording the event all his life.

The next year, de Perrot returned to the church. Roger again responded to the invitation, convinced that he had not lived for Christ in the preceding year. He made other public affirmations of commitment through the years that helped solidify his faith, and his father strongly encouraged his spiritual development. Roger was a participant in the International League for Bible Reading, an organization that promoted the daily intake of Scripture. On yet another visit by the evangelist, the town drunk, a man by the name of Rochat, was converted and became a faithful church member and singer in the choir. Unlike many other Reformed thinkers, Roger did not believe the "invitation system" was necessarily bad (if not abused).

Roger's father was a devoted pastor, well loved and appreciated by his congregation. One evidence of this affection was related to the particular difficulty Albert's blindness caused him at night. When the church added an evening meeting, an elder would gently lead him out of the church following the service. His preaching was textual in style. He prepared a typescript of a sermon, which a family member would read aloud to him until it was thoroughly familiar. Though he could see neither Bible nor sermon because of his blindness, he kept the open text of Scripture before him as he preached (the passage was known to him by heart). Albert also catechized the young, usually between the ages of fourteen and sixteen, before they were confirmed and admitted to Communion. He employed a catechism that he had written himself, based solely on the words of Jesus, entitled *Il Enseignait* ("He Taught"). Roger's brother was catechized by Albert at the church; Roger and Mariella only received some of the catechism at home (the family moved before they had opportunity to complete the training in the normal fashion). Thus, Roger became a communicant member when he was eighteen. Albert also was occupied with pastoral visitation in the homes of church members and with private instruction in Greek held at the Nicole home.

Albert once hosted a missions conference at the church. The missionary speaker was a black pastor from Angola named Mouholo. He illustrated his presentation with displays of items from the country, including a tarantula. Mouholo was well received by the congregation. Monetary collections for special events were typically small at the church; in fact, when the offering bag on the end of a pole was passed down each pew during *regular* services, the gathering usually was not substantial. Albert made a shocking announcement when the missionary completed his message: "I expect the offering tonight to be two hundred francs." His parishioners were stunned. But more than one third of the total was given by Albert, who donated (unbeknownst to his wife) seven gold coins Bertha had been saving in a closet. The incident taught the church (and Roger) a lesson about generosity in Christian stewardship.

The congregation's ideas about church finances were again tested when Albert challenged the church rummage sale, the favored way to make up for budget shortfalls. As pastor, Albert considered the practice worldly and not in keeping with the spiritual nature of the gospel. He tried unsuccessfully to convince the elders to stop the practice, and to encourage the people to give regularly and generously for the needs of the church. But he was no sore loser: he dressed Roger and Mariella in traditional mountain garb and allowed them to sell pears they had grown at exorbitant prices at the sale. Eventually, the church saw the wisdom of Albert's approach and abandoned the practice. Such vignettes further reinforced the graciousness that was to characterize Roger's life and ministry.

Albert did face two notable crises at the church. Seven years into his tenure, a female member who had studied at a liberal seminary began to cause turmoil. She tried to use her influence with her husband, a young elder at the church, to fill the pulpit with liberal guest preachers. There was a division among the elders, which led to disunity among the congregation (particularly, pitting older against younger members). The divisive woman's husband announced his unilateral invitation to a particular liberal preacher for a service; Albert announced that the man was *not* welcome, and that if he preached, the church would have his pastoral resignation (note from Roger: "don't play the resignation game"). Roger's father in turn invited a South African commissioner from the Salvation Army, a man who was "really ringing the bell" with his tremendous evangelical sermons. The messages on Jesus' experiences in Gethsemane were especially dramatic and memorable.

The other difficult situation arose when the Salvation Army preacher noted his disapproval of the Laufer Psalter, a hymnal prepared by one of the liberal seminary professors. The hymnal, though containing some six hundred hymns, had noticeably left out many that were decidedly evangelical. Albert, obviously, was opposed to it and the Salvation Army commissioner commented, "I've seen it, and it does not have 'Just As I Am Without One Plea' which is a truly great hymn. It is an enormously damaging collection." The troublesome woman said, "It *is* in there," and the guest preacher loudly rebuffed her in the presence of all (actually, two versions of the song were in use at the time, and the unfamiliar adaptation *was* in the hymnal). This led to even more hard feelings.

A New Testament professor from the liberal seminary representing the synodical commission came to remonstrate with Albert. For a whole hour he criticized what the commission viewed as an unsupportive attitude. He objected particularly to a statement Albert had made, "If I had a hundred sons, I'd send none of them to the seminary; instead, I'd send them to the Bible Institute to study with Dr. Saillens." The division in the church grew, and the resulting tension led to Albert's physical sickness that nearly proved fatal. He wrote a long letter to his mother about the ordeal, but he kept the day-to-day details from the children. Albert was ultimately vindicated: the troublesome female church member was eventually institutionalized for severe mental illness. Medically, Albert needed a change of climate from northern Switzerland. He made the move to Lausanne, to the great sadness of many of his parishioners (the choir came to sing to him under his parsonage window). There he taught for a year at the Emmaus Bible Institute as a professor of homiletics, doctrine, and biblical introduction. Roger's observation on that time in his father's ministry revealed a deep filial respect: "Dad was a good two cubits above other professors—that Bible Institute really lost out when he resigned."

Education was prized highly in the Nicole home. The seriousness of study was emphasized, and the order of "school first, then play" was strictly observed. Long before the current popularity of homeschooling, Roger received his tutelage at home until age eleven. Roger's first grade teacher in Sonvilier was Hélène Borle, a private tutor of kindly temperament in whose home Roger and the daughter of the eighth grade public school teacher were instructed. Roger was a diligent young scholar, excelling in all areas except writing, which gave him no small challenge. After a year of instruction under Miss Borle, another tutor named Miss Jacot (the daughter of an elder at Albert's church) came to teach him privately at the Nicole home. She guided Roger's schooling with a strong emphasis on academics through the second grade.

After Miss Jacot, Roger's principal educator was his father. Albert taught both Roger and Mariella in the disciplines of history, geography, French, and Latin; mathematics, however, received little attention. For geography lessons, Albert would employ his collection of some fifty thousand postcards. His favorite method was to provide a pile of these postcards for his young pupils to sort by countries and provinces, with the aid of a geographical dictionary. As a result, Roger developed a keen interest and facility in geography, which perhaps contributed to his lifelong love of philately. Roger and Mariella received a two-volume French encyclopedia ("I almost fainted with joy when that thing came out of the drawer where the presents were kept") in 1925, and Roger was given almanacs every year for Christmas. While the two younger Nicole children were enjoying a rigorous home education emphasizing history and Latin declensions, Jules Marcel was commuting by train to a school in another town. His only real academic weakness was French, which he overcame with the assistance of a tutor. Jules Marcel graduated with a B.A. in 1925, then went to Paris where he studied at the Bible Institute of Nogent-Marne and the Sorbonne (with a specialization in classical languages).

Albert Nicole noted during Roger's fifth-grade year that his younger son was weak in math. A professor of mathematics named Charles Perret was employed to give Roger six private lessons of one hour each. Perret, who held a doctor of science degree, helped Roger *to think mathematically*, a skill that proved tremendously advantageous in his later theological studies. After five of the contracted six lessons, Dr. Perret told him, "I believe that you are current with your classmates in math. I am going to show you something in advance of the program." He was behind his peers in math before; now, and for the rest of his early education, Roger was *ahead*. Later, when his fellows were studying geometry, he was working trigonometric problems; though calculus was not even supposed to be taught in his classical course of studies, Roger was advancing in that discipline as well. By the time he was nineteen, he was studying differential and integral calculus on his own and participating in mathematics competitions. This progress in arithmetic was augmented by his sincere love for the discipline, which led him to take an additional course in math each summer while on vacation. Roger actually read mathematics texts recreationally, commenting, "In math there are no external factors which modify your results; it is a super-sensory activity in which you are reaching pure truth—a wonderfully rewarding exercise for the mind."

Professor Perret had taught Roger how to extract square roots. He found this process of uncovering hidden mathematical relationships mentally gratifying. At the age of fifteen, Roger developed a method for extracting not only square and cubic roots, but even fifth roots and beyond, based on the Newtonian binomial. When he showed this to his current instructor, the teacher was dubious, but nonetheless encouraged the enthusiastic young scholar. Roger studied for a year at Gymnase de La Chaux-de-Fonds before the family left Sonvilier for Lausanne. At this secondary school, Roger enjoyed the company of other children and found that his home education had prepared him quite well for future academic challenges. He also recalled a memorable event of childhood folly that led to a rather severe illness:

> I had very weak health in my childhood, perhaps due in part to the privations suffered during World War I. Anyway, I was extremely susceptible to colds. If I became overexerted, I would often break into a sweat very quickly, catch a cold and sometimes even develop bronchitis. So I spent quite a number of days in bed as a child. During the time I was at La Chaux-de-Fonds, there had been snow one day, and for some idiotic reason, I filled my beret with snow and actually put it on my head to wear. The other boys thought I was very brave for doing this. Of course, I caught a severe cold with a high fever for more than a week. A spinster lady, the daughter of the chief elder in my father's church, said to me, "You are supposed to be intelligent, but this business about the snow is absolutely stupid!" What could I say? I certainly could not respond, "Oh, no, it was a very smart thing to do!"

CHAPTER 3

1928-1938
Lausanne and Paris

When the family moved to Lausanne, Roger attended a summer camp. He recalled that it was a good experience, especially for his social development and spiritual growth. While attending the camp the following year, he sensed that God was calling him to a ministerial vocation. Meanwhile, his parents were participants in the Swiss Keswick movement (Albert preached at some of the conferences). At one service, quite independent of each other, Albert and Bertha stood at an invitation to dedicate their children to God's service. There were no conditions placed on this consecration, even if their progeny should be called to the ends of the earth as missionaries. Thus, Roger was being set apart unmistakably for his future ministry.

Roger was exempted from Switzerland's compulsory military service on medical grounds when he turned nineteen. Under the government system, after an initiation of four months, two weeks of military training was mandated annually until age thirty-two. Those exempted had to pay a special tax in place of the military service. Even into his late forties, a Swiss male was on alert status. This gave the citizenry a national pride in their marksmanship. A popular anecdote spoke of an exchange between a Swiss national and a German: "We have a military of six hundred thousand men!" to which the German replied, "What if we come and invade you with one million two hundred thousand men?" The Swiss replied nonchalantly, "Two shots each!"

Swiss education involved two levels prior to the university. Primary education continued through the fourth grade, with secondary education following thereafter. Roger's academic prowess continued to manifest itself upon his arrival in Lausanne. The school was stricter than the Gymnase at La Chaux-de-Fonds in all areas except math, but Roger was still at the top of his class. In fact, for the entire seven years of his studies there, he never lost "first of class" status. He took French, spelling, literature, Latin (six hours or more per week), Greek, German, physics, chemistry, history, philosophy, gymnastics, geography, natural science, drawing, and mathematics. Roger was awarded the B.A. from Gymnase Classique in Lausanne in 1935.

Gymnase Classique was considered the second most demanding school in Switzerland, after Zurich. The grueling schedule of classes prepared Roger well for the Sorbonne. The highest mark was 10, but students that received an 8 could feel well satisfied. In fact, in the last year, a student who had achieved an average of 8 would be exempted from taking oral examinations. In 1935, Roger had maintained an average of 9 and was the only student who was thus exempted. No student during the previous five years had done better academically than Roger. He did have to take written examinations in Greek, Latin, German, analytic geometry, and French. The French essay was on Voltaire with the subject "All types of writing are good except boring writing." He was, by his own admission, "bookish" during his studies: during his last three years at Gymnase Classique he read one thousand pages a year in German alone. Roger's parents allowed him to have friends over for visits to allow for his social development, but only one at a time.

Roger Nicole was a beloved professor to his students throughout his teaching career, communicating a sense of Christ-like compassion and genuine concern in addition to theological knowledge. This quality derived in part from the positive examples to be emulated, and the negative examples to be avoided, of his own teachers. One such professor, Dr. Vaney, held a doctorate in mathematics from the University of Paris with Highest Congratulations (like *summa cum laude*) but had little classroom control, a fact which the students exploited by "goofing off." Another math teacher, Dr. Mellet, had been a civil employee in

Moscow, presiding over that city's streetcar system; he maintained better class discipline than his colleague Vaney. Charles Gilliard was one of Roger's "best ever" professors. In his teaching of history, he demonstrated the subject as a combination of causes, not merely dates and famous words; there was, for Gilliard, a *logic* in history that the professor was concerned to unveil for the student. He had a working knowledge of original source documents, and Roger enjoyed his three hours per week with this gifted scholar. "Some of my best professors—and some of my worst—I had in history," Roger observed.

When readers familiar with Roger Nicole think about him, the subject of inerrancy naturally arises. His stalwart defense of biblical integrity is legendary. Few individuals know, however, about a crucial formative experience he had in a philosophy class. Roger relates,

> In my last year, before the baccalaureate, I had a situation that was a very significant crisis of faith. The professor of philosophy who taught one hour per week in my classes had been a devotee of biblical criticism. But when he applied for ordination, he and another very distinguished candidate were refused by the Free Church of the Canton de Vaud because they were considered to be tainted with unbelief. He did not become a minister, but instead became a professor of German and of philosophy. During his lectures in philosophy, whether he realized it or not, he sought to justify his own standards before the class, and he made it a special point to undermine the principle of authority. Outright commitment to a book or a person, without benefit of reexamination, was unworthy of a true thinker, according to this teacher. In order to prove that point, he undertook to point to some errors that he felt were obviously present in Scripture, showing that people who had committed themselves to the Bible as the Word of God were doing the wrong thing, and were failing to exercise the proper discipline intellectually.
>
> The supposed errors that he chose were of such a nature that I could easily go to my father's library in order to find an explanation of what the Bible actually said there (in response to those who asserted that errors must be present in the Bible because of the involvement of human authors, Roger answered that "as sinners, in human activity we are *prone* to error, but we

are not *obliged* to error"). Therefore, I could return to class and show that what he claimed to be an error was, in fact, explainable in proper terms. There was with me another student who was a Roman Catholic and who obviously was also enduring difficulties since he felt that the tradition of the church and statements *ex cathedra* of the Pope were binding on his faith. There was also another student who was a member of the Plymouth Brethren, the strict type, who also believed in the inerrancy of Scripture as I did. We were therefore under considerable pressure because we respected this man very much. He was a man of exceptional ability. He had proven himself teaching German, at least as far as I was concerned, and now he was in his own field of specialization, the realm of philosophy. This was a discipline in which unquestionably he had a great deal of credibility.

And so throughout the term, from September to December, I was mainly concerned about this particular issue, the principle of authority. And while I could find an explanation for the errors that the professor mentioned, there still seemed to be some significance in his outlook on the problem of authority. Again, he had made it plain that anyone who abandoned his right of reexamination was really neglecting his responsibility as a thinking human being. Louis Gaussen's book on biblical inspiration, *Theopneustia*, helped me considerably at that time, but it did not resolve the original problem of the propriety of accepting the Bible simply as the Word of God, and not to give legitimacy to a reexamination of anything it teaches. The professor taught at the Gymnase in Lausanne, which was a secular school, so he was not bound to hold to any particular view as long as he was capable in the subjects that he taught, and that he certainly was. His name was Henri Miéville, and shortly after I graduated, he became Professor of Philosophy at the University of Lausanne. In essence, he was promoted from a professor in the secondary line of education to the highest level. And I would say he was highly competent for that. He published books that contributed to the philosophical corpus and which validated, in his view, his position.

Well, I sensed very deeply that if this professor was right, and that I was not permitted to accept the Bible as the Word of God without any further discussion, I would have lost my whole basis for faith. I would have no standard fence to prevent me from coming down into an abyss. I could sense myself being cornered, as it were, to maintain my faith contrary to what the professor said, or to move on and be suspended over the abyss, not knowing how deeply and how far I would go. I was a Christian, I knew myself to be converted, I had already sensed the call to ministry, and so this was a very, very serious problem for me. I spent as much as 30 hours a week just researching in this area, answering the problems and dealing with what other people had thought and written about authority, but without coming to a really decisive answer. So at the Christmas vacation, when my brother came back from the Paris Bible Institute where he was teaching, to Lausanne, where I resided, I told my brother, "I have a problem in philosophy. I want to talk with you about it." And my brother said, "Well that would be fine." And I said, "I have a problem on the matter of authority," and I explained to him the situation with the professor that I just described. I came down with the notes I had taken in class, opening my notes to the chapter dealing with the problem of authority. My brother wouldn't read THAT, he said, "What did he say before?" And I said, "Never mind what he said before, this is where my problem is, this is where it sticks." My brother said, "I want to see what he said before." I said, "Well, go right ahead, here are my notes for the whole course." And there was a point in which I had a chapter called "The Criterion of Truth" so my brother said, "What did he say there?" "He said what is very obvious," I replied, "that the criterion of truth is coherence; truth is tested by whether it fits with everything else." And my brother said, "Did you accept that?" And I said, "Of course, I accepted that, what else could I do?" And he said, "That's where your mistake came in. You have accepted a criterion of truth which he cannot prove, but which in your case eliminates the possibility there might be an element of truth that is beyond your check and that is, however, binding." My brother added, "When somebody talks about the criterion of truth, he is obliged to go beyond what he really can prove, because then he has to assume the truth of his approach in order to check whether his criterion is right. And if you have another criterion, he cannot dislodge you."

Now this was a very simple remark, yet so profound to me that we did not even have to go to the problem of authority. It was like a big flash of light, and suddenly all the clouds that I had in my mind were dissipated. I spent my Christmas vacation working up a new epistemology in which there might be a supreme criterion of truth that is what God has said, and a number of subordinate criteria of truth that would involve the feelings and the will as well. It would not just be an intellectual matter, but there were other factors that were part and parcel of what God has given us to test the truth. When in January the classes resumed, I went to see the professor and I said, "I think I have found the answer to the problem that we had during last term." I said, "I have come to the conclusion that my supreme criterion of truth must be Scripture, because this is God's Word, and then there are other criteria that can be applied in other matters but this has priority over everything else." And he looked at me and said, "You are impossible."

For me, that was a declaration of liberty; I was like a bird that had been in a cage and now the door had flown open. This was an experience of immense significance for me because it led me to discard rationalism, though not for lack of a sound alternative basis, but to discard it as a foundation. Everything became subservient to the Bible, and of course, that has been a foundational principle that has affected my whole career. The inerrancy of Scripture has been one of the major emphases in my teaching and writing career. And it goes right back to that moment. People may say that I had a psychologically traumatic experience, and that now I was attempting to defend my view even as the professor was trying to defend his. Maybe so, but this is what happened and this is the principle on which I feel I have the proper right, and even duty, to set the Word of God over any other kind of authority. This was a most important experience, affecting the total course of my life. I completed my degree happily; there was no great problem after that. But that one term was horrendous, because I was really tormented, feeling as though taken in a vise. I knew where the truth was, but I couldn't justify it. Conceding in the question of the criterion of truth, I had provided the professor with undue leverage. He had been unwise in his choice of errors he pointed to since I could resolve them. This was not a question of discussing concrete errors, but a question of methodology. And this incident was very significant on another level: it reinforced my confidence in my brother. In a very simple manner he just cleaned up the plate. He did exactly the right thing, asking, "What did he say before?" I didn't realize that I had unconsciously accepted what was said before, and that I should have never accepted it. And this was proven by the fact that when I told the professor, he didn't say "Well, I'm going to show you this is wrong." He said, "You are impossible." He gave up. Jules Marcel said, "In philosophy, don't make any concessions before you know what you are doing." It was a tremendous experience of liberation; I had a great Christmas that year. That was the end of the year 1934. I graduated in 1935, six months later with my 90 average. So the relation with the professor was not damaged, for I still had him for German. I did very well in German. I was reading 1,000 pages of German a year, so I was undoubtedly his best student in German. I still speak it now fairly fluently, although I have forgotten some of it. This was significant for my theological studies and also for my degree at the Sorbonne.

Roger Nicole was already something of a standout when he arrived at the University of Paris: he and a close family friend, Philippe Blocher, both had baccalaureates, whereas most students accepted at the Bible Institute of Nogent-Marne (where Nicole was also enrolled) had only a primary education. His three years as a resident student at the Bible Institute marked his first experience of living away from home:

Even though I was apart from the home, I was still very closely tied to my family: I was going back home for Christmas, for Easter vacation, and for the summer. This was the time I was enjoying mountaineering. During vacation my parents always went to an area of Switzerland that had a lot of mountains, so I had mountaineering experience most of the time with my brother, but in the final years even sometimes by myself. So that out of twelve months, I spent still four months at home, and only about eight months at the Bible Institute. Then at the Bible Institute my elder brother was teaching there, so on Sunday afternoons we would go on a long trek for 4-5 hours of walking and we had a chance to talk about all kinds of things. That was good for me too.

Because of his classical Greek background, Roger was excused from the New Testament Greek obligation at the Bible Institute. Since there was no attendance requirement at the University, Roger registered for many classes, dropped those not deemed necessary, and spent most of his study week at Nogent-Marne.

The studiousness that Roger had developed over his young lifetime stood him in good stead at the Sorbonne (University of Paris). Roger was growing in his eagerness to know Scripture, and he studied and memorized passages diligently. During his first year at the University of Paris, he labored at Latin and Greek, with a full program of study also in the summer. The second year was devoted to French literature and to philology. Grading was extremely severe. The scale ranged from one to twenty, with twenty being the best; an average of 10 was needed to pass. Specific proficiency certificates had to be earned in each discipline as prerequisites to the M.A. for teaching. A final examination was the only basis for grading the students. In a typical class of six hundred students, three-fourths would be flunked in the written examinations.

After the subsequent oral examinations, the class would be further reduced to one hundred twenty students. Of these fortunate remaining students, ninety would "just pass" with a grade of 10-12; twenty five would achieve a mark of 12-14 ("fairly good"); and 5 would receive a grade of 14-16 ("good"). Only rarely would anyone make a grade of 16-18 ("very good"). Roger received a "fairly good" in Latin, Greek, and philology (on one particular oral exam in philology he actually received the coveted mark of 18); he managed a "good" in French literature, a discipline with which he struggled as compared to those who were natives of France. Roger's studies in philology helped him learn the diversity of languages necessary for a lifetime of scholarly work. He developed great facility with English, Latin, Greek, French, German, and Dutch. He could work well with Hebrew, though "vocabulary was lacking."

This was the basis for a memorable experience from his time at the Sorbonne. During the 1930s, the theater was considered "off limits" to conscientious evangelical Christians. Films were not considered scandalous (in fact, Roger recalled seeing a film about the growth of plants, as well as one about the 1936 Olympics), but going to the theater was censured because of the known immorality of the actors. Three of the plays being studied by Roger's French literature class were to be performed for the students by the best actors of the stage. A definite advantage at examination time was to be gained by attending the performance. But for Roger to attend the theater would have been considered by some to be a compromise of his evangelical convictions. In the end, Roger decided not to go, though he definitely needed whatever help he could potentially gain in French. Roger recalled, "I was studying to prepare for a lifetime of service to God; I decided I must not compromise to gain advantage." Later in his life, Roger would become a teetotaler with alcohol and tobacco in America, though this had not been his conviction in Switzerland. He always sought to manifest a sense of responsibility to the larger Christian community. His irenic and statesmanlike spirit was evident in his assertion that whenever there are two genuine believers who disagree, they can always agree to pray.

On the written exam, Roger was given an essay question from *Gargantua and Pantagruel* by François Rabelais, dealing with the monastery of Thelema as a demonstration of the freethinking morality of the satirist. The examination lasted four hours: 1 hour 50 minutes to write, break with a baguette, then another 1 hour 50 minutes. Roger ran out of time, but turned in both rough and final copies. Students were not allowed a single mistake in spelling; Roger scored a sixteen. At the oral examination, Roger witnessed a fellow student's ordeal with a Victor Hugo question that did not go well. Roger drew Blaise Pascal ("right up my alley"), whose connections with mathematics and apologetics made him an easy subject for Roger. He scored a "good" in French, placing him in the 99th percentile among students in Paris at that time. Roger learned a valuable lesson: he had decided to honor God and his Christian commitments by not attending the theater before the exam, even though it would have given him a great academic advantage. In turn, God blessed him with a written essay in his area of proficiency (Rabelais/morality) and Roger was given a verbal exam in a subject with which he was very comfortable (Pascal/mathematics and apologetics). Roger commented, "I was God's servant, not the servant of the M.A. Of course I realize that I don't fit at all in the ninety-ninth percentile of Sorbonne students examined in the course of 'French Language and Literature.' This obviously to me was a pure gift of God, proving to me concretely that God can and does take care of those who make obedience to Him a true priority."

Roger received the M.A. from the Sorbonne in the fall of 1937, as the storm clouds of war were gathering ominously on the horizon. No formal ceremony attended this prestigious event in his life; in fact, students could expect to receive their diplomas only several years after graduation. Roger received his diploma nine years later, duly signed by the French secretary of education. At the Bible Institute he completed the whole program and taught French for a time to missionaries preparing to minister in Africa, and he studied English for six months in anticipation of going to America. Roger desired to go to Gordon Divinity School in Massachusetts for advanced theological study because, like his brother, he wished to study "in a school of faith rather than in a school of doubt."

Concurrent with his studies at the University of Paris, Roger earned a certificate from the Bible Institute of Nogent-Marne. His time at the Institute was bittersweet, for he had a difficult relationship with the director, Miss Saillens. He was, however, able to study with his brother, who taught on the faculty. This was a trial of sorts as well. Roger greatly loved and respected his brother, but he was very severe on Roger academically, requiring near perfection. Roger's classmates even interceded with Jules Marcel on his behalf, pleading for some leniency. The conflict with Miss Saillens had much to do with Roger's independent spirit ("one must go his own way and not kowtow to authority figures") and his prodigious knowledge. She was intimidated by the young theologian, fearing that he might try to embarrass her in front of the other students. When Roger's parents, who were good friends of Miss Saillens, learned of this, Mrs. Nicole assured her that "Roger is better trained than that." Roger and his best friend, an evangelist by the name of Georges-Ali Maire, decided on their own initiative to brush up the front porch and grounds of the Institute. This project served two purposes: the tension between the director and Roger was eased, and a lesson was reinforced which was to characterize Roger's entire career as a scholar and Christian statesman: be pleasant even to those with whom you disagree.

Georges-Ali Maire was Roger's roommate at the Bible Institute the first year he was there, and since he was Swiss rather than Belgian or French, the two developed a close friendship. When Roger came back to Europe, he would visit Georges and "it wouldn't take a minute for us to rejoin as if we had been together the whole time; we never got estranged from one another; we always had a perfect understanding." Georges had a significant disappointment in that he had intended for a long time to go to Laos, which had mission work by the Plymouth Brethren, but when he had done his work at the Bible Institute, somehow since he was not part of the Brethren movement, they did not accept him for missionary appointment. Roger was there to offer consolation. Then Georges went to be a missionary in Savoie, just south of Lake Geneva. It was a mainly Catholic area, he had an effective gospel work there, and it was also the birthplace of some of his children. After that, World War II came, and during the war he was back in Switzerland working as an evangelist in the town of Colombier. Roger fondly remembered,

> He had a very fine ministry, a wonderful family with six children, one of whom sadly died when she was sixteen. His two sons went to Africa as missionaries and two of the daughters were married and were involved in Christian work, one in Switzerland and one in French Canada. The oldest girl, who was very supportive when her mother was extremely ill, married a postal employee who was a member of the church where Georges ministered. Really his whole family grew in the Lord, and so it was a wonderful example of having a family in which the members really were close. That was extremely important for my life because it was the first time I got *that* close to people who were not part of my family circle. In our family my parents did not favor much contact outside with other kids. My friendship with Georges was a marked change for me. I was greatly challenged by him and he says I am the one who taught him how to do mental work, how to think; I was working on my master's degree at the same time I was going to the Bible Institute. I said, "Let's take two hours for work, then we'll take a quarter-hour for rest." He had been a watchmaker of great skill, a trade with which he supported his family for some time. Georges was older than most students when he came to the Bible Institute, about twenty-nine. His fiancée was doing work at the Bible Institute to help pay for his expense, so I knew her also. This happened between 1935 and

1938. I was present at his marriage. I came down from Paris to La Côte-aux-Fees there in Switzerland for this occasion.

Philippe Blocher was another significant friend to Roger during this time, though his influence was marked by some sadness:

One friend I had in the Bible Institute who was not that close, but became closer, was Philippe Blocher. Philippe was studying at the Bible Institute but he was not living there. He was living with his mother (his father had been the pastor of the largest Baptist church in Paris and probably the largest in all of France). Philippe's father had married the daughter of Dr. Saillens, who was the president of the Bible Institute. When Philippe's father died in 1929, Mrs. Blocher took over the pastorate, and she was very conscious of the possibilities of ministry for women. In fact, she was a significant figure in my journey towards biblical egalitarianism. For fifty years I was not an egalitarian in the full sense; only in the last 35 years or so has this really matured. I had some strong incentives not to be egalitarian, because the sharpest conflict I may ever have had with a professor was with this egalitarian woman who was very overbearing. I was trying to oppose her wherever I could, even to the point of saying, "I think that Esau was better than Jacob because he was more forthright" and she challenged me on that. Well, it is not really difficult to find fault with Jacob! She herself was serving as a pastor and was very sensitive on that point. This woman was a superb preacher, very biblical and quite powerful in her use of Scripture. She was being criticized harshly, and sometimes in an unchristian way, by some people who were very staunch conservatives. And she was taking it out on the class, giving a better grade to the women than, say, to me because I had a degree from the Sorbonne and, even though my work was better, she would give a lower mark to me simply because I was a man. It did not really do me any harm, but it tended to put me in a confrontational mood. What *did* move me toward egalitarianism was the total teaching of the Bible.

Philippe Blocher went to Spurgeon's College in 1936 and he found there a whole lot of biblical criticism that had come in and undermined his confidence in the Bible, even to the point that a professor thought Isaiah was not really talking about Christ. So he went into business rather than ministry, where his exceptional gift would have been very beneficial. This shift was very significant for me because, by contrast, I was getting reinforced in my belief in the Scripture. I remember I wrote a long letter to Philippe to try to get him back, and I showed it to my brother, and my brother said, "Do you have a copy of this for yourself?" I said, "No, I haven't thought about that." He said, "You've got some good stuff in there; maybe you better not just send it there and be done." That shows that I was moving in the direction of inerrancy, without having the close inspection of particular parts of the Scripture, just in a general way. Philippe Blocher's course was for me an example not to follow.

CHAPTER 4

1938-1945
Gordon Divinity School

Having completed his studies at the Bible Institute in the summer of 1938, Nicole prepared earnestly for his education at Gordon. He was acquainted with the school because of his brother's experience, but it was no easy task to get there. Nicole had to make the trip to the consulate in Zurich to apply in person for his visa. The paperwork was done swiftly (by July 1938) and he hoped to get an invitation to the consulate in August. The first two weeks of August passed, but no summons was forthcoming. Nicole was required to produce a small mountain of documents. His parents had funds to help with this process, but they were frozen by this time in Germany. Passage was booked for Nicole on a ship to America, and his mother had gone to Frankfurt to await him. At the last moment, the consulate in Zurich required a birth certificate from Charlottenburg (being a Swiss citizen, he had obtained a birth certificate from Geneva, but this was administratively unacceptable). Nicole eventually obtained the document, but too late for the scheduled passage. He arrived at Gordon a month late for the start of the semester.

The challenges were to continue for Roger Nicole upon his arrival at Gordon. He only had six months of English training prior to this, supplemented by tutoring from Jules Marcel. Roger practiced his English skills with his brother during their mountain-climbing excursions, but the elder Nicole only answered "So do I!" to everything Roger said. The peculiarities of the English idiom ("hot dog" and "cut it out") gave Roger particular trouble. And though he started the semester at Gordon late due to circumstances beyond his control, Roger received no special dispensation from his professors. He was responsible for the entirety of the book of Romans; complete summaries for Dr. Byington on the history of doctrine; and he was required to preach in English for his homiletics class. Nicole met these tests with typical aplomb. The registrar asked him to preach at a gospel mission at Thanksgiving—after only two months at Gordon—at which time Roger knew "I had to sink or swim."

Nicole had a strong desire to earn his living through pastoral ministry. The Bachelor of Divinity (B.D.)[2] degree at Gordon was designed to be completed in three years. Since he already possessed an M.A. from an esteemed university, the administration was willing to allow him to finish in two years. Nicole insisted on completing the program in one year. The directors were dubious, but by November they consented, on the condition that he study full time with no outside employment. Two months later, due to his extraordinary progress, the administration agreed even to let him work if he wanted. No French churches were open, however, until May 1939. This was also the time when Nicole made an important acquisition not related to citizenship or academics:

> I got my first car in 1939; it was a 1933 Chevy. I bought it for $75. It was very useful for ministry. Before that I was walking all through Worcester. There was a member of my church who was a student at Gordon College, so I could get rides with him. Later on, he taught me how to drive, so I eventually received my driving license. That was a significant development for me, since nobody in my family had a car. My father could not have been driving, obviously, because he was practically blind.

Nicole's commitment to the inerrancy of Scripture was further refined in the writing of his B.D. thesis. Sixty-seven years later, the process was still clear in his mind:

> In the beginning of 1939, I had to prepare my thesis in order to receive the B.D. degree. I chose to deal with the attitude of Jesus toward the Old Testament Scriptures in particular, but

---

[2] This is equivalent to the currently offered M.Div. (Master of Divinity) degree.

also relating to some extent to His stance on the New Testament. I chose this topic because I felt that His attitude toward biblical revelation must determine my attitude, and so I decided to title the thesis "Jesus and the Bible in Relation to the Inspiration of Scripture." That led me to discover B. B. Warfield, a very important factor in my further development as an inerrantist. In fact, the first thing that President Wood (my advisor) told me to do was to "check on Warfield." Of course, there was this great book, *Revelation and Inspiration*, in the 10-volume set of Warfield's works. Here I found in much greater depth what I had seen only briefly sketched in the work of Gaussen. I found in Warfield a very careful study of particular elements in the doctrine of inspiration, grounded in the proper understanding of what Scripture itself shows about it. This was a broader scope than what I wanted to cover, but it gave me great confidence in the propriety of studying inspiration on the basis of the Bible itself. Since I wanted to take particularly the attitude of Jesus on the subject, I was led to consider three approaches.

Nicole's first approach was to examine what Jesus expressly said about Scripture in those passages where Scripture itself was the object of attention. This would include passages like Matthew 5:17-18, "Do not think that I have come to abolish the Law or the Prophets; I have not come to abolish them but to fulfill them. For truly, I say to you, until heaven and earth pass away, not an iota, not a dot, will pass from the Law until all is accomplished." Other passages of that type were John 5:39, "You search the Scriptures because you think that in them you have eternal life; and it is they that bear witness about me" and John 10:35, "Scripture cannot be broken." He also considered the passages about Jesus after His resurrection, where He upbraided the disciples on the road to Emmaus for their lack of insight into the Old Testament revelation about Himself. He noted that Jesus developed what the whole Old Testament taught concerning Himself—Law, Prophets, and Psalms. Thus, he studied those specific passages in which Jesus dealt with the Scripture itself and expressed in what ways it is subject to trust on the part of those who want to follow Him. A careful consideration of those passages provided a crucial foundation for his thesis.

His second line of investigation considered the instances where Jesus simply quoted Scripture. He wanted to determine how often Jesus supported His own teaching by elements that were found in the Old Testament. What he discovered was that Jesus was invariably affirming the veracity and historicity of Old Testament Scripture. Jesus sought to accredit His own teaching with the people who heard Him by appealing to the Old Testament for support.

Third, he considered the ways in which Jesus positively fulfilled the Scripture. Jesus fulfilled Scripture in the perfect obedience to the Law under which He came. He also did this through specific events in His life that actually fulfilled elements found in prophetic Scripture. Nicole was interested, for instance, in why certain prophecies *must* be fulfilled as they were (e.g., Matthew 26:54) in the life of Jesus.

Thus three avenues of very strong support of Scripture by Jesus were examined in his thesis. Particularly on Jesus' use of quotations, it was important for his study that Jesus not simply *mention* the Scripture, but that He mention it in a way that observes that this is God's Word. An example would be Matthew 19:4 where He queried the Pharisees, "Have you not read that he who created them from the beginning made them male and female and said . . .?" (Genesis 2:24). Clearly, this was not a statement of God in the Old Testament. It was part of the narrative of Moses, but Jesus claimed that God said it! Obviously, it was Moses by the direction of the Holy Spirit who said this. But Jesus, in quoting as He did, chose not merely to allude to Scripture, but to indicate the kind of confidence He had in the Scripture as being the Word of God. Nicole studied very carefully at this point the introductions to the quotations by Jesus.

Having done that, he considered elements from the negative perspective, where someone might aver that Jesus seemed to acknowledge some limitations in the Scripture. The most important instances of this category were the discussions on the Sabbath and the relative purity of foods, as well as the end of Matthew chapter 5, where Jesus seemed to set aside some Old Testament laws. Jesus was in conflict with the Jewish leaders at that time about the Sabbath, and that might seem to abrogate the law of the Sabbath as it is contained in the Old Testament. This led Nicole to consider very carefully all the discussions about the Sabbath, and he found that there were three things for which Jesus was under attack. First, Jesus condoned Sabbath violation in permitting the disciples to pick wheat as they were passing by. Second, He commanded violation in telling the paralytic at Bethesda to pick up his mat on the Sabbath. Third, He personally violated the Sabbath by performing healings on that day. Furthermore, He indicated a limitation to the Sabbath law by saying things like "the Son of Man is Lord of the Sabbath." This would, in the minds of some, be a rejection of the law of the Sabbath as part of Scripture. Such would give the impression that He had the right to change that law, as if God had not given it irrevocably.

Nicole found in his research that none of those elements really were present. In fact there was nothing that prohibited healing, especially healing by faith, on the Sabbath. So the supposed violation of the Sabbath by Jesus was really a violation of the Jewish *interpretation* of what is involved in the Sabbath rest, rather than a violation of what Moses actually enjoined (Deuteronomy 23:25). Second, in connection with the disciples passing by and eating the wheat on the Sabbath, it is clear that Jesus did not suggest that it was permissible to harvest on the Sabbath; that would be a clear violation. Rather, He taught that when a person is very hungry then it is not really a violation. Jesus took as a precedent the way in which David ate the showbread in the temple. The interest was in the survival of God's anointed, and that was more important than a ritual prescription that ordinarily should be binding. Thus the statement that Jesus presented at that point indicated a certain gradation in the Law, where in a conflict one portion would have precedence over another portion. He showed that of course this was the case because the priests in the Temple were working on the Sabbath. That was a pivotal part of His answer: there was some sort of consideration that had priority over a mere attachment to the principle of "do not work," and it was the notion that priests may work on the Sabbath with impunity. When He said that He was Lord of the Sabbath, what Jesus meant was not, "I have the right to rest or not to rest on the Sabbath," but "I am the One Who came from God to tell you how to interpret the Scripture." His meaning was, "I am Lord of the Sabbath, rather than the teachers of the Law, because I am the One Who really understands what God wants." So the situation of the Sabbath clearly does not violate the respect for and acceptance of the Scripture by Jesus.

Another line of investigation was the situation when Jesus discussed the laws of purification. The Jews had multifarious rules about how to purify things, and Jesus encountered their hypocritical fastidiousness in Mark 7 and Matthew 15. In those texts the question was "Why do You allow Your disciples to come into a meal without washing their hands?" Of course there were some laws of purification delineated in the Old Testament Scriptures, but they were not violated on this occasion; there was nothing about the ritual washing of hands before a meal. There were special purifications for the priests, as well as for an Israelite defiled by covenantal uncleanness. But this was not involved in the case with Jesus' disciples, so in connection with that Jesus made the statement that seemed to set aside certain laws held dear by the Jews. He declared that what enters into a man is not what soils him; rather, it is what comes out of a man that is really the source of the stain that God detests. And Mark adds the parenthetical note "thus he declared all foods clean." Here was apparently a direct conflict with the Scripture, for the Old Testament surely states that there are certain foods that are clean and others that are unclean. Incidentally, Peter was faced with this same truth in Acts 10.

Nicole determined that in the incident of the disciples' inattention to hand washing, Jesus was dealing with the transitory character of some elements in the law that were given as object lessons to the Jews. They failed to understand that God wanted them to obey the physical requirement, but He also sought to teach them spiritual truth through their obedience. What God taught is that the world has some things that are not clean, and the one who is his servant needs to observe that point. But the uncleanness that is most significant in the eyes of God is the uncleanness of human hearts; that is the source of all kinds of evil. The uncleanness of the body by comparison is relatively irrelevant, and it is merely an object lesson rather than a permanent disposition. Therefore Jesus showed how immature was the application of the Pharisees, as presumptive teachers of the Law, developing more and more uncleanness in small things (even far beyond what the Law prescribed) and how they were ignoring the fundamental uncleanness which is really most distasteful to God. Jesus dared to suggest that the Pharisees had made void the Word of God by their tradition. So this passage, far from saying that the Old Testament is irrelevant (and some things can therefore be omitted in it) says that the Old Testament is the Word of God, and what the Pharisees had developed was the tradition of men, which really ought not to be pressed.

Finally, there was the great passage in Matthew 5, in the Sermon on the Mount, where it seemed that Jesus repudiated the Old Testament law at several points, at least according to some interpreters. This was the instance when Jesus declared that it was commanded them of old not to kill, not to commit adultery, not to divorce, not to forswear oneself, not to take vengeance, and to love one's neighbor while hating one's enemy. Nicole noted that one should begin that study by observing that this follows another explicit statement by Jesus that He was not going to bypass the Law, but that all would be fulfilled even in the smallest details. Surely no one but a fool would then proceed to repudiate forthwith some of the Ten Commandments written by the very "finger of God!" Any interpretation of those passages which would show unity between what He said and Old Testament truth should have preference over a consideration that He somehow bypassed the Old Testament. Specifically, there were six elements that Nicole examined for the B.D. thesis to see if in fact Jesus repudiated the Old Testament law.

For the first point, the commandment not to kill, the repudiation would actually be, "You go ahead and kill if you want—I free you now from the obligation to have restraint!" But Jesus did not say that. What He did was to ask in effect, "What is it that leads people to murder?" Obviously, it is hatred, it is jealousy, it is anger and Jesus said if one is angry, that one is subject to judgment. To call one's brother *raca*, or fool, is to actually trespass God's law. So what Jesus was condemning was not only the finished act of murder, in which the physical life of a human being is taken away, but also the feelings and attitudes that in the worst cases may lead to murder. So the Law ought to be understood, not merely in the most superficial way, as simply forbidding murder in a physical sense; rather, the Law has to be understood in the light of human relationships to other people, whether hostile or supportive. Here Nicole noticed that, instead of bypassing the Law, Jesus insisted on rightly understanding the Law. This was not done in a mere letter-like application, but also with an understanding of the foundation of God's giving of the Law and what God manifested as His own attitude toward people who are sinning. Jesus was not saying, "Go ahead and kill." That would be an obvious repudiation. Jesus was saying, "I want to show you that if you really want to understand this portion of the Law, and if you really want to please God, it is not enough that you don't go around committing murders. You must squelch within your own heart the dispositions which in the worst cases do actually lead to murder." As Nicole put it, "God condemns murder, not only in its *fruitage* but also in its *rootage*."

The same thing was true of course with adultery. Jesus did not say, "Go ahead and be promiscuous if you like." On the contrary, He understood that what is first and foundationally wrong is the lustful look outside of the marriage relationship. For a man to look at a woman and covet her sexually is to have already violated what God wants. Nicole commented that "dirty thoughts are not pleasing to God; therefore, it does not have to be a finished act that violates the marriage covenant. The danger, the root wickedness, is the kind of disposition that leads ultimately to adultery in some of the worst cases. This is very plain."

Next was the situation of divorce, and that was studied not only in Matthew 5, but also in Matthew 19. There he found that Jesus made a statement that seemed to abrogate the Law when He said in essence, "Moses, for the hardness of hearts, gave the prescription that a bill of divorcement was required to dissolve a marriage." There appeared to be a toleration of divorce in some cases, and that seemed to be contrary to the law of marriage. In that connection Jesus related Himself to two interpretations of divorce law already present in the Jewish world at that time, Rabbi Hillel's and Rabbi Shammai's. Jesus lined up with Shammai, agreeing that the law of divorce was given in order to restrict divorce and not to expand divorce. One had to have a *bill* of divorcement, which meant people who could not write had to wait until the next day in order to get that written down. This would serve, in effect, as a "cooling off" period. Furthermore, the woman could not simply be sent back to her father without consideration of whether this was permanent or just a temporary fit of anger. Also, it involved the question of the dowry—if the woman was repudiated, probably the dowry she brought into the marriage would have to be returned. All of these were elements that "slowed up" the process and helped prevent the breakdown of marriages. So clearly, Moses did not take the initiative of bypassing the law of God; instead, in God's name he provided that particular arrangement which in the worst cases might be necessary because people just could not get along, or else when one of the spouses might be considered a threat to the children.

This was obviously not a bypassing of the Law. This was a recognition that marriage is a fundamental establishment of God that has to last as long as both partners are alive, though there are, sadly, certain circumstances in which a separation occurs. Such separation does not leave the parties free to remarry, however, if the divorce was for something other than adultery. In such a case both parties have to remain unmarried; the marriage is still binding on them, even though they may not be together. This prescription was given because people are sinners, and because therefore the marriage union (which was meant to be a development of peace and blessing for both parties) can become sometimes unbearable in terms of the sinfulness of one or both of the partners. This passage, therefore, reaffirmed the authority of the original text of Genesis 2 as being not only a statement of Moses or of Adam himself, but as being really what God has said for all time. That defines authoritatively the nature of marriage, but the presence of sin has at times damaged what would have been ideally a permanent relationship as long as both parties are alive. This example is a validation of the Old Testament Scripture as limiting the random tendency in the Ancient Near East for a husband to dismiss summarily his wife, and that without consideration for her own interests and rights. This case is somewhat more complex than the first two, but it still manifests a support of Scripture in taking the Genesis passage as fundamental for an understanding of marriage, rather than anything the scribes and Pharisees tried to say. Concerning the reason why a principle might have been given "because of the hardness of hearts," it could be argued that God established some sacrifices because of the hardness of hearts. Surely if Adam and Eve had remained faithful at the beginning there would have been no need of sacrifice of any kind. So some of the Old Testament Law represented a gracious condescension by God to a sinful humanity that had already damaged the most basic principles of the Creator/creature relationship.

According to Nicole, the next case was very easy—"don't forswear yourself." Jesus said in essence, "Can't you see here? God is interested in the truth per se, and not only when it is preceded by a solemn formulation that binds you." He taught elsewhere that persons should not swear by heaven (cf. also Matthew 23:16-22)—there is obvious confusion about what is a valid binding, and people are looking for ways to get away with lying. This was a very wrong emphasis in what the Pharisees taught, and Jesus countered that God wants the truth to be spoken all the time—"let what you say be simply 'Yes' or 'No'"—not only when there is present a specific formula to declare, "I am not going to lie now, you can be sure, I really mean it!" So on that account Jesus did not mean that any kind of oath or swearing was always and in all cases forbidden. Later in the New Testament record the apostle Paul called God as his witness, so the Quaker interpretation that this means never to swear, not even in court, is without substantial foundation. What Jesus was protesting was not the propriety of some solemn oaths being given at times, but rather the tendency of people to consider themselves free to tell lies when they had no specific oath to bind them. That is really the same heart principle as the prohibition against murder. When God commands, "Don't forswear yourself, but keep your oaths," He is not merely attempting to strengthen the significance of oaths; He is showing that the divine interest is in truth under any circumstances.

The fifth element involved the *lex talionis*, the concept of "an eye for an eye and a tooth for a tooth" (Exodus 21:24; Leviticus 24:20; Deuteronomy 19:21). Jesus taught, however, that one should not take vengeance at all. Here Nicole perceived this was a passage that seemed to involve a contradiction. The Old Testament Law clearly taught an eye for an eye, and that implied vengeance. Then Jesus said there was to be no vengeance; this appeared to be opposition. At this point the commentator Adolf Schlatter helped him. Schlatter wrote that the original statement was meant to limit the level of penalty that could be imposed because of some damage committed. But the tendency in human beings is to take a bigger vengeance than the original damage. The inclination of sinners is to want not an *eye* for an eye but a *neck* for an eye! There is a limitation involved here, one that establishes the principle, not of personal retaliation, but rather of guidelines for the judges to assess the penalty for damages committed. The intent was obviously to determine what kind of tort exists at the level of the court, rather than an official permission for people to avenge themselves up to a certain point.

So Nicole deduced from this passage in the Sermon on the Mount that God is not pleased with the principle of vengeance on the part of individuals. That truth is found in Proverbs and later in Romans (Prov 20:22; 24:29; Rom 12:14), so Jesus was teaching that the original statement in the Torah did not validate a right for people to retaliate. Rather, it was an expression of the kind of limitation that must be present even in the way the court establishes what may need to be done in order to correct a damage that was caused by one person to another. God Himself will avenge as a judge. God does not like the spirit of retaliation in the hearts of people, and He is not interested merely in limiting this, although the Old Testament could perhaps be understood in that way. He is interested in the suppression of bitterness in the hearts of people, so that when a wrong is suffered, vengeance does not prevail. God wants persons to have a peaceful approach. This is developed in the teaching of Jesus that if somebody is in need of one's cloak, something else should be given as well; if one is slapped by a person on the right cheek, the left should be offered as well. Jesus showed that the Law really condemns the spirit of vengeance, but once again the pride of the Pharisees had misinterpreted that and instead considered that this provided an official right to vengeance, albeit in a limited way. Nicole noted that the commandment "prevented the vengeance from snowballing, because if you have a neck for an eye, the next person will say, 'You killed one of ours, now we are going to kill five of yours,' and the vengeance grows worse and worse. In that scenario, there is always some more grievous offense to be repaired, and then people go beyond the bounds, and that precipitates the perpetuation and increase of evil."

The final element was the consideration of loving neighbors and hating enemies. Here it seemed that Nicole had "finally met a real defeat, a statement of Jesus that was directly contradictory to the other statements." Instead of hate your enemy, Jesus said to love your enemy. Nicole's first consideration at that point was to discover where the concept of hating one's enemy was commanded in Scripture. The Bible teaches in Leviticus 19 the principle of loving one's neighbors, but there is no corollary commandment to hate one's enemies. This is found neither in Leviticus nor anywhere else in Scripture. Of course what the Jews understood by the love of neighbors meant love for *Jewish* neighbors; outside of that, Israelites were free to hate as much as they wanted! Jesus demonstrated here that an enemy is a neighbor as well. Persons are obligated to love that enemy, unconditionally. It was an inappropriate extrapolation of the law to love one's neighbor to say, "My enemy is not my neighbor, so I have no obligation to him." That was a restriction of the Law that was not present in the Law. Some might object that in Psalm 139 there is the statement, "Do I not hate those who hate you, O LORD? And do I not loathe those who rise up against you? I hate them with complete hatred; I count them my enemies." But here it is not so much people that hate *me* (the individual) but people that hate *you* (God); these are the ones that believers have to shun, or at least not to imitate. Hatred in that sense is the hatred of evil, but it must not be transferred to *people* considered to be evil. The demands of love apply even to enemies, and therefore Jesus said believers are to love their enemies and bless those who persecute them. He distinguished between the Law as it was explicitly stated ("Love your neighbor") and an interpretation of that Law ("Your neighbor is not every person, but only some persons") by the Jewish leaders.

Thus, Nicole discovered that in this section of the Sermon on the Mount, there was not a single repudiation of the Law. This should not be surprising, since "Jesus stated incontrovertibly that he was *not* coming to do that!" Objectors might say, "That is not Jesus, that is Matthew reconstructing this passage!" Nicole's response was, "Well, Matthew was not an imbecile either! Matthew would not set himself in flat contradiction to the assertion of Jesus that he came not to abolish the Law but to fulfill it." And that fulfillment of the Law was due to a resolute understanding of the law in terms of God's purpose, rather than simply in terms of some limitation in the actual circumstances of living. Jesus showed that the Law has its origin in God Himself and is reflective of His character, and it is therefore not just like human laws that are made "in order to corral human beings." By giving the spiritual explanation of what the Law involves, Jesus made the highest possible recognition of the Law as being essentially spiritual. This is reasonable, since God, the Lawgiver, is a spiritual being.

Nicole noted at this point that "New Covenant Theology" is wrong in thinking that the Law of God is no longer binding for the Christian. He commented that "fortunately, the proponents of New Covenant Theology do recognize that these principles I have mentioned are present in the New Testament, and therefore they are not throwing away the whole bit. What they *are* throwing away is a unity between the Old and New Testaments in interpreting the will of God." Thus, Jesus is the One Who provided the right understanding of what the Law implies, and He certainly did not reject the Law! He validated the Law for Christians as a means of living a life well pleasing to the God who has saved them. So, the performance of the Law is not a meritorious function by which believers accredit themselves with God. That would be contrary to justification by faith alone. Rather, the observance of the Law is a careful examination of God's own intent for His people, with a desire to live a life that is in accordance with His purpose and with His truth. True faith does not hesitate to go beyond the letter to understand the spirit and apply it to daily life.

Nicole stated that those last two elements (not taking vengeance and loving one's enemies) so definitely affirm the Law, that when people want to object in some way to the Old Testament, "I do not even mention them because I know *they* will. And the moment they do, the Lord has delivered them into my hands, because it is absolutely crazy to interpret this passage as rejecting the Old Testament. Instead, this passage is a most moving acceptance of the Old Testament, and provides a bedrock hermeneutical principle." That concept has to do with a proper understanding of the Old Testament as going beyond the mere letter to reveal God's outlook, along with the human responsibility to fulfill it. An example from domestic life illustrates this truth. Suppose a man's wife tells him she does not like the dust she sees on a particular picture in the living room. Of course, because the husband knows and loves his wife, he understands that she does not mean she is only concerned about the dust on *that particular picture*. She is indicating her desire to live in a neat, clean home without dust on any surface. The astute husband interprets this in terms of her disposition: what is it she likes and what is it she dislikes. When someone is in love, they want to provide what the beloved likes rather than what the beloved dislikes. That is what makes for a harmonious relationship in marriage. If the wife sees dust on the picture and comments about it, she has already indicated that she does not like it on the object *over there* either!

This is what Nicole found to be so significant at this stage of the thesis: Jesus interpreted the Old Testament Law in terms of God Himself being the Lawgiver. That is especially true when He says *Moses* gave you this (the prescription for limiting divorce). Clearly, that was not an initiative of Moses, who bypassed the purpose of God and violated it; rather, it was a remedy that God Himself had provided to handle the damage done by sinful human hearts to the beautiful institution of marriage. His thesis conclusion after all this was that in fact Jesus unequivocally, throughout His whole career, supported the authority of the Old Testament as coming from God. This was apparent in what He said expressly, in what He did in his own life, in what He quoted and how He quoted it, and even in the passages that some people interpret as being a repudiation of Old Testament teaching. All this was "of one piece" and represented a commitment to Scripture that was given by inspiration of God and was vested with the authority of God Himself. Nicole's thesis was entitled *Jesus and The Bible in Reference to the Doctrine of The Inspiration of the Scriptures*. It showed God to be the author. The conclusion actually reads as follows:

> According to Jesus' attitude, we believe that the whole Bible in the original texts has been written by men under the supernatural influence of the Holy Spirit, so that they were preserved from any error and any omission in any departments as to the thoughts and as to the words, yea as to the tittles, in all the sacred writings. Thus, while there are differences in function of its parts and in the mode of inspiration, the whole original Bible, is invested with all the authority and inerrancy of God, with all the peculiarities of men.

That statement was the summation, not only of his B.D. thesis, but also of Nicole's own formulation of a doctrine of inspiration based on the ground of what Jesus had said. The B.D. thesis was actually the very beginning of his theological attempts, and would form the foundation of a career lasting some seven decades hence. He remembered gratefully,

> The thesis passed examination, I received the B.D., and it was stated that I had gone through the New Testament and had found *every* passage that was relevant to this topic. I really had not bypassed any important issues at all, but whatever was relevant to the subject had been considered, positively and negatively. Therefore, I had really done a competent piece of work. For me, this has been absolutely fundamental to my faith and to my theological career, because I examined everything we know about Jesus, and without any kind of question or uncertainty or vagueness, the Scripture is presented as the Word of God and treated as the Word of God. And *that* is the issue for me—it does not matter to me what anybody else has to say, be they graduates of Harvard, Oxford, Cambridge, or the Sorbonne—I am going to be on this subject together with *Jesus*! I think I know what He taught and I am committed to Him and to His truth—that has been for me the rock, in opposition to what Henri Miéville (the philosophy professor Jules Marcel helped him with) had taught. On this point I am unshakable! The conclusion of my B.D. was a confirmation to my mind and soul several years after that crisis event. I feel I went down to the depths of the subject, and there was nothing that I saw there and bypassed. I found nothing that gave me pause, or caused a reexamination of my faith. Of course, I find difficulties in the Bible; there are passages I do not understand. But the crucial point is this: the Bible remains the supreme authority, and it cannot be challenged in anything it says. To dispute anything taught in God's Word, I think, is a supreme arrogance that is absolutely unacceptable.

This was his first "throw" so to speak, in which Nicole was attempting to set forth in a correlative manner what he saw on a particular subject. The impact on his future career as a theologian cannot be overestimated. In 2002, when it was planned to publish some of his writings in book form, he mentioned that this was really the most basic thing that he had done. The publishers suggested that he prepare the B.D. thesis for inclusion in the works, but he felt that there were too many areas that would need thorough expansion (because of development and maturing through the decades), so it was not included. The B.D. thesis is imperfect in many respects, Nicole admitted. The English employed is that of a person who had less than a year of use in the language. Though he had people who helped him with grammar and syntax, the language is clumsy at some points. In some ways, it demonstrates theological immaturity, but the basic approach is there, and it is that which has sealed his basic orientation.

Benjamin B. Warfield is the theologian who did with the accomplished qualities of a thorough scholar what Nicole was attempting as a young student, and it was he who gave the young theologue the inspiration and challenge that when any doctrinal matter is examined in detail, the Bible proves true. Warfield wrote several major articles addressing various facets of this subject. One is entitled *The Real Problem of Inspiration*, which demonstrates that the real problem of inspiration is the failure of its acceptance by people! Then he has a study about the Greek word *theopneustos* entitled *God-Inspired Scripture*, explaining the God-breathed nature of the Bible.   Within that same article, Warfield examines thoroughly all Greek expressions ending in *–tos*. He "absolutely demolished" a scholar by the name of Hermann Cremer (the author of a biblical theological dictionary of the New Testament), a relatively conservative German, who at this point thought the word *theopneustos* meant *inspiring* rather than *inspired*. Warfield showed very powerfully that it could not be interpreted that way; what it says is "breathed out *by* God." Another article that helped Nicole greatly dealt with the use of the phrase "oracles of God" in Scripture. The last article that provided clarity was *"It Says:" "Scripture Says:" "God Says,"* a study in which Warfield showed, in a way that was essentially beyond challenge, that the forms in that title are equivalent expressions of biblical authority. Nicole stated that while "I have heard people say that Warfield was wrong in his implications, I have never heard people claim that Warfield failed to prove his point." Warfield would work to such an extent that he arrived at a definitive formulation, and that is the part that Nicole found extremely inspiring.

Nicole's preparation for a lifetime of teaching continued with the pursuit of the Master of Sacred Theology (S.T.M) from Gordon. This study strengthened his already firm commitment to the full veracity of the Bible. He theorized that the most difficult question about inspiration came in the quotations of the Old Testament in the New Testament. The problem for investigation was the way the quoting was done, to determine if there was a proper reproduction of the Old Testament statement, as coming from God, and therefore needing no modification whatsoever. If this was not the case, then it was necessary to show why a kind of freedom in quoting is evident, in which some changes could be made, in which a variety of versions could be used, and in which there was liberty in making, say, a change in the pronouns from "us" to "you." There were critics who claimed that if the authors of the New Testament believed in verbal inspiration, they obviously would be obliged to reproduce the Old Testament in absolute accuracy. Any such freedom in this respect, they claimed, would indicate a certain vagueness about the nature of inspiration, a freedom that God would surely have prevented them from using.

Another problem for plenary inspiration is that its adversaries claimed, sometimes very pointedly, that the New Testament writers were quoting Scripture in a way that is not in accordance with proper exegesis, and that they were using Old Testament wording in ways that are not appropriate for proper understanding of what the Old Testament actually stated. A good example of that claim would be found in Hosea 11, where Hosea says, "When Israel was a child, I loved him, and out of Egypt I called my son." And then Matthew 2:15 reads, "This was to fulfill what the Lord had spoken by the prophet, 'Out of Egypt I called my Son.'" Matthew relates that to the decision of Joseph and Mary to return from Egypt to Palestine, and that does not seem to fit the Old Testament Scripture at all. Some people would say that Hosea had no idea that this could be used later on in that sense as Matthew does; therefore, the interpretation of the Old Testament here given is highly arbitrary.

Nicole felt that this needed to be examined. He had to research how the quotations in their wording related to the Old Testament Scriptures to which they alluded. Also, he needed to investigate how the meaning of the Old Testament Scripture was observed in order to be fitted as the New Testament writers did. He undertook this rather enormous task, one that perhaps the school should have prevented him from attempting because of the wide range of the more than 230 quotations involved. The title of the thesis was *A Study of Old Testament Quotations in the New Testament With Reference to the Doctrine of the Inspiration of the Scriptures.* He made a study of the quotations and developed a chart (included as a foldout in the rear of the thesis) of how each of the books of the Old Testament was quoted in each of the books of the New Testament. This represented a mammoth amount of work, since his study had to include every quotation in the New Testament. Unless they stated explicitly, "I am now quoting," the New Testament writers were obligated to use neither precisely the same meaning nor the same wording as the Old Testament. Also, if it was very close, and he could recognize that they were quoting (either directly or summarily), but they did not employ a formulation such as "God said this in the Old Testament," then Nicole affirmed their right to simply state the matter and summarize in their own terms. He recalled that this was what he often did during the interviews for the present biography: at times he quoted the words of Jesus verbatim, and at other times he simply paraphrased. Nicole noted that "this kind of thing is certainly done by all sorts of people who believe strongly in inspiration, be they preachers, theology professors, or interviewees. But the fact is I am not inspired of God in the way that the New Testament writers were, and neither are the preachers, theology professors, or interviewees."

The quotations of the New Testament writers had to be consonant with a perfect control by God of how and what they were writing. So the method of quoting, the literalness of it, the freedom of it, needed to be very carefully studied. Nicole felt under less obligation to validate the hermeneutics of the New Testament than he felt to validate the wording of the New Testament as reflecting the belief in Old Testament inspiration by New Testament writers. He went through all the quotations of the New Testament, not omitting a single one, not even those that were merely allusions. He did make a distinction in meaning in terms of allusions and quotations, so the 230 that he mentioned are *quotations* that are introduced in some way by "this is what was said" or "so was fulfilled" and expressions of that kind. There are some "orphaned" quotations where there is no place in the Old Testament that clearly corresponds to what the New Testament quotes. The quotation "He will be called a Nazarene" in Matthew 2:23 is an example. Those certainly were the objects of his study, too. He developed the matter more fully in connection with Matthew, Romans, and Hebrews where there are abundant quotations. He did not focus on the book of Revelation, where there is obviously the densest amount of allusions to the Old Testament, but not formulated as quotations. In Matthew, particularly, there is a strong emphasis on fulfillment, so Nicole had to examine in what sense this takes place.

Having studied the quotations themselves, he needed to give careful attention to the introduction of the quotations. He checked whether it was with a verb referring to speech, or to writing; or again, whether to human authors or to God as the author. In the quotations themselves, he found that since they were writing in Greek and the text quoted was in Hebrew, they had to translate, unless they wanted to fill their book with Hebrew passages. In translation a certain amount of freedom exists, and there are several different forms of language that can acceptably translate something. That particular principle explained most of the differences. The New Testament writers used extensively the Septuagint, a translation that was made by human beings not corrected or guided by the inspiration of God. Of course in the case of the Septuagint there was a form of language that appealed to the people who would read the New Testament, because they would remember some of the things written in the familiar Greek idiom. At the same time, that did not authenticate the Septuagint as being by *itself* the Word of God; rather, it is the Word of God only to the extent that it properly represents what the *Hebrew* said.

Nicole considered the problem that developed, and demonstrated some principles showing, for instance, that Luke was inspired when he quoted Stephen, but that if Stephen did not quote accurately, Luke could not be charged with wrongdoing. The rules of scholarly quoting today are in place because of printing, and printing did not exist when Scripture was written. Paraphrase is perfectly legitimate; allusions are different from quotations; Messianic prophecy has to be recognized as somewhat veiled; personalities of the writers must be respected; the Holy Spirit is entirely free—all of these are principles by which some variation in a quotation could be explained without being an invalidation, either of the original text quoted or of the New Testament writer and the way in which he quoted. The result was that in all that large body of quotations, there was none in which there was a departure that was so significant as to raise questions about either the belief of the original author in the inspiration of the Old Testament, or in which the inspiration of the New Testament writer was in question. For each quotation examined, he wanted to know who used the quotation, how it was used, how often it was used, why it was used, and how it was introduced. He discovered, as he had in the B.D. study about Jesus' own view of Scripture, a tremendous confirmation. Here in fact is not an argument against inspiration, but the way in which the New Testament refers to the Old is overwhelmingly affirming of the authority and inspiration of the Old Testament Scriptures. The Old Testament was presented as God's Word, even to the point where one letter might be sufficient to establish an argument as in Galatians (see Gal. 3:16).

He found that an objection which at first he could not resist because he lacked the data, now, upon thorough examination of the data, was no valid objection at all. The New Testament writers quoted in ways that recognized the Old Testament Scripture as God's Word, authoritative in whatever is asserted there. Where there were questionable cases, as in Matthew's use of Hosea 11 and Paul's reference to Abraham in Galatians 3, he appealed to the principle that when the inspiration of God applied, there may be a meaning in the text that goes beyond what the original author could have envisioned, because this is God's statement as well as the human author's statement. One has the case of Caiaphas: John explains that Caiaphas claimed that it was advantageous for one man to die for the people rather than the whole nation to be destroyed. John makes the statement, "He did not say this on his own, but as high priest that year he prophesied that Jesus would die for the

Jewish nation" (John 11:51). That prophecy was true: it was advantageous that Christ should die, rather than all the people He was going to save. That is certainly something Caiaphas had no intention to suggest at all.

In Matthew 2:15 there is a kind of parallelism in God's design for his people. The parallelism of the Exodus is meaningful not only for the journey of the people of Israel in the days of Moses, but there also is a sense in which God continually calls out his people from a world of bondage into a world of freedom. In a real sense the Exodus is true of believers individually, of Christians as a whole, and more significantly even, of the actual events of the life of Jesus. So Matthew was able by inspiration to recognize in the statement of Hosea, not only a statement concerning the Exodus of Moses, but also a statement of God Himself characterizing the nature of His redemptive activity. Even geographically there was a parallelism appointed by God, which would not have been the same if Joseph and Mary had gone to Babylon. There is a clear sense of an overarching providence of God that covers the Scripture and finds correspondences that may not have been thought of by the original authors. Preachers do this regularly in their sermons. There is a total outlook of the redemptive activity that is quite evident, and this redemptive activity has forerunners as it were, prefigurements, and in a certain way Abraham leaving Ur of the Chaldees in order to go to Haran is already a sign of the "pilgrim's progress." That is really what John Bunyan has done in his famous allegory: to take the pilgrim's progress, with a supposed geography, as a description of the spiritual development of somebody who goes through the Christian life.

Without going into lengthy discussions of hermeneutics (Nicole did not feel the need to validate the interpretation given by the New Testament authors in every case), he was particularly concerned to have a right understanding of how New Testament writers used the Old Testament in the way they quoted it. Patrick Fairbairn's *Typology of Scripture* and *Hermeneutical Manual of the New Testament* were particularly helpful to him in this study. Fairbairn made the point that the New Testament writers were really disciples of the school of Jesus, that they had heard Jesus discussing Old Testament passages at some length. Disciples like those who walked with Jesus on the road to Emmaus had heard Jesus describe in detail the allusions to himself in all of the Old Testament (Luke 24:27). So those people, being under the discipleship of Jesus, would carry out what Jesus had done (and probably in many cases using the same particular passages Jesus himself had used), reproducing the way Jesus had used these passages in order to show His own ministry. The form, for instance, that the Tabernacle and the Temple had was meant to be instructive, and the material used is always very precious material, the best there is in that order: best cloth, best wood, best metal. The arrangement of the Holy Place and the Most Holy Place—all of that is meaningful in terms of our relationship to God. The sacrifices were manifestly a preparation for the ultimate sacrifice of Christ. Nicole deduced that where at first one might perceive a fanciful arrangement, in the final analysis there is the possibility that there is instead a prefigurement intended by God based on the way the people looked at things at that time. He warned interpreters not to discard typological considerations, because there *is* a basic pattern of redemptive activity that is carried through from Genesis to Revelation, and this is all the activity of God the *Redeemer*. What is contained in the Old Testament, as Paul said, is written for our instruction (Rom 15:4; I Cor 10:8, 11), so one has to be careful in the way application is made outside of what is actually stated in Scripture. He did not find that Paul quotes differently from Jesus, and he found that what Jesus quoted fits very well with the general pattern of the rest of the New Testament.

A hallmark of Nicole's teaching was his willingness to deal with difficult passages in the Bible. He did not bypass in his S.T.M. studies the so-called "orphaned" passages, for which no clear Old Testament reference can be located (Matthew 2:23; Luke 11:49; John 7:38; I Corinthians 2:9; Ephesians 5:14; James 4:5). "He shall be called a Nazarene" is an example. He examined a number of possibilities of interpretation that would validate the propriety of what the New Testament affirms. Some commentators suggested that Jesus, in coming to live in Nazareth, typified the humiliation that was characteristic of the Christ. He was not in the center of the religion of Israel, which was Jerusalem; He was in a despised province (and actually in a despised city) that was part of a large current of military movements. The people of Nazareth had a bad reputation on that account, and so Nazareth, the very name of it, fit with the humility of His position. Others pointed to the Nazirites, which would have some correlation in the Hebrew, where they had committed themselves to a certain pattern because of their acceptance of God. Still others claim that Jesus, in coming to Nazareth, identified Himself with folks that were despised and humiliated, and so in that sense the humiliation of Christ is foreseen and foretold very clearly in the Old Testament. This is also manifested in His establishment of a dwelling place and carpentry shop in Nazareth. Some interpreters urge that the name Nazareth is not the basis of the statement. In this case, as in others like it, Nicole would not commit himself to one explanation but would list several among which the reader may choose.

Some of the Master's thesis material has been published in three different places. First, there is an article that Nicole published in the *Gordon Review*, which was taken out of the thesis, as a kind of summary explanation that could be given about the use of quotations.[3] Second, he gave another presentation on New Testament interpretation in the little book *Hermeneutics* published by Bernard Ramm.[4] Third, in an article published in the first volume of *The Expositor's Bible Commentary* edited by Frank E. Gaebelein, Nicole attempted to deal particularly with some of the difficult passages where the New Testament use may at first appear out of line with the Old Testament context only to be found in fact quite harmonious to it.[5]

Nicole's advisor for this thesis was Professor Merrill C. Tenney who gave him masterly supervision and required that he should use the Harvard-Andover Library in his preparation. This was his first contact with a first-class theological library. The potential for discovery there was a tremendous challenge to him. This is reflected in his bibliography of 97 titles devoted to Old Testament quotations in the New Testament: 26 in Latin, 5 in French, 22 in German, 43 in English, and 1 in Dutch. Nicole received the S.T.M. in 1940, and was honored to be valedictorian for that year's graduation. He gave

[3] See Bibliography C1
[4] *Ibid.*, D5
[5] *Ibid.*, B14

a brief message on "speaking the truth in love" (Eph 4:15), a passage that continued to provide a personal challenge throughout his career.

In 1940, Gordon Divinity School decided to offer a Th.D. degree rather than the S.T.D., which was thought to be partially honorary. Rev. Earl Kalland and Nicole were the first candidates for the new degree. The attendance requirement at classes was quite limited and Nicole completed it in 1941. This left only the dissertation for him to complete a terminal degree.

Clarence Bouma of Calvin Seminary came to teach at Gordon during the fall term of 1940. He was to have a profound impact on Nicole's thinking in terms of Reformed theology and apologetics–"in his one course he managed to influence me more thoroughly than perhaps anybody else." Nicole approached Bouma for specific pastoral counsel beyond the classroom doctrinal instruction. Not only did Bouma provide helpful insights about a particularly challenging situation, but he also prayed with Nicole personally. Bouma's consistency and organization of thought appealed to Nicole, who in the 2002 publication of his collected writings dedicated the work to his brother Jules Marcel and to Bouma as "my two most influential theological teachers of my youth."

President Nathan Wood, who was his main doctoral dissertation advisor, impressed Nicole as a "genius." He taught classes in a seminar style, allowing students to make presentations on which he commented. Wood was tolerant and gracious, but he never compromised on the truth. He used vivid and stunning illustrations in the classroom. He was a very spiritual man who was intensely devoted to Gordon, having led it through various status changes: from Bible school to Bible college, and from Bible college to include a seminary.

The major emphasis was placed on the dissertation research and writing. Nicole had observed that certain difficulties in the structure of theology had been encountered through the centuries of development of the Christian view. The relationship between the divine and human natures in the Person of the Incarnate Logos; or again the relationship between God's sovereign plan and the reality of human responsible decisions were notable examples of this situation. Nicole posited that when the plane of divine life enters in contact with the plane of human life, there originates a point of contact that is transcendental with respect to finite reason. Even in mathematics, which approaches pure thought, the introduction of infinity demands a new set of rules that would be inappropriate with merely finite values. An example of this would be the equation $\infty + 50 = \infty - 50$, an equality that would normally lead to the conclusion $100 = 0$. But of course that result is absurd. Another instance of this mystery would be in the equation $y=1/x$. A hyperboloid formed by rotating the hyperbola on an axis would have an infinite area but a finite volume—one could not cover with paint the *outside*, but one could fill with paint the *inside*.

In theology, similarly, the consideration of God's infinite nature in His relation to our finitude generates an infinite factor that appears in conflict with our finite comprehension. This may be called an antinomy, not in the sense advocated by Immanuel Kant, as an evidence of the inadequacy of human knowledge of noumena. Here the reference would be not to a formal contradiction, but to the inadequacy of finite minds to comprehend the infinite, so that the truth would manifest a tension that cannot be resolved in finite terms. Nicole agrees at this point more with Cornelius VanTil than with Gordon Clark—there *are* mysteries that cannot be understood by finite logic and that only have their resolution in the ultimate, the infinite.

In the history of doctrine, the effort to resolve such a tension has led many thinkers to curtail one or both parts of the tension, so as to achieve rational harmony in finite terms at the expense of actual, biblical truth. As Nicole puts it,

> The study of this insight led me to recognize five such antinomies. Supremely there is the incarnation of the Logos with divine and human natures simultaneously present in the Person of Jesus Christ. Then there is God's coexistence of immanence and transcendence in one created universe. The tension between renewed and sinful natures in the regenerate person was listed, although this is scheduled to disappear in the *eschaton*. Another example is the coexistence of divine

foreordination and of responsible decision of rational agents. This same tension is present in inspiration with the reality of divine and human authorship of the sacred text.

The Th.D. study required Nicole to examine the whole Bible to trace the tensions averred and the affirmation of the transcendence of the divine thought (e.g., Isa 55:9; I Cor 1 and 2). For this purpose the entire Bible was read within two weeks with appropriate noting of relevant passages. Then a survey was made of works on systematic theology where the existence of the tension was acknowledged, even if not systematically developed. A special consideration was given to theologians who presented antinomies as a key to their theology (Erich Przywara, Emanuel Hirsch, Karl Dunkmann, Jules Bovon, W. P. McKay, Robert Govett, Thomas Richey and Charles Marsh Meade). In order to ensure appropriate completeness, Nicole spent a whole day each week at the Andover-Harvard Theological Library, poring over books in category 629: Systematic Theology as a Whole by Protestant Authors. For every author not in that library, he went to the library at Union Seminary in New York, where he spent about three weeks in rigorous study; for every author not in the previous two libraries, he went to Princeton Seminary's library.

He consulted theological texts in French, German, English, Dutch, and Latin; until 1943, his file of bibliographic cards from this research was likely the largest collection on Protestant systematic theology in the world. This work led him to conclude that the principle of mysteries/antinomies was prevalent in Protestant theology. He earned the Th.D. *summa cum laude* in 1943. It is worthy of note that when Gordon Divinity School came under attack from some alumni, President Wood used Nicole's dissertation, entitled "An Introduction to the Study of Certain Antinomies of the Christian Faith," to defend the school's orthodoxy and scholarship. The thesis concluded that "the points of contact between the divine and the human plane of life are of a nature that transcends human reason. The study of any one of these points of contact, if properly conducted, will manifest the existence of two planes, the divine and the human, seemingly in absolute opposition to each other and thus mutually exclusive, and yet both essential integrant elements of the Christian system."

Marcel Bonard was the pastor of two French Baptist congregations in Massachusetts—one in Worcester and one in Manchaug from 1934 to 1939. In April 1939, he went to New York as a candidate for a vacant French pulpit, and in his absence Nicole filled the pulpit. When Bonard accepted the pastorate of the New York congregation, both Massachusetts churches called Nicole on May 1. The home mission secretary of the American Baptist Convention extended the call to him. "I'm not a Baptist," he said. The secretary asked, "Are you opposed to believer's baptism?" Nicole replied, "No." Then the secretary asked, "Will you preach the gospel?" He simply said, "Yes." That was the extent of his formal examination by the denominational hierarchy.

His compensation of fourteen dollars per week (later twenty dollars) was derived from the two churches, the Baptist City Mission Board, and the American Baptist Convention. He completed his B.D. studies in May 1939, and though he had a return ticket to Europe, he stayed in Massachusetts for the summer "to get to know the people." He continued as pastor of both churches for seven years, pursuing simultaneously his studies for the Master and Doctor of Theology.

Having never been scripturally baptized, an assistant at the Worcester church immersed him (1943). Nicole recalled that there were three members from that congregation who were inmates at the insane asylum. He made pastoral visits there faithfully, but only at the end of the day: "I could do no other ministry work after visiting there." While visiting a female inmate, a long-time member of the church, Nicole and an asylum staffer noted that she murmured to herself incoherently. While the pastor read Scripture, she continued to mutter. But when he prayed at the end of the visit, she was utterly silent. After the 'amen' she resumed her murmuring. Nicole commented that "she was a wall without any windows, but God came in from above—prayer was a breakthrough."

The two churches had a rich history. A large influx of nearly two million French-speaking persons from Quebec had occurred in New England from 1870 to 1930. The primary reason for this was economic (textile and leather mills in the United States could provide both jobs and housing). The Catholic Church in Quebec exercised excessive control over the lives of people. It was a settled policy of the Catholic Church not to emphasize educational attainments. The only courses taught in French at the university level were designed to prepare prospective physicians, lawyers, and priests. The priests exerted pressure on their Catholic constituents to conform. Some priests at the time could go so far as to prevent the delivery of New Testaments sent through the mail, with the rationale that it was better for the common people to remain ignorant of the Scriptures. They believed that the less contact persons had with heretics (Protestants), the better. When these formerly oppressed Catholics arrived in New England, they were often very approachable and receptive to gospel witness.

There had been a substantial French-speaking mission throughout New England as a result of this massive French immigration. In 1920, there were as many as twenty-five French Baptist missions there. But by the 1940s, the missions were in decline (only seven remained, one of which was in Maine, and since its pastor preferred English to French, he chose to anglicize that congregation). The remaining six missions—still supported financially by the American Baptist Convention at the time—had only one pastor for every two churches. The simplest explanation for this downturn was that the mass arrival of Canadians had largely ceased. Also, second generation Canadians were capable of speaking English (which their parents encouraged) and therefore joined English-speaking congregations.

When Nicole was called to the pastorate at Worcester it was the second largest French-speaking congregation in New England; still, half of its membership was by this time already gone. The church was located in a once predominantly French area that had lost much of its French character by 1939. One could travel half a mile before hearing a single word spoken in French. Though ninety percent of the members were strongly committed French Canadians, the church was poorly attended for prayer meetings, and the Sunday evening service was comprised entirely of young people and carried out in English.

Nicole's other congregation, in the village of Manchaug, was born as the result of a severe quarrel among the Roman Catholic residents. A textile company had built two large mills, a number of small cottages, a grocery store, and a Catholic church for the expatriate French Canadians who comprised its workforce. The priest at the church had abused his office, airing confidential information revealed to him in the confessional. Among the outraged congregants was a medical doctor, who along with several others, sought relief from the bishop of Springfield, who utterly ignored their complaints. There was at this time, however, another Roman Catholic priest who was not in fellowship with his own church, and who offered to provide spiritual care to the disgruntled members. Thus, two Catholic churches were operating in Manchaug. The dissident priest, Mr. Ribourg, had been receiving instruction at the First Baptist Church of Worcester, and was baptized by immersion there at the beginning of the twentieth century. Having gradually weaned his parishioners from their Roman Catholic outlook, Ribourg arranged for a baptism to take place, during which some forty persons were baptized. A fortnight later, fifteen more were immersed upon their profession of faith in Jesus Christ.

There was a significant remnant that desired to remain Roman Catholic, even with a loose-lipped priest, so they returned to the original Catholic church in the village. Friction developed among the workers at the mill, and since the owners did not want religious quarrelling on the job, they fired the French Baptist group. Thus, these were expelled from their homes, refused credit at the store, and denied their half-price milk distribution. This effectively cut the church in half or more; those who remained in spite of the restrictions, along with those who later returned, were the members of the French Baptist Church at Manchaug. Since ninety-five percent of the parishioners lived in that village, Nicole was able to pay pastoral visits to his entire congregation in a single afternoon.

Nicole was part of the movement within American Baptists toward a more conservative direction. He was, after all, the son of one of the "dangerous men." He joined with those reacting to the encroachment of liberalism within the church; he was a part of the protesting group. "Among *Protest*ants it ought not to be a terrible thing to be *protesting*," he observed. He had a somewhat hostile approach at first, but then he considered how they could help the church in the situation, and particularly the churches that were sound but which were in a union which *itself* was not sound. The analysis of it would involve having cooperative people, but if they did not feel they could cooperate, then they would be prepared to leave on their own, rather than be dismissed, and particularly not to take a church along with them. Nicole related the humorous "humbling" of a particular liberal antagonist:

> The liberals were very overbearing, notably Dr. Thomas Roy who was pastor of First Baptist Church of Worcester. He was uniting with the Unitarians in the summer. He actually had people like Harry Emerson Fosdick come in and preach. When an evangelical would come as a candidate for ordination, he would attempt to embarrass the ordinand in one way or another. One time he was asking a candidate about the Second Coming of Christ and how it would come about: would it come about in Boston on one day and Chicago the next day? The fellow seeking ordination was fairly sharp ordinarily, but he got a bit of mud on his face in this instance. Another time we had two people come up for examination who had considerable theological training. One was myself. Dr. Roy tried to embarrass me at the ordination committee meeting. He wanted to raise questions about people who had such a view of the Trinity, that there was only one God appearing in different phases. Well, that is obviously Sabellianism. He raised the question there, and I had written in my statement of faith not only a positive affirmation of historic orthodoxy, but also a repudiation of errors that I thought were dangerous in church history. I had specifically listed Sabellianism there as a dangerous error! So, I said, "I have put in writing my repudiation of Sabellianism, and anybody who knows anything about the history of the church knows that what you are describing is Sabellianism. I don't think I can be accused of promoting that!" He had shown an enormous lapse on church history there, so he kept quiet the rest of the meeting.
>
> Then at the actual ordination council, I had made a statement that I was glad to be a part of the American Baptist Convention, and to support it as far as it agreed with my outlook in faith. Where it did not, I felt it was my duty not only to disagree, but to warn my people not to spend their money and prayers in a direction that was contrary to their convictions. In my statement of faith for ordination I had to say something about

my relationship to the denomination. Dr. Roy said in a rather nasty way to me "What would happen if everybody in the denomination took your stance?" To which I replied, "Mr. Chairman, we would have an apostolic church!" The whole council laughed, and Dr. Roy realized that with some guys, he was going to get smothered.

The next man that came was Warren Young, who had a Ph.D. from Boston University. Well, Dr. Roy on the committee tried to attack Young, saying that in the Johannine writings you have the doctrine of the Logos, which really came from the philosophy of Philo. This was certainly not acceptable from an evangelical view. Warren Young said, "I am very interested in what you are saying, because I just made a study of Philo in connection with my work under Professor Brightman, and so I would be very interested to see at what point you find a connection between this and John!" He mostly shut up after that, though later he tried to get Young again. As chairman, Dr. Roy said that any question might be asked as long as the questioner knew the answer himself. He asked Young a question about how the deity of Christ and his humanity were united. Warren Young looked like a dunce at times, just sitting there with his mouth open, as if he were a hick, easy to intimidate. Young asked Dr. Roy, "Well, do *you* know the answer to that question?" Dr. Roy replied, "No, I don't know the answer; I don't believe that!" And Young reproached him for violating his own rules of questioning. So we tamed Roy a little bit, both Young and myself, within about a month of each other.

When Nicole came to the United States he was hoping to become independent of his parents in terms of finances. He had never earned his own living before. He was doing some tutoring while in school (during his last three years of education in Lausanne). His parents permitted him to teach as many as three hours per week, and he was getting some money for that, but this was not turned in for the family budget. Instead, these funds were included in his savings account, so he was not contributing financially to the home. When he went to the Bible Institute, his parents continued to support him, though in the last year he did teach French to some English-speaking people who wanted to be missionaries. And he also did some typing of his brother's notes in church history that were to be used by the Bible Institute. So, he was contributing a little to his own support but not very heavily. When he came to the United States his parents gave him a letter of credit for one thousand dollars, but he only used about three hundred dollars of that. He was hoping to have a position teaching some French, or else to be the pastor of some of the French-speaking churches that existed in New England.

From Friday to Monday morning, he was living in a rented room at the home of an elderly lady in Worcester, Massachusetts. She was a widow and an affiliate with a Plymouth Brethren assembly. This very sound and pious lady was named Mrs. Vanderpyl. She charged him three dollars per week for the room, eventually agreeing to supply him with his food as well. She had a number of rooms that were rented to various people. Her deceased husband was of Dutch descent and had been a buyer for one of the department stores in Worcester. He was a very fine person, also of the Plymouth Brethren persuasion. When he died, in order to subsist, she had to rent a portion of the three-story house that she had. Mrs. Vanderpyl received some supplemental income by using her car to give rides to folks who needed transportation around town. She lived in a frugal manner, "from hand to mouth," and it was apparent that she was not accumulating money. She charged very modestly for the meals.

As Nicole came downstairs one day to get hot water for a shave, there was a young woman there who was applying to have a room. Mrs. Vanderpyl said, "This is Miss Cyr, she wants to have a room, and her native language seems to be French." So she was very pleased to have someone who could speak French with her. This was Annette, Nicole's future wife. Between the two of them, the landlady and Nicole, a faithful gospel witness was begun to Annette. She had been born into a very pious Roman Catholic family, but was having at this time serious concerns about some aspects of the Catholic faith. She spoke nothing but French until age nine. One of her aunts, who was unmarried, was actually going to Mass every day, and quite often Annette accompanied her to the church in New Bedford. All of this was in French, and the whole environment was steeped in the Catholic Church. Her father died when she was not quite two, in the worldwide influenza epidemic of 1918. Annette was the only child. After some time her mother, who was a widow working in a textile mill in New Bedford, decided to remarry. This decision was made in part to provide a home for her daughter and also to secure some kind of assurance for the future. She felt she was too much under the influence of her late husband's family, the Cyrs, and wanted some more independence. She remarried, but this was a very unhappy choice. Her new husband was not a very sophisticated man, and his horizons were low and limited. He was, to his credit, a diligent laborer, but this was confined to moving dirt and working with a pick and shovel. So, Annette had very little intellectual stimulation, in contrast with the Cyr family, in which she had people who were very well developed, with a good understanding of things and of the world—with a broader vision. Upon remarrying, Nicole's mother-in-law moved to the vicinity of Worcester. Annette grew up there, learned English, and for a time the family lived in an Italian area, so she learned some Italian as well. So Annette was at least fairly capable in three languages: French (native), English (with no accent), and some Italian.

The atmosphere in the home of Annette's upbringing was not very good. When the Depression hit, the new husband of Annette's mother lost the home. They had owned their home but were obliged to dispose of it because they could not meet the mortgage payment, so they lived in rented property after that. Annette's stepfather was strict in many respects and made the home a very unpleasant place. So at the age of 16 she was led to go out and work, thus giving her some respite from an unhappy home life. During all that time she was very faithful in the church. She was involved with teaching some of the children at church, and the regular contact she had with the priests provided ample opportunity also to ask questions. Purgatory was one of the questions that bothered her. She was concerned about the destiny of her father in purgatory. She had paid for Masses for his rest and she was praying for him every day. She approached the priest and said, "I have been thinking about my father for so many years. When will I know that finally his soul has been removed from purgatory and that he has gone to heaven?" The priest replied, "You cannot know that! Nobody knows that." Annette said, "Suppose that he is already in heaven and I am still praying for him and having Masses for him?" "Well," the priest said, "then God would use that merit for other people."

Annette made a list of books (she was in high school at that time) that she wanted to read, and the first book was the Bible. The priest looked at the list, and the first book he crossed out was the Bible. He said, "That's not for you." That displeased her considerably. Thus, by the summer of 1940, she was having some serious questions about the Church. Meanwhile, she had been told some things about Protestants that were simply false. Among other things, she was told that Protestants did not believe that Jesus was born of a virgin, nor did they believe that Jesus was God. So they were accused of undermining the faith in a tremendous way, in a way that would be true for liberal Protestants, but that was not true for Mrs. Vanderpyl, or for the Plymouth Brethren or for Nicole. So one of the first things that the two resident witnesses had to do was to show her that Protestants were not estranged from the Christian faith, but that they had some essential beliefs in common with Rome. This was very important for her to see, especially the Protestant affirmation that salvation came through Jesus Christ.

In connection with his witness to her, Nicole gave her an English Bible, which he knew she would use more readily than the French, because her training in reading was now in English. This was the first Bible she ever had held in her hands, and she began reading the Bible very assiduously. Increasingly, she became more detached from the Catholic Church and realized some of the things in it were not in accordance with Scripture. She came to a better conception of her own faith. Although she was believing in Christ before, now her faith was delivered from some accretions which made it very difficult for her. Under those circumstances, Nicole encouraged her to come to his church and worship. There he expected his people to say, "Well, we have somebody here who is fresh from the Catholic Church. We are going to receive her very enthusiastically." But it did not turn out that way. Folks were leery, and they began to realize their pastor had an interest in her that was more than just church-related. Their desire was that he should become engaged with somebody from their own company. They were disappointed that a woman from the outside had "caught Roger's eye." Annette did not receive a very warm reception at the church.

Since the congregation was not very hospitable, Annette did not feel encouraged to join the church. She went with Mrs. Vanderpyl to the Plymouth Brethren meetings regularly, so her faith was nurtured in a sound conservative Protestant outlook with the Scripture as the basis. She read the Bible voraciously, ingesting the entirety of God's Word rather quickly. She was greatly challenged and stimulated by this exercise.

Plymouth Brethren did not speak of "the church"; instead, they referred to their gatherings as "assemblies." They felt that the church as a structured entity had already failed by the time of II Timothy, though it was still present in Paul's first epistle to Timothy. They believed neither in official ordination of clergy, nor in having an appointed person to preside at the meetings. Mrs. Vanderpyl belonged to a very small group where a man named Gleason was more or less in charge. Gleason was handling every service that they had on Sunday mornings, and his pattern was to read a biblical passage and then provide commentary and application. He and his family, Mrs. Vanderpyl, an older couple, and Annette were all that were present in those meetings. There was spiritual nurture there all the same, but also an extreme narrowness that was sometimes present among the old type Plymouth Brethren. Nicole commented that they have broadened very much indeed in modern times, so that many of them have fine and flourishing congregations, and the Plymouth Brethren sustain Bible institutes for deeper study. This particular group was of the narrowest type, however. They did cultivate a lively faith and a commitment to Christ, and they placed a great emphasis on prophetic Scripture (order of events, Rapture, Tribulation, things of that kind). Mrs. Vanderpyl, for instance, was discussing who might be the Antichrist and how he could not be Benito Mussolini because, as she said, he had to be a Jew. There were all kinds of details in her map of future events. Nicole tended to avoid discussion on this. She was disappointed that he did not carry the same particular eschatological outlook, although she realized he had a good solid grounding in biblical studies. She was the person who typed his Th.D. thesis for Gordon Divinity School.

Life for Nicole at this time was a flurry of activity. He was doing his pastoral work in the church. He was continuing his theological studies at Gordon. While Annette and he were growing increasingly fond of each other, the possibility of marriage scarcely entered the picture because of the great difference in their backgrounds. Annette enlisted in the United States Coast Guard, so she had three years of service during World War II. She trained first in New York at Hunter's College, where they had the basic training session. Then she was given further instruction at Cedar Falls, Iowa. She was stationed first in Seattle, then later in Boston. When she was at Boston, Nicole often had occasion to see her. The couple could share a meal together, near the Coast Guard tower, but even at that time their courtship was really not a very public matter. In fact, it was kept quite private, because they had no assurance that in the end they would be married. She reached the rank of Yeoman First Class, equivalent to staff sergeant in the army. She was doing very well in the service, and was for about two years boarding with an old retired teacher of Norwegian origin.

With the arrival of 1946, one of the most signal events of his life took place: Annette and he were married before a justice of the peace on June 18. This was necessary in order to have the right surname on her passport, Nicole rather than Cyr, so that they could cross the Atlantic for his father to bless their wedding. They took the trip to Switzerland on a ship called *Ile de France*, which was a German ship that had been expropriated by France at the end of the war. It was still run like the troop transport ship it had been, with no individual cabins, only rather large dormitories. So he was in the men's dormitory and his wife was in the women's dormitory. They were married in terms of the civil situation, but without being able to be together as a honeymooning couple. Then they had a very embarrassing situation. The officials in charge of cargo failed to take their trunk on the ship, so the things they had for the European wedding ceremony were not available to them. They waited a few extra days in Paris, but the trunk still did not arrive. Then they went on to Switzerland to be with his parents, but again the trunk was missing. The time had been announced for their wedding in the church, but neither one of them had any clothes except what they had with them. So they went for a vacation time in the mountains of

Switzerland, then finally, on July 14, 1946 (Bastille Day for the French) his father blessed their wedding. Roger and Annette celebrated two dates: June 18, when they were married before the justice of the peace, and July 14, when they were married before God by the ministry of his father. Incidentally, this whole affair angered Nicole's aunt very much because she had gotten a special dress to wear for the wedding. After all this disruption, the trunk finally arrived late in August.

At the end of May 1946, before the couple left for Switzerland, Nicole resigned from his position as pastor of the churches. He had found for the churches someone who could carry on the ministry in French, a man by the name of Paul Duchesneau. He also had been an affiliate of the Plymouth Brethren and had been serving quite a while in Canada. Duchesneau was willing to take the leadership, and so he carried on through the end of 1946 and the full year 1947 as their pastor. He had a very different relationship with the people than did Nicole. He was a married man when he came to the church; Nicole had been a bachelor. There was a closeness, a sense of Nicole being "one of the people" that did not obtain with Duchesneau, and Mrs. Duchesneau was fairly hard to get along with, being somewhat dictatorial. At the end of 1947 he resigned and the churches were really in a difficult situation. So they appealed to Nicole to come back and to be their pastor again. He told them he was involved in the work of the school too heavily to be their regular pastor, that they should have someone who is able to be there with them more than he was able. He said that he would be an interim for them, but with the hope of finding a French-speaking pastor as soon as practicable—that interim pastorate lasted for about eight years, from the beginning of 1948 to 1956! Nicole happily recalled that the people opened their hearts very well to his wife, and the difficulty that they had before did not surface. He thought it was a good thing for them to have that intermission of a year and a half with someone else, and so he decided he could probably do the job with the time that was available. He continued to meet their pastoral needs of preaching, although with much less visitation than he had done before.

There was a Canadian member of the church, a very good-natured fellow with great physical strength, who, when Nicole was receiving a gift at Christmas, said it was not right to give only the pastor a gift and not his wife. So he arranged to have a gift for Annette, which he was giving to her personally. This man's wife had been against Nicole's marriage to Annette, and had been extremely critical at an earlier point. The man had become fonder of Annette than he was of Roger, though Roger had done a lot for him pastorally. He was given to drink, and for a while Nicole went to his home every day, to read the Scripture with him and help him overcome the temptation to drink. He had quite a strong contact with the man, and as a result he was more generous than others about the pastor's marriage. Others in the church were very critical, probably because they thought their pastor was making a mistake. But the Lord proved he made no mistake with sixty years of blissful evidence!

Annette matured exceptionally well through the difficulty they faced with the church not accepting her before. And it helped prepare her for the maturity needed for the task of being a professor's wife. A pastor's wife already has some difficulties: the church expects her to be at the level of her husband, and they project upon her demands that are often unfair. They also expect to get another person working full-time without any additional salary. This should be safeguarded against, so that she gets to be a member without feeling "pastoral pressure." But at least a pastor's wife does get exposure to the people and to fellowship opportunities. She is involved in the "current of things." The wife of a professor is not like that. She does not get to see the students very often. She has little inkling of how her husband is or is not accepted. The wife of a pastor is there when he preaches; she can see the response—not so with the professor's wife when he teaches. If professors get together as couples, the professors still have a tendency to "talk shop" and the wives can feel isolated. They can actually be quite lonely.

During the 1940s Nicole worked to move the two churches in Worcester and Manchaug from mission to full church status. He helped them to write a constitution and a statement of faith, and they became full members of the American Baptist Convention. In due course the candlesticks of those churches became extinguished because there were no more French people moving from Canada to the United States.

The dual pastorate was crucial for Nicole's continued development as a professor of theology. Most obviously, it is advantageous for a seminary teacher, responsible for the training of future ministers, to have some practical ministry experience among God's people. Nicole was challenged to preach, with his already capacious knowledge, in a manner comprehensible to congregants at both Worcester and Manchaug who rarely had a high school education:

> In my work as pastor, because of the smallness of the churches and because I was a bachelor, I had a very close relationship to my parishioners. That helped me more than I could have thought, because in some way I got to share their concerns, and then I could preach in ways that were significant to them, rather than to develop ideas and theological conceptions of which they had no idea. The people had a very sound faith. One elderly lady who hardly knew how to read resisted a previous pastor to his face because he did not believe in the Virgin Birth, so she said, "That is wrong!" And she was right, not the pastor. The personal affection that developed helped those people to get from me in ministry what they needed; their friendship was a very good experience for me in the pastorate. Of all the people in both churches, maybe only a small minority had even high school educations.
>
> One man who was the organist for the church in Manchaug and who also played in a band outside the church (and was thus out late on Saturday nights), had a high school training but was not a very spiritual man, nor was his family. In the Worcester church, I had one fellow who was going to Gordon College, so of course he had high school training, as did his sister, and maybe in their family others were high school trained. The treasurer of the church at Worcester also had high school. That was the very top level of education, so you had people who had a hard time reading. In order to be effective with them you needed to be at the level where they were living. Otherwise, it was like showing fruit at the top of a tree: it might be very appealing to look at, but it is not going to do them any good if they can't get it! I was there to reach *them*; I had no right to insist that they reach my range of thinking. I had made the commitment to spend the summer of 1939 getting to know the people in the churches, with the expectation that after that I could be at the same time studying for the master's and perhaps later the doctorate. When the war was declared in September of 1939, I could not return to Switzerland.

His famous ability to illustrate spiritual truth was strengthened during this time as he used anecdotes and illustrations familiar to former Quebec citizens. He learned also the unique difficulties of being a student-pastor and a professor-pastor, a fact that his later students would greatly appreciate. Finally, Nicole was exposed to "some of the most spiritual and devout people I ever served," individuals who, especially at Manchaug, suffered much for their faith in Jesus.

There were many privations during the war, with ration cards being issued by the government for food and gasoline. Nicole's parishioners had very little gasoline. Since he was a pastor he had what they called an "X card" which allowed him to purchase gasoline without limitation. As a result, the congregants were quite inclined to ask him to drive them to various places. On one occasion, some people from his church who were five miles outside of Worcester ran low on gasoline. It was a Sunday night, about 8:00, and they called him to see if he would be able to give them some fuel. He went, recalling,

> Ordinarily, that would be a crazy request of your pastor. When I arrived, I soon realized that they knew nothing about siphoning. And they had no siphoning tube of any kind. They finally got a vacuum cleaner tube, so I tried to get the tube in the fuel tank and inhale to get the gasoline moving—and I got a MOUTHFUL of gasoline; gas is not my favorite drink! I was almost sick with that stuff. Annette was outraged!

Nicole had another memorable experience related to automobiles at this time. Both smiles and frowns attended his next car purchases:

> A very nice thing developed for me in that period. There was a man who had been in the First World War, and as a result had a nervous reaction. He owned a nice car that was not very heavily used. He just couldn't get a license to drive. The last time he went to get a license he drove right into a field with the employee of the registry. The employee opened the door and said "Goodbye! I'm not going any further with you!" So the man decided to sell his car at very low cost. I knew his pastor

well, and I got the car, a beautiful 1936 Chevy, so much better than my 1933 Chevy. I sold my 1933 for $80. I was married by this time, and we were living on a hill in Roxbury near Boston. There was a terrible ice storm, but I had to go to the school. I managed to get the car out of the garage in the snow, but the car started to slip, and there was no way of stopping it at all. It came down to the bottom of the hill, and there was a large avenue with an elevated train. Just as I was coming down, a huge truck passed by and I went BANG into his hind tire. And that ruined the car. So I had to buy a 1939 Chevy after that, and it was much more expensive and never as good. So I had that disappointment: my beautiful 1936 was beyond repair. The radiator was leaking like a sieve.

During this period, Nicole enjoyed a close friendship with one of his classmates at Gordon, Irving Howard, who was pastor of a small church about five miles from the Manchaug church. Nicole got in the habit of going to the prayer meeting in Manchaug on Wednesday evenings and then from there retiring to Howard's home. He would stay overnight there, then on Thursday morning he would leave with him. Howard was studying at Harvard and Nicole was doing research in the Harvard library. Howard provided great intellectual challenge to his friend—"he had a very broad outlook and a range of acquaintance with the world that was quite beyond mine." His wife was "a lovely person." The couple had two little girls who would come into Nicole's room and wake him up on Thursday mornings, bouncing on the bed. Unfortunately, Howard became attached to a parishioner in an inappropriate way, a woman who had an exceedingly sick husband. Howard broke covenant with his wife, and then Annette and Roger were brought close to the wife, and Annette was a great help to her. The Nicoles continued the friendship with the wife, but Howard was estranged. In this country, he was Roger's best friend at the time and probably Roger was his best friend also.

CHAPTER 5

1945-1960
First Years of Teaching

Gordon College engaged Nicole to teach French in 1944. This began a vocational relationship with the school that was to last for more than forty years. T. Leonard Lewis was president at the time and Burton Goddard was the dean. Nicole remembered President Lewis as a man of fine spiritual stature, democratic leadership, and a good sense of humor. Of Dean Goddard, he commented, "His was the example of self-effacement. He was interested in the promotion of others rather than himself." Nicole was also impressed by the relationships among faculty members, most of whom were in their forties or younger—"not an old beard among them." They shared lunch together nearly every day, and whenever disagreements arose, they were resolved without anger. Nathan Wood, the departing president, asked Nicole to teach his course "The Discourses of Jesus" to the sophomores. By 1945, he was teaching French and German during summer school. That was the first time they had a summer school at Gordon, and Carl F. H. Henry came to teach in the summer school. He was a very good friend of President Lewis, and Nicole had quite a bit of contact with Henry, who was interested in the young professor's theological outlook. Henry spoke to the president and said, "You ought not to have this guy teaching modern foreign languages; he is really somebody you need in the divinity school." The friendship of Carl Henry was very important for Nicole, and the camaraderie was strengthened because Henry was coming every summer for four years, from 1945-1948, and spending eight weeks or more at the school. That provided quite a bit of interaction on theological issues and other subjects. President Lewis had been teaching theology, but his administrative responsibilities prevented him from being in the classroom as much as he should, so he delegated the teaching of theology to Nicole at that point. The first course he taught at the divinity school was "Mysteries of Christianity." In 1946, he became titular Professor of Systematic Theology at Gordon Divinity School.

Nicole described the early development of Gordon Divinity School as an institution distinct from the college:

> In 1945, the Divinity School took its wings beyond the college. It had been started in 1921 for the needs of students who were graduates of Gordon College but who did not have enough preparation for regular ministry beyond very small churches. The school decided to buy a property that had been owned by Jewish people in Brookline. It was a superb location, available at low cost considering the excellence of the property, and very adequate for our student body of about sixty. The school bought this, and that was the first time that there was one building owned by the Divinity School, which was not tied to the College. That also meant that the faculty was specifically Divinity School faculty. Out of sixty students, probably forty-five were Gordon College graduates, and maybe fifteen or so were from other schools.
>
> That building was purchased in 1945, and some of us worked on it to make it ready for a separate school, including Carl F. H. Henry who was there as a summer teacher. He came for four summers, and during that time he was doing his Ph.D. at Boston University. He had a Th.D. from Northern Baptist Seminary, and so did the president, but that was a school really not qualified to give those degrees. They had neither the facilities for that, nor the library, and they scarcely had a faculty that was adequately equipped. And at Gordon I'd have to say there was a professor in biology who was the only one with a Ph.D. in science, but he was at the College, not the Divinity School. Tenney was working on his Ph.D. at Harvard, but he got it in 1944, and I got my Th.D. in 1943 so I was really ahead of him in the doctorate. Those professors were competent, Tenney especially, but there were people who greatly objected. One fellow came from Wheaton and said,

"What's the matter here? At Wheaton, all of those guys would have Ph.D.s and here what have we got?" He was not satisfied. I however was well satisfied with the training I got; they were capable people, good teachers, and President Wood was a genius in some ways. You could be challenged at Gordon if you wanted to be challenged.

It was good for the Divinity School to have an existence that was physically separate from the College. We got a portion of the books that were in the College, but since they were still doing training in New Testament, etc., we could not just take all the theological books from the Gordon library. But we took a good portion of them. And Dean Goddard brought in his own library of about 5000 volumes for loan to the Divinity School (they were marked with a white circle to indicate his ownership), but he never got those back; they became part of the permanent collection. We were developing the library, and at that point we had two professors besides me who were very interested in that and extremely capable in buying books, Edward Dalglish and George Ladd. We were making raids in various places, so we were building up the library, even before I became librarian. I had discovered in a 1942 visit to Union Theological Seminary thousands of duplicates that could be bought at a very low price, often less than 25 cents per volume. On three occasions I bought lots of 2000 duplicates for 10 cents per volume from seminaries in Bangor, Maine, Pittsburgh and Princeton. I also purchased more than 1000 volumes from the Lausanne Free Church Library. I was especially concerned to build up series of theological periodicals for the Divinity School library and also to increase its collection in English. Obviously there were also books in other languages, some of which I purchased for my own collection.

When I became librarian (which responsibility involved no increase in salary) there were only maybe five theological schools with libraries of 100,000 volumes. In nine years, from 1951 to 1959, I used a $1000 per annum budget to increase our holdings to 30,000 volumes. I was appointed librarian because of my ability to purchase books at good rates. Besides, I am a "bookish" guy! It was understood that my efforts to increase the holdings at the Divinity School library would not demand a halt in the development of my personal library. I got to know the folks from the organization of theological librarians, where I could obtain a lot of duplicates from those contacts. It got to the point where they would say at meetings, "Hello, Roger, we don't have any duplicates."

At this time, Nicole was teaching systematic theology at Gordon Divinity School. There were some students coming from Wheaton who were in his class, including Ray Buker, who was the son of a missionary. Buker's father was a very strong supporter of the Conservative Baptists. Nicole was not a Conservative Baptist; he was an American Baptist. He remained in the major Baptist movement because he had not been interfered with in his attempt to serve the Lord and to proclaim the truth. There was "nothing to push me out of the American Baptists, though others were in fact pushed out." In his teaching at Gordon, he made biblical inspiration a key emphasis, because he felt that students who grasped that would not "go into dead ends and side areas that really tend to stultify the ministry." He was especially eager to establish the doctrine of inspiration on the witness of Jesus.

The Conservative Baptists had a seminary, located first in Portland, Oregon, and then in Denver, Colorado. Buker's father was teaching missions at the Conservative Baptist Theological Seminary in Denver, and apparently his son must have talked to him about Nicole's teaching. They thought he was the person who really taught inspiration in the most effective way, so they wanted him to come to their seminary and give some lectures on the inspiration of Scripture. Unfortunately, this whole episode was completely misunderstood by a very rancorous group within the General Association of Regular Baptist churches who said, "Now, the Conservative Baptists are looking to someone who is a member of the American Baptist church for inspiration." They insisted that the Conservative Baptists cancel the invitation on that account, but Nicole did give those lectures at that time (1952). Whenever he lectured on inspiration, his starting point was always the same— "What did Jesus say?" That has been very significant throughout his whole ministry. Also in the *Standing Forth* book there is a whole group of articles that deal with inspiration. For Nicole, inspiration is a basic place where one cannot alter the divine authorship without terrible damage. A failure here undermines the whole theological enterprise.

Colleagues at the Divinity School provided for Nicole both Christian fellowship and intellectual challenge. Burton Goddard was called as dean of the Divinity School (Hudson Amerding, later president of Wheaton College, became dean at Gordon College). Nicole remembered,

> Burton Goddard is probably the most self-effacing person I have ever known. He was single-minded in advancing the kingdom of God, yet he was also concerned to advance the people who were working with him. He was a wonderful example to me in so many ways. The school faced some difficulties in 1947, particularly related to loss of key faculty members. As soon as E. J. Carnell received his prize for apologetics, he accepted the invitation to go to Fuller Seminary. With Carnell's departure we lost a very brilliant fellow. Then George Eldon Ladd had some difficulty in some of his classes because he imposed requirements at Gordon that would be more appropriate at Harvard, and the students revolted against that. Both President Lewis and Dean Goddard tried to help Ladd, but Ladd resented this enormously, and in 1950 he accepted the call to Fuller. So we lost two professors right there.
>
> Later on Paul K. Jewett left us in 1955. Jewett had written his doctoral thesis at Harvard on the theology of Brunner, where he nailed Brunner on the matter of inspiration. In some ways he was impressed by Brunner, and I think that sort of fermented in his mind. He was very uneasy with the attempt to maintain theological positions which were difficult to support. While Jewett was at Gordon he was struggling quite a bit with the question of the age of the earth. He had a very good friend who was a carbon-14 scholar, and for whom an old age for the earth was almost beyond dispute. I always held that the earth was old, and I had gotten to the point where I felt I could reconcile this with a Scriptural outlook. Jewett was of the opinion that the Bible and science were in a serious conflict. I think if he had stayed at Gordon, I could have been able to safeguard him from the extremes he went to; at Fuller, he moved on in his own way. He went for a sabbatical in France,

and was studying at the Institut Catholique in Paris. Their view of inerrancy was jaundiced, and when he came back he published *Man as Male and Female* (Grand Rapids: Eerdmans, 1975), in which he said that Paul in I Timothy had been influenced by his old rabbinic training, and was putting forth a rabbinic outlook on women. In Galatians, Jewett surmised, Paul said there is no male or female (Galatians 3:28), but then he fell back into a rabbinic type of approach that really was not inspired (I Cor. and I Tim.). When you start picking passages of the Bible and say they are not inspired, you are in trouble! In fact, the faculty of Fuller rebuked him: they gave him the most serious censure available short of firing him.

Gordon was really bled by Fuller: Jewett, Ladd, Carnell, and later Glenn Barker. We provided for them four of their key people. Barker was at Gordon for seventeen years before going finally to Fuller. Fuller insisted on having professors that were premillenarians, and Carnell tended to be amillenarian. When he accepted the invitation, I said, "Are you a pre-mill?" He said, "Oh, I guess so!" The salary was about double at Fuller from what it was at Gordon. They wanted to make Fuller the supreme seminary whose scholarship would match the best anywhere and yet also be evangelical. Dr. Harold John Ockenga (1905-1985) was much in favor of that, so he served as president. Then doctrinal defections began at Fuller, and at one point they lost Wilbur Smith, Carl Henry, and Gleason Archer, because they disapproved of looseness found on the commitment to Scripture.

Gordon Divinity School experienced further challenges during the 1950s. When Paul Jewett left they needed two professors to replace him—he had been teaching Philosophy and Church History. The school called William Kerr for church history and Lloyd Kalland for apologetics. Kalland was a very capable organizer and would have even been qualified to be president, according to Nicole. He was theologically sound and he had proper academic preparation. His strengths were in the area of personal relationships. As president, Ockenga delegated most of his internal duties to Kalland as his assistant. And Kalland distinguished himself as associate to the president. William Kerr built strongly in church history and missions. His studies at Northern Baptist Seminary were greatly deepened in his work for the Ph.D. at Edinburgh.

In 1951, a situation developed which caused the school to have a considerable difficulty. Gordon had purchased in 1947 a huge lot in the northeastern part of Massachusetts. A man named Frederick Prince, the owner of railroads and stockyards in Chicago, had a fortune of some two hundred million dollars. He did not wish to dwell in Massachusetts because the taxation was exorbitant for him. So he decided to establish himself in Rhode Island. He purchased a very impressive property in Newport, Rhode Island. He also owned land of about one thousand fifty acres in Massachusetts. Prince desired to give that to the United Nations so that they would establish themselves there. They did not accept his offer; instead, they decided to go to New York City. So he offered the land to Harvard University. Harvard said, "What kind of funds are you giving us in addition to this land so we can maintain it properly?" Harvard did not get the land either, so Gordon received it for $125,000. Prince himself put in one-fifth the price and four trustees put in $25,000 each. There was more than a thousand acres as one large block altogether. Prince, in addition to having some buildings there, built a chapel for the school in memory of his wife.

Thus, the College had a huge property for a campus and the question was, "How are we going to move there?" It was taken in order to relocate the College, which was "really cracking at the joints." But how could they move the College there? They had no proper buildings equipped to receive the College and to provide for dormitories. Gordon had a very desirable piece of land and was making no use of it. This was a source of consternation with the townships involved because this was now land that was out of the tax rolls. Both the College and the Divinity School were losing face.

At the initiative of Glenn Barker, the suggestion was made that if the College could not move, perhaps the Divinity School could. The Divinity School did not need to have many dormitories because their students were mostly commuters. Nicole recalled the specific details of the move:

> When everything was weighed out, it was decided that the Divinity School could move. Thus in 1951, the Divinity School relocated. We had a thousand acres in Wenham, Hamilton,

Essex, Manchester, and Beverly townships. It was like a large island going over the boundaries of various towns. Mr. Prince had bought various farms that were being abandoned—he was quite gifted in real estate. It made for a remarkable campus. We did have to do some pioneer-type work with this because there was no building that was in superb shape. The Divinity School had to have some places in which resident students could stay, so we had fifteen mobile homes brought in. There was an old hostelry there, which was in very poor shape, but we had nine different apartments in that. A lot of people were coming by car to their classes so we needed some parking areas.

That was the time that the trustees decided to give one acre of land to faculty who had been there for some time. And the Divinity School professors had the first choices because we were there and we knew the place. So we got some extremely valuable lots that way. The first three years, I commuted thirty miles from Belmont. Some other professors were commuting, such as Edward Dalglish and Frank Littorin. Paul Jewett built a house there on the campus. Burton Goddard, who had been renting for some time, built his own home there. Annette and I had a house built for us on a lot the school gave us, and we moved in on Thanksgiving 1954. The house, with all the developments that were made after the original planning, cost less than $20,000. We had $10,000 available because in selling our former house we made a profit of $5000, and we pocketed the equity we had developed by paying on the mortgage. Thus we had a building mortgage of 4.5%. When the house was built, I went to the bank and said, "You really have no risk anymore and perhaps you could lower my mortgage." And they lowered it to 4%. So, we started paying in 1954 for twenty years, after which time the debt was wiped out.

There were very few restaurants nearby, so the professors would bring in their lunch and eat together. Thus they had a faculty meeting, so to speak, every day, Monday through Friday. There was nothing that arose that the faculty could not discuss together prior to having some official decision. They developed a very good understanding of each other as a faculty. There was a tremendous unity among the professors, one "that probably no other faculty elsewhere had achieved." When President Forrester came in 1960, he felt threatened by the unity of the faculty. He tried to diminish that as much as he could. But with Dean Goddard they really achieved a tremendous level of cooperation together in organizing programs and deciding how they would deal in relationship to churches. Incidentally, this served the advancement of Calvinism, because both Jewett and Nicole were strong Calvinists, and Glenn Barker had been won over from another line of thinking at Wheaton—he came from a Keswick approach. The students benefited from the fact that the professors were correlating in their classes with what the other professors were teaching.

Roger and Annette's move to a home on the Gordon Divinity School campus provided the occasion for a discussion of one of Nicole's favorite subjects: books. His appetite for collecting and his doctrinal interest converged in the assembling of his personal theological library. As a youth he enjoyed visiting the stores of second-hand book dealers. By the age of 19 he had assembled a collection of some forty volumes on mathematics. For his 1938 journey to the United States, however, he had little else than an English Bible and the three volume German commentary on the New Testament by Adolf Schlatter. In its more final form, Nicole's personal collection included a special emphasis on systematic theology, including some 400 titles on the atonement. The most ancient volume was a copy of Heinrich Bullinger's *Decades*, printed in 1552. There were 10 volumes from the 1500's and more than 100 from the 1600's. An estimate by a specialist from Chicago reached the sum of $450,000 – which had been acquired for less than $50,000. Not included in these totals was his assortment of detective literature and subjects other than theology, which numbered approximately 5000 volumes. He recalled,

> In moving from Belmont to Hamilton, when we had developed the house in 1954, I had a mover to move our furniture, but I decided to move my books by renting a truck and using some of the students to help me. The new house had dimensions of 40 feet by 45 feet, all under one roof, plus a garage of 10x20, and a little porch of 10x8. The full size of the basement was 40x45; the attic was also of similar size. It was understood that Annette should have complete control of what to put in the main floor of the house, and that I would have the attic and the basement for my

books. I had some bookcases that I had made, but I also had a large number of wooden boxes used for citrus and other fruit, 144 of those from Florida packing houses, and 80 more from California that I used for bookcases. Often, I could store the books two rows deep in these boxes. I had a considerable space for my library, which at the time of moving was not all that large (though it enlarged continuously to the point of being some 20,000 volumes when we moved to Orlando). This was done in about four truckloads from Belmont to Wenham. In addition to that, some transport of books was made by myself in my car.

I had a considerable task getting the boxes set up so they would stand properly with the books, then classifying the books so I could find what I needed. For 35 years, from 1954 to 1989, that was sufficient. When I came to Florida, I had some books that I abandoned, but there was also a large amount I brought here. The moving company, whom we used for our Florida relocation, decided they could use their biggest truck, and that in addition to my books they could put in some furniture on top. I showed them everything to be moved, and they started putting my books in the truck. They had not even finished loading my books in there, and they realized the truck was full. They could not even get out of the driveway turning right as they needed to, because the truck was so low it would have scraped the ground. They turned left to accomplish this so that they did not have to have a declivity. Far from being able to get the books *plus* some household objects, they found my books alone filled up that truck.

As a result, we had a very unsatisfactory moving. I had chosen the moving company because of their low price, but they did not arrive on time, did not load on time, did not bring to Florida on time, and there were some items missing, particularly some parts of our bed frames. It took about a month before everything was finally together. They must also have lost two boxes of books or more. Termites then damaged four boxes when the books were stored for a time at Reformed Theological Seminary in Maitland. I had altogether 800 boxes of books, both wooden and cardboard. Our home in Apopka had four bedrooms, a living room, dining room, and two baths. The major part of the library was housed at RTS, though I kept some books at home. When the seminary moved from Maitland to Oviedo, the moving of my books was again a considerable problem.

I always recommended to the students to build a good library, because they might be in small churches where resources would be limited to the books they had gathered. So I told them to think in terms of a library of 1000 volumes. This was manageable to move, and once they reached the mark of 1000, they could stay at that, but improve the quality. My advice was to buy an older encyclopedia, maybe 20 years old, which would have adequate data on the core material, and to get a *World Almanac* every five years for the more current data. At least one set of commentaries on the whole Bible should be purchased, so that they would not be lacking on any part of the Bible. If a parishioner came in with a question, they would have at least one commentary to cover that. My advice in recent years has been to get the *Expositor's Bible Commentary*, edited by Frank Gaebelein. That is the one I keep in my bedroom. Then I would advise, in order that they would not lose what they have painfully acquired in seminary, to take one Bible book or theological subject, and keep up with that in terms of current scholarship, buying all the books and commentaries and periodicals related to that, so that they would be on a footing even with professionals. They could speak at pastor's meetings as specialists, and the expense would be limited because the study would be focused. Get a good dictionary. Secure a good book on medicine. A number of translations of Scripture should always be available for reference.

I would encourage the church to provide some money each year, which would not be taxable, which could be used to keep the pastor in good books. Edward Dalglish said some of the libraries of our pastors are so infantile that *The Bobsey Twins* is practically a classic. In building the library at Gordon, as well as my personal library, I depended quite often on buying the libraries of deceased ministers. I approached the widow, asking if she had any intent with respect to her husband's books. Many times the widow wanted to sell the books, but if she approached a book dealer, the offer was so ridiculously low that she was unwilling to sell. She knew, after all, something of what her husband had paid for those books, and the privations that the family had suffered at times so he could have them. The widow might remember with a sigh that her husband as a pastor had bought books when what the family needed was shoes! My approach was to offer more than most book dealers could, so that the widow would get a little extra. My way of looking at it was, I knew there were books I wanted to buy, and I figured what I could pay for those, then I offered that price for the whole bunch. The books that I did not want I could not afford to pay money for. I told the students that their ministry would not rise much above the level of their library.

Thus I could help build the Gordon library (and my personal library) through these acquisitions, and still be able to sell extra copies to the students so their libraries could be built up at low cost. I found these libraries through notices of alumni that had died, as well as newspaper obituaries. I found books at the Salvation Army and other thrift stores. One professor, Dr. Mercer, was going to move and did not want to relocate his entire library. He had dealers come from New York to make an offer to buy some books; the offer was so low he said that he would rather give them to the Salvation Army, which he did. Well, I found these and thought, "A great scholar has died." But when I called to speak to the widow, Dr. Mercer answered and said, "I am Mrs. Mercer's husband!" I asked if he had other books he would be willing to sell and he did.

I was impressed by the spiritual dimension of the ministry of the librarian in the seminary. He is the one who has under his control the treasury of things that have been accumulated in the body of Christ, which can be made available in our day. The librarian has in his hand the treasuries of the past, even as somebody who is selling cans of fruit and vegetables has some of the treasury of earlier harvests on the shelves. In some ways it is better to get fruit fresh (this was the conviction of D. Martyn Lloyd-Jones), but without books we just cannot go back to the freshness of the 2nd century.

In 1955, finally, the College managed to move. They had two buildings prepared for them as dormitories, then "we had to divide the lot as it were, College and Divinity School." It meant retrenchment for the Divinity School, because various places they had used were turned over to the College. The College was getting more money because the tuition was higher, and the enrollment was higher, and it was essential for them to get accreditation because otherwise the Divinity School could not be accredited. The College received accreditation in the 1960s, and immediately after that the

Divinity School also was accredited. That occurred in the days of President Forrester.

The Gordon Review was started by some of Nicole's colleagues at Gordon College. Other schools had their own theological journal, and it seemed appropriate that Gordon should have something of the kind. Lloyd Dean was very active in this as first editor, as was the professor of church history, Milburn Keene. They wanted an attachment to the Divinity School as well. The periodical was initiated in February 1955 and was intended to be a quarterly. Nicole had a portion of his master's thesis reproduced in it as a contribution from the Divinity School. For some time it continued, but at an early point Milburn Keene died, and Lloyd Dean left the school because the salary was inadequate. He was engaged by the pharmacy school to teach philosophy, but the dean of the college arranged such a schedule that he could not carry it all. Professor Huttar from the English division of the College was very active as editor for a while, but then he left to teach at Hope College. By default, Nicole became editor in 1959. The school did not budget enough funds to support the review—"the school barely had enough to run itself." There were other schools interested in this struggling project. A consortium of fifteen evangelical schools took over, renaming it *The Christian Scholar's Review*. There were some controversies about the infallibility of Scripture that were dealt with in the review. Nicole wrote an article about inspiration, dealing with B. B. Warfield versus Dewey Beagle[6] (Beagle said there were some *hymns* more inspired than some parts of *Scripture*). The review broadened further after the consortium took over; it is still a well-regarded review at the seminary and college level. *The Gordon Review* lasted until spring 1970; it was changed to *The Christian Scholar's Review* in Fall 1970.

The statement of faith for the Divinity School was very brief and somewhat vague. Theological soundness was safeguarded primarily through the soundness of the president, Nathan Wood. He ensured that only persons of sound evangelical faith were appointed. The school decided to develop a more thorough statement of faith, and since Nicole was the one who was trained in theology they

---

[6] See Bibliography D11

asked him to write a first draft. Ultimately he worked with a committee to compose a final draft. Then, once that was improved and finalized, the committee submitted it to the faculty as a whole, and then to the trustees. The statement of faith that Gordon has is essentially the one Nicole prepared, with a few stylistic changes.

Nicole noted that Gordon Divinity School always sought to have a friendly relationship with the churches, and to provide graduates who would be in harmony with their outlook. As a result, they had within the student body and also in the faculty people who belonged to denominations that did not always get along very well with each other. Particularly the American Baptists and the Conservative Baptists were at odds, and Gordon had both American Baptist and Conservative Baptist students. Frank Littorin was a notable representative of the American Baptists on the faculty, and Nicole also was in that body, although not as approving of it as was Littorin. Then there were Conservative Baptists like Glenn Barker, and Paul Jewett who came from the GARB (General Association of Regular Baptists). There were Presbyterians like McLeod and Goddard. Thus there was a variety of denominations represented in the faculty and in the student body.

Gordon's approach was that they were preparing people for the service of God *in churches*, so they did not want to have a narrow-minded ecclesiology. They wanted to see a variety of churches receiving the benefit of pastors with their training in Bible, history and theology. They wanted their graduates to function as cooperative people in the churches in which they served. One approach the school attempted to avoid was to have graduates who went into churches with the intent of moving those congregations out of their respective denominational relations. That tactic tended to follow a law of diminishing returns: "one or two like that, and the school is blackballed; and if we are blackballed, we can't do the job." Gordon wanted to be known for being sound in theology, but also for being in a cooperative mood, unless there were matters of conviction that cooperation violated. Their approach was that if a student was in a denomination, and the denomination had an approach that violated the student's faith, the best thing was not to move the church out of that connection. Rather, the student should move out of the connection, and then join another body in line with his or her convictions:

> If you attempt to move churches out, you are putting a black mark on yourself, both as a person and as a church worker. And evangelicals are not going to be eager to have you because they don't know when you are going to take the church out of *their* fellowship. Somebody who does that is obnoxious, not only for the people that he leaves, but also for the people that he joins. We at Gordon attempted to collaborate with the churches.

The school had a committee of placement, because churches would approach them to get the names of candidates whom they could call when they were without a pastor. They trusted Gordon Divinity School to give them recommendations that would be profitable for the church. They often did not trust the Convention because they thought the Convention would give them recommendations that would be beneficial to the Convention. For about ten years Nicole was chairman of that committee (the president and the dean were also a part). He knew precisely what was wanted in that regard. And he fully agreed with the principle that there was no dividend in sending people to raise trouble in churches.

In 1949, Roger and Annette were privileged to have a two-month visit from his parents and sister. Some time before this the couple had bought a house in Belmont, moving away from Roxbury ("which was a slum"). Annette had actually found the apartment in Roxbury before their marriage, and this had been their home for three years. The home in Belmont was a very nice place, located in a suburb near Harvard University where members of the Harvard faculty were living. The Nicoles had bought this two-family home on advantageous terms because of Annette's service in the United States Coast Guard. The income from the rent of the second apartment and of Annette's job in the Lincoln Laboratory enabled them to develop a significant equity. Nicole's father feared when they bought a house that they would have concerns of upkeep that would hinder their ministry. He came to see that by having a mortgage, Roger and Annette were putting money away for the future through the equity that was being built. His parents saw the range of the couple's activities, they saw the new home setup, they visited the churches, and Albert was even one of the speakers at the annual reunion of French Baptist churches in New England. Bertha Nicole said, "Well, it was hard for us to accept that you would be away, but now that we see what you are doing and the kind of reception you have here, we can see that this may truly be God's will for you." They recognized that there was a range of opportunities for Nicole in America that Europe could not have provided for him. That was very important for his parents, and it was a great relief for them to feel that they could view it that way. In 1954, they moved to Hamilton, MA, near the Gordon Divinity School into a new house constructed for them on a design that Annette had prepared. It was a beautiful four-room building with large picture windows and substantial basement and attic.

It was difficult for Annette to live so far from Roger's parents, since her father had died when she was a small child. Her mother was very good-hearted, but living on a level quite different from the Cyrs, to whom Annette was also related. She had missed a father badly, and she felt that now Roger's father would be her father. In the first year of their marriage, they had a rather difficult honeymoon. They were not able to adjust easily to marriage, just the two of them. She did not see his parents in the best light during the first visit to Europe. When his parents visited America, they got to know Annette better, and yet there remained some reservations that caused for Annette a trauma that Roger was not able to see at first.

Albert and Bertha Nicole were more influenced by the principle of "class" in society than was Roger. They experienced some difficulty because of that. Nicole's mother was of an elevated class in society, because she was a "de Neufville" (having the "de" before the name was indicative of class privilege). She did not belong to the hoi polloi; in fact, she was of the very upper levels. Albert felt very strongly about the dignity of a university professor. His own father, Roger's grandfather Jules, was a highly esteemed university faculty member. Roger's parents had a difficulty in seeing Jules Marcel's marriage and Roger's as the extraordinary blessings that they turned out to be:

> If God puts you in the cream, that does not mean you have the option to stay out of touch with the milk; that is what the ministry is. My father had high ambitions for our family, and I

think that precluded him in some way from appreciating at first the true value of the gifts of Annette. When I am at our home here at Village on the Green, I can see she has more gifts for interacting with people than I do. With all the knowledge I have, it doesn't get me next to people the way Annette is doing. I have learned myself to appreciate her more than I did before. I believe I would have been 50-65 percent less effective without a good wife like Annette.

The congregation, to their credit, was very concerned for Nicole, for they had become close as pastor and people. They were looking after him as an unattached young fellow away from his own family. They *were* eager for him to get married, thinking it better for the pastor to be married rather than single. Nicole agreed with this assessment himself! But they wanted him to have the right person, and they did not feel Annette was the one. Some of them had daughters of marriageable age, and they were perhaps hopeful he would choose one of those. This period was a "cloud in the sky" for Annette and Roger that made their early days of marriage somewhat difficult, but God blessed them through it. In 1946 (during the 1 ½ years he was not pastoring), he was privileged to baptize Annette into the membership of James Street Baptist Church, which was very near their home (a quarter mile or less) in Roxbury. Michael Strom, a Norwegian, was pastor. In 1954, the French Baptist church at Manchaug united with the English Baptist church in that village (this was possible because fewer and fewer persons there depended on the French language for their spiritual needs). Services continued at Worcester until 1956. In that closing year, Nicole came to the church only every other Sunday for an audience of three: one exceptionally spiritual woman who only knew French, and two others who knew English. He felt he was released from this when the godly French-speaking woman died. He continued to serve as an interim in half a dozen churches, sometimes for as long as a year. This period of interim preaching assignments was very interesting:

> Starting in 1956, I was able to be more diverse in pulpit supply, serving churches in Connecticut, New Hampshire, and Maine. I was also able to do temporary interim pastorates. The first interim pastorate was in Concord, Massachusetts for about a year. This was a church with a lot of internal division, and I am

thankful to say that during my ministry there they drew closer together. Next, I served in Exeter, New Hampshire at a church of Advent Christians for at least six months. Then I was ministering in Nashua, New Hampshire at a Conservative Baptist church with a very fine spirit and several dedicated Christians. The pastor, unfortunately, had been in an affair with a church member and had to resign suddenly. The woman from the affair eventually came back, but was received rather coolly. The elders of that church were very fine, and it was overall a thriving church with a very sound evangelical commitment. I had an opportunity to minister to a lady who had requested anointing with oil and laying on of hands by the elders (James 5:14). I helped the elders do this in a proper manner, examining her intentions and her heart preparation.

Annette was able to attend services with me during this time. We would often eat at the homes of the church members. If there was an evening service, I would rest during the afternoon (they would have a room for me to rest, since I had already developed narcolepsy). While I rested, Annette ministered to the people in her own delightful way, and could tell me important matters later as we rode in the car. Her gifts developed and she helped me tremendously. In East Rochester, New Hampshire I served a church that was very divided, but at least had spiritual deacons. We got very close to those people. They had approached a pastoral candidate from Gordon. The church extended to the man a unanimous call, which was remarkable considering their internal strife. This fellow was confronted by two calls at the same time, and he took the *other* church. The folks were severely disappointed. They eventually called another man, and I said I thought he would be even better than the one who rejected them.

I ministered also in Manchester, New Hampshire, at an American Baptist church that was quite evangelical. I was there for more than a year. This was the one town in New England where there was a large contingent of French Canadians. Some who could not understand English were still coming to the church where I was preaching.

Nicole decided to have a French service for those few folks in the afternoon one Sunday per month, in the hopes that a separate

French congregation might develop. Then a pastor from Boston took a Sunday, also preaching in French. Finally a member who had been a schoolteacher took one other Sunday. The last Sunday of the month they had French preaching tapes. The church recently celebrated its twenty-year anniversary, for which Nicole taped a message on the answering machine. He served as interim in a church at Woonsocket, Rhode Island. Interestingly, his brother had been pastor there for a year when he was a student. Nicole was there after the pastor retired. This was a church that Gilbert Bilezikian eventually served as well. In Worcester, Nicole served as a co-interim in a Swedish Baptist church with Wesley Roberts, a Jamaican professor of church history at Gordon. They struggled with having a black interim pastor. Finally, he ministered in Haverhill at Second Baptist Church, "a dying place." He was preaching every Sunday, and performing weddings and funerals. His goal was to "keep some oars in the water of the pastorate, not just in academe."

Nicole had some French students from the school who joined with him in ministry from time to time, going door-to-door giving away New Testaments. One of these, Samuel Benétreau, became a professor of New Testament at a fledgling seminary near Paris, Vaux-Sur-Seine, and wrote commentaries on I Peter and Romans. Another was Gilbert Bilezikian, who became pastor of a church near Albany, New York (Loudonville Community Church) for five years. From that post he went to Wheaton College, where he had a productive teaching ministry for twenty years. He also served as president of a college in Lebanon (Hagazian College), but had to return because of the condition of one of his children who needed special attention. Bilezikian is a leader in the biblical egalitarian movement. While he was in Lebanon and his wife was in this country, meeting all kinds of difficult situations, he was amazed at the amount of work she could accomplish, and this led him to reconsider what he thought the Bible taught about the roles of men and women. He concluded that the Bible had room for women that was much larger than what society permitted. So in the light of the special ability his wife had shown, he was led to revamp his understanding of the place of women in God's purpose, both in the home, in the church and in society. He is also the co-founder, with

Bill Hybels, of Willow Creek Community Church. "He is a very fine brother," Nicole noted.

Gilbert Bilezikian had the following to say about his former professor,

> "While I was a student at Gordon [Divinity School], I met a young Baptist man, very gifted, Jean Valla. There was also Samuel Bénétreau, who became a notable figure in the French Evangelical movement. I also took classes with Roger Nicole, brother of Jules Marcel Nicole. He had an astounding memory. He was thoroughly committed to Calvinism. We have continued our Christian friendship in spite of differences which developed later."[7]

In the summer of 1947, Nicole was invited to Western Baptist Theological Seminary in Portland, Oregon, as a guest lecturer. He made the long trip with Annette by train, three days journey to Chicago, across Montana, down to Spokane, then to Portland. He had a course of six weeks there, dealing with theological developments in the 19th century and influential leaders like Friedrich Schleiermacher and Albrecht Ritschl. The seminary was eager to keep Nicole there at the conclusion of his course. Their professor of theology was getting old, and though he was a good man in many ways, he was "remaining somewhat on the surface." They were eager to assure their future, but Nicole was not interested in relocating there, because he felt he would not have the library resources there that he would need for future studies, while in Boston he would have research materials in abundance.

Nicole had several faculty colleagues who were doctoral candidates at Harvard, "where they did not care if you were an evangelical; in fact, they did not care what you believed." When elected professor at Gordon Divinity School, he felt that he needed a doctorate that was acknowledged even beyond the confines of the evangelical landscape. He was convinced that the Gordon Th.D. validated his evangelical conviction, but that it did not prove his academic abilities for teaching at the seminary level and outside

---

[7] The original quotation by Bilezikian was in French. The translation here provided is by Nicole.

evangelical circles. After teaching the summer course in Portland, Nicole became a Ph.D. candidate at Harvard (he passed the language exams that same year). His area of study was history and philosophy of religion, because "church history helps us avoid the danger of deviations in theological trends." He commented that he did right choosing history rather than theology, because the overall brilliance evident at Harvard was coupled with fundamental departures from the faith: "At Harvard, I saw firsthand a vision of the desert when the Bible is abandoned." He described graphically the spiritual condition, not only of Harvard, but of the whole New England region:

> Harvard was not a school of faith; it was a university of doubt! I was well grounded in my commitment to the inspiration of Scripture, and though I knew that if you go into the chill winds you may get spiritual pneumonia—I was willing to take that risk and to trust God to keep me sound and not let me get carried away by the studies I was pursuing. I would have to say that my contact at Harvard reinforced me in my evangelical faith, because I had the chance to see first hand the kind of desolate situation you have when the faith is gone; it was a burnt ground. Unfortunately, New England was as a whole a burnt ground spiritually. It had been damaged enormously by the unbelief found in Congregational work which had become essentially Unitarian (in fact that is how Unitarianism started, with Congregationalism going down the drain).

He was received very well at Harvard, and he also earned several scholarships. In fact, he noted, "I never paid a cent to them—they gave me everything. Harvard was even paying my medical insurance for a while! How gracious God was to me in all of that." He came to Harvard already with a master's degree from the Sorbonne and a doctorate from Gordon. The Ph.D. required eight credits of coursework, and then the thesis. He explained:

> My class requirement at Harvard required 8 credits of 8 different classes, but also you had to manifest competency in 6 different disciplines. For two of them you could take a course, so that you would not be examined on them. I took my Bible discipline by course. I had two courses in New Testament by Professor Henry Joel Cadbury (a Quaker with defective views on the resurrection),

which I attended as an active participant, and the mere attendance was enough to satisfy that requirement. Then I took one course in Old Testament Introduction by Charles Taylor, who was dean of the Episcopal school in Cambridge. He was a very excellent professor and I had great respect for him. Taylor was very fair, and gave me highest marks for my work, even though I made it clear that I did not accept the critical outlook. That was my Bible arrangement. One other requirement I met by course was two classes in Islam (I needed to study another religion beside Christianity) by Dr. Thomson who was quite strong in Arabic, and very knowledgeable in Islam.

After that I had to be examined in one phase of Christian doctrine, one era of church history, one phase of development of the church at the practical level and one phase of development of doctrinal approach. My chosen doctrine was atonement; my period of church history was 325-451 (the Christological controversies); my development of the church subject was the progress of free churches in Europe as contrasted with state churches, and on that I had all kinds of data that even Harvard did not have because my father was an actual participant in that; and my doctrinal development related to Dutch theology in the 19th and 20th centuries. My general exams were taken in 1955 and I had no difficulty with them. I was supposed to have Paul Tillich as the examiner, but he was out of town at the time the exams were scheduled, so they got Professor William J. Wolf from the Episcopal school, who had written a book on the atonement called *No Cross, No Crown*. Professor Paul Tillich was absent. When I saw him afterward, I said, "You should have been there at my examination." He said, "What were you examined on?" I said, "On the atonement." He said, "Oh, I dislike the thought anyway!" So, I thought it was a very nice thing not to have Tillich as my examiner!

I took one course on Modern Dutch Theology which gave me two credits out of eight and I did not have to sit through a single class for that. I took two inane classes in theology with a humanist; he was one of the worst professors I ever had. Then I had two courses in theology with Dr. Dillistone who was teaching at the Episcopal school. I had one seminar on Arianism with Dr. George Williams. He had members of the class to represent various elements of the Arian controversy through a dramatic presentation. I was privileged to be Athanasius. Fortunately, play-acting was not embarrassing to me. Williams was quite likely to become suddenly very severe, and the student who was playing Arius was not well prepared. Dr. Williams just blasted him heavily. Thankfully, he was never that critical of anything I did in the course. Then, on the final day, he had invited us to come to his home, and present the play about the Nicene Council. He said to me, "You are Athanasius. I want you to do a good job on this. It is not only for my course, though naturally I am interested in that too. But some of these fellows do not have an inkling of what the score is, and you are the one who can get them right. So, as a witness for the truth of God, I want you to do a good job." This was surely an unusual thing at Harvard! Dr. Williams had a tender heart for minorities, and evangelicals were certainly a minority there. He even lobbied to have an evangelical professor at Harvard.

Nicole successfully completed general examinations in 1955, defended his thesis over a decade later in 1966, and received his Ph.D. in 1967.

For the Ph.D. at Harvard, Nicole determined to write a thesis about Moïse Amyraut, a seventeenth century French theologian, who in contrast to Calvinism assumed that there was a universal redeeming intent in the death of Christ. Nicole opined, "Now, if this is what you hold, it is manifest that the purpose of God was not realized, since there are people who are lost. So if the death of Christ was intended for all people, and some people get lost, then there is a frustration in the design of God. One advantage of definite atonement is that the death of Christ corresponds precisely with the elective purpose of God. All who are redeemed, and no others, in the end are saved by virtue of the substitution of Christ." The supporters of Amyraut had attempted to broaden the Calvinistic view by including in the redemptive purpose of God those who were unsaved. It is that particular problem which Nicole thought watered down the original Calvinism of the Reformation and produced a weakening, especially in the French Reformed understanding. This outlook made it easier for Reformed people to turn back to Catholicism. Some adherents of this defective view took refuge away from France and entered into relation with other Reformed churches, thus tending to weaken them as well. So, Amyraut had quite an influence, not only within France but also without, by virtue of the persecution in France which thrust people out of the country into England, Scotland, the Netherlands, Germany, Switzerland, and ultimately the United States. Some of these people had been severely damaged by the challenge of the Amyraldian movement. On that account, people who have a somewhat liberal view of Christianity consider Amyraut to have been a hero who managed to escape from the rigor of original Calvinism and provide a broader base for the Christian approach, a base that would not be sectarian but universal.

Nicole discovered at the beginning of his Ph.D. studies that most other people who studied in this area supported Amyraut. He was particularly qualified to study Amyraut since he knew French, Old French, and Latin well enough to have direct access to the original sources. But he had from the very start a fundamental objection to Amyraut, because in his judgment Amyraut had watered down in an inappropriate way the intent of one of the Persons of the Trinity. That was a very serious defect, in Nicole's estimation. The title of the dissertation was "Moïse Amyraut and the Controversy on Universal Grace—First Phase." The reason why it was "first phase" was that the controversy started in 1634, and the first phase ended about 1638. In 1637, there was a national synod held at Alençon, France, in which Amyraut was accused of having turned to heresy, along with a friend of his named Paul Testard. They were charged before the synod of having developed an inappropriate view of predestination, and they were therefore also charged with a faulty outlook on the intent of Christ's death. The synod was in a very uncomfortable position, because on one hand there were very vigorous protests as to the way Amyraut and Testard presented the doctrine, and on the other hand, Amyraut and his colleagues at Saumur were the representatives of the most brilliant theological seminary in France. There were other seminaries, but they did not have the reputation of Saumur. One of these schools was in Sedan, which was not technically part of France. Sedan, whose people spoke French, was an independent principality, surrounded by French territory. Later it was annexed into France, so now Sedan is the name of a French city. The seminary in Sedan was in rivalry with Saumur. Saumur attracted the larger number of students. If the national assembly in Alençon declared Amyraut heretical, they would have put a black mark on their most notable seminary, one that was very effective in the preparation of ministers. And that would also harm the people who graduated from Saumur, who would be thought to be somewhat deviant. On the other hand, if they just let it pass without doing anything, they would show themselves insensitive to very strong protests that had been heard, both from within France and also from the Netherlands and Switzerland.

Concerned Christians had sent urgent messages to the synod, warning of the dangers of the Amyraldian error. Church leaders in Geneva, especially, wrote to the synod, or more particularly to the organization of the French churches, speaking against Amyraut. One of Amyraut's main opponents was a man of tremendous influence in France, Pierre du Moulin, who actually in due course wrote three books against Amyraldianism. The members of the synod were "really at a sticky wicket at this point." Their solution was to say, "We are not going to make a real condemnation. Those people appeared before us, and they professed a sound faith, but we had to warn them not to use certain language that might be misunderstood. And we would suggest that the discussions that developed in this respect are not helpful to the churches. We request that these things not be discussed because the discussions produce internal breakdowns, and it is not to the help of the church which has to suffer persecution from the government of France." In 1598, there was the Edict of Nantes made by Henry IV, which granted Protestants the right of existence in France and actually provided help for churches, ministers, and even an army. This ensured that Protestants would have some military power so that they would not be at the mercy of Catholics who were ruling over the French army in general. This seemed to put an end to the "Wars of Religion" that had decimated France from the time of 1520 or so, when the first martyrs of Protestantism were killed in France until the latter sixteenth century, when a Protestant prince actually became the king of France. Henry IV abjured his faith and joined the Catholic Church (having famously said, "Paris is worth a mass!"). He shifted, and then became honestly a Catholic.

The king of France had to be Catholic, because the majority of the French populace was Catholic, though perhaps as many as one third were at least in sympathy with Protestantism. There was erosion of the Edict of Nantes, and Protestants received less and less of the permissions they had been granted. The king even approved a number of measures that were injurious to Protestantism. So in 1637, when the synod at Alençon met, Protestants were already a battered group, entrenched in order to resist the considerable Catholic pressure. They really did not want to weaken their whole position by saying, "We will just throw out our best school." So the synod concluded that Amyraut and his friend Testard should be sent back to the exercise of their function, but with a warning not to deal with the topics that had caused difficulty. There were others who were told not to deal with the controversial subjects, and since the synod had the right of controlling what was published, they exercised considerable control over the dissemination of ideas. But Amyraut started writing some paraphrases of various parts of the Scripture, including the book of Psalms and nearly the whole New Testament. In those paraphrases, obviously, he wrote in such a way that supported his own view. They were overtly slanted, but you could not expect otherwise from a man who had thought this matter through as completely as Amyraut considered he had.

Amyraut's opponents felt that the instructions of the synod were not being observed, and that in some way the Salmurians were continuing a kind of insidious warfare against the sound propositions of Reformed theology as expressed by men such as Francis Turretin. A German who had moved from Geneva to Leiden, Frederick Spanheim, was especially distressed by these developments. Another man with a tremendous influence at this time was André Rivet. Rivet was a professor in France and then became a professor in Leiden, at the best Dutch seminary. From there he was called to be the private tutor for the children of the governor of the Netherlands. Rivet also had misgivings about Amyraut, and he had written to the synod at Alençon against Amyraut. Spanheim produced a series of theses about the intent of the work of Christ in which he said that there were people who, being orthodox otherwise, were attempting to claim a universal intent for the death of Christ. Well, to say "orthodox *otherwise*" was to say that they were *not* orthodox at this point! Those theses of Spanheim were formulations of doctrine which the professor wrote and which the student, to graduate, would be required to defend as an exhibition of his ability in theology. The writing was not done by a tyro but by an expert, and the tyro, through the exercise of defending the theses, would be prepared to handle official attacks on the truth. The theses then were published (at the expense of the student) separately as little pamphlets. So the theses of Spanheim were thus published, receiving a wide circulation.

Of course the Amyraldians took great exception to that. And Professor du Moulin in Sedan was also making statements about "two people" who were raising difficulties. He called them by names that resembled Amyraut and Testard: "Thaumassin," from the Greek *thaumazo* (to admire), corresponds to the Latin "A[d]miraldus," and "Capito" evokes Testard (*caput* is the word for "head" in Latin; the Old French for head is *teste*). Obviously, these were names whose connection anybody who knew how to read could make: "This is Testard and this is Amyraut." With his extremely witty and biting rhetoric, du Moulin caused great offense in the Amyraldian camp.

So Amyraut attempted to defend himself by publishing a defense of the doctrine of Calvin concerning predestination and reprobation. It was soon evident that this pretended apology of Calvin was really an attempt to defend Amyraut himself against the accusations made by others. That was considered to be a direct violation of the decree of the national synod at Alençon, so at that point Spanheim began to write a systematic objection to the work that had started the controversy. This started as a small presentation on predestination and its major dependencies, but he continued writing, and his publisher made the mistake of starting to print what he was doing without knowing where it would end. And it ended by being a volume of 2700 pages, which had to be divided into three volumes for circulation. When this appeared in the Netherlands, in Latin, it was really a direct violation of what the synod had decided, but the synod had no control over what the Dutch people were writing. Then Amyraut felt that it was his turn to answer, so he wrote a response of about one thousand pages to defend his point of view. He wrote this from 1545-1546, so it was eight years after Alençon.

Nicole limited himself to the first phase of the Amyraldian controversy for lack of time. Meanwhile, he had a student named Brian Armstrong who got interested in Amyraut through some discussions they had together, so he wrote a rather notable book entitled *Calvinism and the Amyraut Heresy: Protestant Scholasticism and Humanism In Seventeenth-Century France* that has had a wide academic influence. Armstrong was sympathetic to Amyraut. Jürgen Moltmann wrote his thesis on Amyraut, as did François Laplanche, a Roman Catholic scholar who saw Amyraut as interested in rejoining the Catholic Church. This obviously interested him, for other Protestants viewed the Catholic Church as the Antichrist, so Amyraut was for him somebody that was an attractive personality. This was a great thesis, with access to manuscript sources—Nicole found it very helpful in his own study. All the people that he could find were *for* Amyraut, and he was the only one *against* him. He finished the thesis in 1966. Heiko Oberman, his mentor for the thesis, left Harvard to replace Hans Rückert at Tübingen. Oberman was quite a student of the roots of the Reformation in the late Middle Ages. He wrote a book called *Harvest of Medieval Studies*. Nicole made a complete bibliography of the Amyraut controversy through 1660. It has been published and is considered the standard reference for the subject: *Moyse Amyraut: A Bibliography*. New York and London: Garland, 1981. x, 209 pp.

In 1957, Nicole was granted a sabbatical leave to study Amyraut for his Harvard doctorate. He and Annette spent eight months touring Europe. They entered at Southampton, then traveled to London. They toured Paris. The couple met Nicole's sister, Mariella, at Rotterdam. They visited a number of places in the Netherlands, then went to Germany, where they stayed with his cousin. He studied the thesis by Jürgen Moltmann on Amyraut at Göttingen. They visited his homeland of Switzerland. Annette took a side-trip for a time to Italy with a friend. Later, Roger went with Annette to Nice to see his nephew who was pastoring a church. They traveled up to Saumur where he met François Laplanche, the Catholic priest who had done a doctorate on Amyraut (he loaned Nicole a copy of his thesis). They visited Strasbourg. They went back to Paris, then England, then finally home to the United States. While in the United Kingdom, he went to Edinburgh, Oxford, and

Cambridge to study the impact on Britain of Amyraut and Saumur. During this extended trip, he realized he was not Swiss anymore: "They were too narrow; they couldn't see beyond the Alps. I had become Americanized, and had a much broader approach, a more global view than I saw in Switzerland." In 1959 he became naturalized as an American, though his Swiss citizenship did not need to be revoked.

In 1940, evangelicals in the United States (discernible as a loose alliance at least as far back as 1873) were often narrowly confined in their own denominational surroundings. At this time they began to desire and to carry out relationships with evangelicals of other denominations, spurred in part by the proliferation of prophetic conferences and Keswick meetings. This corresponded to a similar movement among European Protestants.

The National Council of Churches and the World Council of Churches were so liberal in orientation that evangelicals felt that they were not appropriately represented. This led them to form two notable affiliations, the American Council of Churches (1941) and the National Association of Evangelicals (1942). Both groups served as centers of communication for evangelicals, but something of a rivalry arose between the ACC and the NAE (which had more members). Many thought that a better contact should be established among those in the academic world who held to the essentials of the faith (evangelical representation among the Association of Theological Schools being meager at the time). Burton L. Goddard, with a Th.D. from Harvard, was an evangelical scholar of note who was greatly concerned to correct this. He sent a letter to several evangelical seminaries, as well as to some individual scholars of influence, suggesting the development of a special organization that would provide a much needed forum for the interchange of ideas and a center of contact which would not involve ecclesiastical standing.

In 1949, at the YMCA in Cincinnati, Ohio, the first meeting of the Evangelical Theological Society was held. This was done during the Christmas holiday, December 27-28, and in close proximity to the Society of Biblical Literature gathering. The diversity was truly amazing: Presbyterians, Baptists, Lutherans, Congregationalists, Methodists, and Charismatics; amillennialists, premillennialists, and postmillennialists; Arminians and Calvinists; ACC and NAE members; teetotalers from tobacco and liquor alongside smokers and moderate drinkers. Five members from the Gordon faculty were present: Burton Goddard, Edward Dalglish, George Ladd, Frank Littorin, and Roger Nicole. There were other Gordon representatives who had either taught at the school or studied there. A committee was appointed (Nicole was a participant) to draw up a statement of faith, which ultimately read simply, "The Bible alone, and the Bible in its entirety is the Word of God written, and is therefore inerrant in the autographs." The statement of faith was later enlarged to include the sentence, "God is a Trinity, Father, Son, and Holy Spirit, each an uncreated person, one in essence, equal in power and glory." The original confession, it was thought, would mark thorough evangelicals and provide a screen against the half-hearted and Roman Catholics. Nicole was asked about the experience of helping to draft the statement of faith. He noted,

> I was privileged to be involved with the formulation of the ETS statement of faith. My studies in this area certainly helped me to be an effective contributor to this. I was there, along with Professor John Murray, who was a much more mature theologian than I. But I was very strong in thinking that we were not going to be able to write a whole statement of our doctrine. Instead, we needed to draft a declaration that would characterize us as evangelicals and which would rule out people who were not evangelicals. The essential element of such a statement, in my opinion, was a strong doctrine of Scripture.

Theodore Engelder, author of the book *The Scripture Cannot Be Broken*, is credited with the motto, taken from John 10:35, that was eventually adopted by the Society and which is incorporated into the logo: (in Greek) "the Scripture cannot be broken." Approximately sixty attendees came to the first meeting. Within one year, the membership was over one hundred; by the year 2005, the roster had swelled to over four thousand.

Nicole remained enthusiastic about the Evangelical Theological Society, despite some of the serious challenges it faced throughout its history. He summarized his experience with ETS,

> Early approval for the Society was remarkable. I felt that God was pleased, and we had success beyond our expectations. The

Society has exercised a wholesome influence on biblical scholarship and has fostered friendly relations between scholars who share a consistent adherence to the supreme authority of Scripture. Inevitably, some who were members (and even some who served as presidents) became disaffected—they thought ETS was too narrow in its outlook. Our regular quarterly journal, *Journal of the Evangelical Theological Society*, has good standing in scholarly quarters. I served the Society as president in 1956, and at the 50th (1998) annual meeting I presented a paper entitled "Musings of a Founder."

The first severe crisis the Society faced was in 1983. Robert Gundry had published a commentary on the first Gospel entitled *Matthew: A Commentary on His Literary and Theological Art* that created quite a stir among evangelicals. The book was heavily influenced by redaction criticism. Gundry propounded a midrashic interpretation of the infancy narratives, mingling biblical fact with fiction in his claim that the journey of the magi (the historicity of which he rejected) was really just the homage of the shepherds, embellished to prefigure Jesus' ministry to the Gentiles. Nicole presented the following motion at the 1983 annual meeting, which was seconded by R. Laird Harris: "As one of the founders of the Evangelical Theological Society, with a heavy heart I move that the Society request that Dr. Robert Gundry submit his resignation, unless he retracts his position on the historical trustworthiness of Matthew's Gospel." As an expression of Christian love, Nicole returned not to his original seat, but to a seat next to Gundry. ETS lost some members at the time. Nicole also recalled that both John Gerstner and Robert Preus would not join ETS at first.

The original formulation of the five points of Calvinism fits a TULIP acrostic rather nicely, thereby facilitating easy memorization of the key elements. But every one of those familiar formulations does in some way open questions and forms a basis for misunderstanding. It is much more important to have a right understanding of the truth than to have a mnemonic approach that helps people to remember the five points. This was the subject of a commencement address given by Nicole at Westminster Seminary in Philadelphia in 1958. He noted that it was rather bold on his part, to come to Westminster, a bastion of Reformed thinking, and challenge a well-established formulation of Calvinistic truth. Professor John Murray was present, and he was a theologian that Nicole supremely admired; in his judgment, while he was alive Murray was the greatest theologian in the world. Naturally, he was very eager to find out what Professor Murray thought about his address. He was "not what I would call overly enthusiastic, but he was supportive. Obviously, this TULIP acrostic is something for English-speaking people—in French, a tulip has 6 letters!"

Nicole's analysis indicated that this acrostic started with Loraine Boettner in his book *The Reformed Doctrine of Predestination* that had a very great influence in restoring Calvinism to a position that some evangelical Christians would think is appropriate. A lot of people believed in universal atonement when that book was first published. The doctrine of definite atonement had very sparse support at the beginning of Nicole's own ministry. He remembered having a real problem trying to commend it to the Gordon students:

I had not realized fully how very damaging universal atonement, in the final analysis, is to the work of Jesus, so this is one doctrine in which I "bathed myself" increasingly. And the more I bathed myself there, the more I saw the other position does not really do justice to the work of Christ. My independent study of the atonement really convinced me of its definite nature. In my opinion, the strongest point of Calvinism is that Jesus Christ died to redeem *his people*. The ultimate issue is the Marriage Feast of the Lamb, and that is the whole purpose of creation as I see it: from beginning to end there is one purpose for God, and in spite of the dereliction from the ideal path he has traced for us, he still carries out his purpose.

T. L. Lewis, president at Gordon Divinity School, died in March 1959. This was a tremendous blow to the faculty. He had gathered them "almost like a father to his children" as a faculty. There had been a great burden on him, serving as president of the college and the divinity school. The divinity school from 1944-59 prospered under his ministry. They grew from a school drawing mainly Gordon College graduates to one that drew from a variegated group (mainly from the fifteen schools of the *Christian Scholars'*

Review consortium). Lewis was only about 55 at the time of his death—"his heart failed from the work." In that same year Nicole gave the Payton Lectureship at Fuller Theological Seminary. Fuller had both the claim and the reputation at the time as being *the* scholarly school for evangelicals. The Lectureship was intended to have speakers with some reputation, even if they did not hold to the school's pre-millennial eschatology. The first lecture series was given by Gordon Clark. John Murray also was invited. Nicole's presentation was on the history of definite atonement. Carl Henry was still at Fuller when Nicole lectured there.

Nicole was invited also that year to participate in the centennial anniversary of Protestant missions in Japan. Oswald Smith, Edward J. Young, the mayor of Atlanta, and Nicole were the main speakers. The failure of Christian missions to gain more than a foothold in Japan was evident to him: "When I was at the train station, I realized that two hundred Japanese persons had to pass by before I could hope that one was a believer in Jesus." In addition to Japan, Nicole visited on this journey Hawaii, Manila, Saigon, Jerusalem, Athens, Rome, Lausanne, Paris, Amsterdam, London, and Edinburgh.

JEAN MEYER   FRANKFURT a.M.
Rossmarkt 12   Haus Nr...

Evangélisons par la parole, par la plume, par la conduite surtout : et arrosons nos labeurs par la prière instante et croyante !

R. SAILLENS, pasteur

Presented by the
Gordon-Conwell Alumni/ae
3/21/86

TENTH PRESBYTERIAN CHURCH

17TH AND SPRUCE STREETS, PHILADELPHIA, PENNSYLVANIA 19103

JAMES MONTGOMERY BOICE, D.THEOL.
MINISTER

February 4, 1975

Gordon-Conwell Theological Seminary
South Hamilton, Massachusetts 01982

Dear Sirs:

I would like to take the opportunity of the celebration of the
thirtieth anniversary of Professor Roger Nicole's service to
Gordon-Conwell Theological Seminary to express my appreciation
and that of my congregation for Professor Nicole's profound
contribution to seminary education, understanding of the doctrines of the Christian faith, and to the task of building up
the churches of our country.

Dr. Nicole is steadfast in his adherence to the absolute authority and integrity of the Scriptures. He is profound in his exposition of reformed doctrine. He is winsome in his speech.
And he is a great Christian gentleman.

It has been a pleasure to meet Dr. Nicole and his lovely wife
in recent years. We pray that the Lord will continue to bless
his life and ministry and to bring much glory to his name through
his servant's testimony.

Sincerely and cordially,

James M. Boice

JMB:cf

WORLD VISION INTERNATIONAL

CARL F. H. HENRY

February 1, 1975

Professor Roger Nicole
Gordon-Conwell Theological Seminary
South Hamilton, Massachusetts 01982

Dear Roger:

Across many of the thirty years of your campus ministry at Gordon
we have had good fellowship, from those early days in the mid-forties when we
haunted the shelves of used book stores and spent ourselves poor trying to
build up reading resources. I recall the pleasant walks near the Fenway campus
when we spoke often of theology and its evangelical responsibilities and opportunities, and dreamed of a powerful Gordon witness for biblical faith in New
England.

You have always been a careful scholar, slowly and steadily working
toward your goals, and unstampeded by the pressure of deadlines that prove so
demanding for some of the rest of us. It was good, when last we met in Lausanne
not many months ago, to find you looking so well, and using your keen mind still
for the things of Christ.

You've shared in various volumes of the Contemporary Evangelical Thought
series and in other works that I've edited, and from the beginning had a part
in giving to Christianity Today magazine some theological backbone. The world
has been better for your literary contributions.

Thirty years on a single campus is a long span of cumulative service
with its own special rewards. Many leaders whose ministry is more nomadic forego
such blessings. I tender hearty congratulations, wish you ongoing years of
effective service, and rejoice to count you ongoingly a personal friend.

Cordially in Christ Jesus,

Carl F. H. Henry

RIDLEY ⁜ COLLEGE

UNIVERSITY OF MELBOURNE

Ridley College
The Avenue, Parkville
Victoria 3052

Telephone 38 1622

21st January, 1975.

Professor Roger Nicole,
Gordon-Conwell Theological Seminary,
South Hamilton,
Massachusetts   01982.

Dear Roger,

I have been informed that there is to be a Convocation at
Gordon-Conwell on February 11 to celebrate the thirtieth anniversary
of your service with the school. This is an outstanding record of
service and I am delighted that the school has seen fit to honor you
in this way.

May I add my little word of congratulation to the very many
that you will be receiving. You have built up for yourself a
reputation first as a Christian gentleman, then as a teacher who
endears himself to his students and as a fine scholar. I do not
wonder that you are so highly esteemed at Gordon-Conwell, for you
are so widely admired beyond it.

My own contacts with you, of course, reflect our common interest
in the doctrine of the atonement and related problems. I regard
your essay on C.H.Dodd and Propitiation as the best thing I have read
on the subject. Through the years our contacts have not been as
frequent as I would have wished. But they have been uniformly
helpful and delightful. I cannot tell you how glad I am that this
mark of honor has come to you.

I trust that it will prove nothing but the springboard for
further useful work. I am sure that you have much to give us and
I look forward to more offerings from your pen.

Warmest congratulations from an admirer in distant Australia.

Yours sincerely,

Leo

Dr. Leon Morris
Principal.

Gordon-Conwell Theological Seminary

SOUTH HAMILTON, MASSACHUSETTS 01982   (617) 468-7111

HAROLD J. OCKENGA, Ph.D.
President

February 6, 1975

Dr. and Mrs. Roger Nicole
Gordon-Conwell Seminary

Dear Annette and Roger:

It does not seem possible that you have been identified with
Gordon College and Gordon Divinity School, and then with
Gordon-Conwell Theological Seminary for a period of years
now amounting to thirty. You both are so young in your
actions and vitality that one would not believe you could
have been teaching and serving with us for that long.

Personally, I have been greatly impressed by the breadth of
Roger's theological reading and knowledge. This has made
a great contribution to the Seminary. His fidelity to the
inspiration and authority of Scripture has fortified our
position as a theological seminary.

His commitment to the Reformed Faith has given the desired
flavor to the theological department.

Both of you have been exemplary Christians, very jolly in
your attitude and outlook, so that you have stimulated
others to an optimistic and victorious outlook in life.

Audrey and I have considered it a great privilege to work
with you for these last six years and to have had some
contacts with you over many of the past thirty.

May the Lord grant you good health, abundant energy and
strength to carry on your fine work at the Seminary and
also for the wider reaches of the kingdom.

With warm regards and hearty congratulations, I am

Faithfully yours,

Harold J. Ockenga
President

HJO/mem

Trinity College

February, 1975

My dear Roger,

      It is my privilege, as well as my pleasure, to find myself invited to join with so many more in wishing you well on this 30th anniversary occasion.   I gratefully recall our first contact in 1959 when, in a typical act of kindness, you wrote to encourage a fledgling author by telling him that you had sat up all night reading his first book, and did not now regret the loss of sleep.   Since the time when, two years after that, we first met in Cambridge, and you and Annette came to visit us in Oxford, I have felt very close to you, though we have never been able to spend anything like as much time together as I would have wished, and I have happy memories of all sorts of kindnesses which you have continued to show me over the years.   Just as I have never worn any cufflinks save those with which you once presented me, so I have never seen reason to hold any views of fundamental Christian truth save those which you teach and defend with such skill, and adorn with so much personal graciousness. So it is with deep respect and great joy blended together that I take this opportunity to salute you as a champion of the true faith, a masterly theologian, a warm-hearted pastor, a beloved man of God, and a precious and honoured Christian friend.   Long may your bow abide in strength!

      Affectionately yours in Christ,

Jim Packer

TRINITY COLLEGE (BRISTOL) LTD
Registered in England No. 1056056

Registered Office:
Stoke Hill, Bristol BS9 1JP

WHEATON COLLEGE

Wheaton, Illinois 60187 • *Since 1860 "For Christ and His Kingdom"*

GRADUATE SCHOOL • 312-682-5069

January 24, 1975

Dr. Roger Nicole
Gordon-Conwell Theological Seminary
South Hamilton, Massachusetts 01982

Dear Dr. Nicole:

Nearly one third of a century has elapsed since our ways parted in Boston, when you became a professor of Theology in Gordon Divinity School and I came to Wheaton College. Now we are both on the way to becoming legendary figures of an academic past who have left their imprint for good or ill on successive generations of theological students. As one teacher to another I join heartily in congratulating you on the achievement of these years, and in the wide ministry which you have exerted by proxy. Echoes come back to me of the effective way in which you have instructed pastors and teachers in the theological truth which you have learned from the Scriptures. You have imparted not only your knowledge, but yourself.

I regret that time and space have precluded the contacts with you that would have enriched my learning, and also that the multi-volumed work on theology which you projected long ago has never become an actuality. Nevertheless, the thoughts written on men's minds are even more valuable, and I congratulate you on the years of useful service and on the indelible stamp that you have left on those who have gone out from your classroom to preach and live the message of Christ.

Accept my appreciation for your achievements of the past, and my best wishes for the continuance of your ministry in the future. You are still a young man, and the best lies before you.

Sincerely yours,

Merrill C. Tenney
Merrill C. Tenney
Professor of Bible & Theology

Office of the Dean
Kenneth S. Kantzer, Ph.D.

Bannockburn, Deerfield, Illinois 60015 / 312/945-6700

February, 1975

Dr. Roger Nicole
Gordon-Conwell Theological Seminary
South Hamilton, Mass. 01982

Dear Roger,

Greetings from a friend from "the old days." They are truly getting to be that for us old timers.

The first time that I remember meeting you was at a Gordon reception on Evans Way held by President and Mrs. Wood at the beginning of the new school year for all the faculty. For me it was a delightful experience and our friendship grew rapidly through the early years at Harvard and at Gordon.

Since that time long ago, the Lord has given you a steady and powerful ministry in His kingdom; and we are all thankful to God both for you and for those into whose lives you have built a love for Him and for His truth as you have prepared succeeding generations of students with the necessary equipment for effective service for Christ in the pastorate, in the school, and in every conceivable ministry in His church. You have been a dedicated student of the Word as well as a committed servant of the Lord, and for this all of us are deeply indebted to you and sincerely grateful to God.

Now that you are "retiring" we pray for God's continued blessing on you and your continuing work for Him. As is true of "commencement" at graduation time, retirement can be just the beginning of a new and productive phase of one's life and work. This is my prayer for you, Roger.

Friends are gifts from above, and I continue to thank God for you.

In Christian love,

Kenneth

Kenneth S. Kantzer

The Evangelical Free Church of America

School of Theology

GLENN W. BARKER, Dean
WALTER C. WRIGHT, Jr.
Coordinator of Academic
Research and Planning

February 4, 1975

Dr. Roger Nicole
Gordon-Conwell Theological Seminary
South Hamilton, Massachusetts 01982

Dear Roger:

On your 30th anniversary of service to Gordon-Conwell Seminary,
I count it a real privilege to be among those who send you greetings.

The years we spent as co-workers in the seminary are years I shall
cherish. Together we watched the growth of the school...from infancy
to one of the top seminaries in the United States. I am glad I was
able to share in that growth along with you.

The contribution you have made, and continue to make, to Gordon-Conwell
is difficult to express in words. Only eternity will reveal the results
of your efforts, but I do know our Heavenly Father has been pleased with
the years you have given to this work of the Kingdom.

The tennis games were par excellent! Needless to say, I miss you as a
partner on the tennis courts. Somehow the courts aren't the same without you competing against me!

Marge joins with me in wishing you God's blessing as you labour in love
for Him. We are deeply grateful that we have been privileged to not only
work with you, but to have you and Annette as dear friends.

Cordially,

Glenn W. Barker, Provost

GWB/a

WESTMINSTER
THEOLOGICAL SEMINARY IN CALIFORNIA

March 7, 1986

Dr. Roger Nicole
Gordon-Conwell Theological Seminary
South Hamilton, Massachusetts 01982

Dear Dr. Nicole,

It is a great privilege for me to offer a word of thanks and tribute
to you for your important influence in my life and ministry. Even
though it is sixteen years since I graduated from Gordon-Conwell, it
seems much more recently that I had the opportunity to serve as your
Byington Fellow and enjoy regular personal contact with you. Except
for that embarrassing incident when I was the only one in class to
misspell Berkhof's name, my memories of our relationship are most
happy. I especially remember your extrordinary kindness in tutoring
me in Dutch and in Latin. Our time reading Dort's Acta Synodi,
Bengel's Gnomon and Bavinck's Gereformeerde Dogmatiek have proved
invaluable to me spiritually and professionally. It was your interest
in the extent of the atonement and the Canons of Dort (the only Reformed
confession a Baptist can sign!) that led me into my own doctoral work
on Dort's Second Head of Doctrine. It was some of your comments in
class on the salvation of infants (Canons of Dort I, 17) that led me to
address that subject when I was inaugurated as Professor of Church
History at Westminster Theological Seminary in California. My continuing interest in the Synod of Dort was certainly presaged in our
cheery (though, to many, obscure) greeting to one another of "Happy
Dort Year" in 1968 and 1969 as we celebrated Dort's 350th anniversary.

I am grateful that over the years since my graduation we have from time
to time been able to renew our relationship. It has been a special
treat to share the platform with you at sessions of the Philadelphia
Conference on Reformed Theology. My only regret is that my lecture
on baptism at the PCRT has not been more fruitful in effecting your
theology on that point.

My prayer is that the Lord will grant you years of health and usefulness
so that your rich insight into His Word may continue to edify the church.
And I thank the Lord for your many contributions to my development as
a Christian and a scholar.

With all best wishes,

Bob

W. Robert Godfrey, Ph.D.
Professor of Church History

R.C. SPROUL

Dear Roger,

As a young seminary student I was taught by Dr. John Gerstner that you were one of the most important Reformed Theologians of our time. That was the first time I heard your name. Over the next four decades plus I came to realize that Gerstner's assessment was quite correct.

God has graced His church by sustaining your life among us now for ninety years. Your witness to this sovereign grace will continue for countless years to come. May the Lord bless and prosper you on this birthday milestone.

Love,
R.C.

CHAPTER 6

1960-1980
Broadening Influence

The decade of the1960s was a time of geopolitical strife and cultural upheaval around the world; it was also an era during which Roger Nicole's international influence was markedly extended. In 1961 there was a meeting in Cambridge, England of the International Council for Reformed Thought and Action. The gathering drew a number of people from the Netherlands, France, Belgium, England, Scotland, and a rather small group from the United States. Nicole was there, together with J. Marcellus Kik, who had been enlisted by Mr. J. Howard Pew to discover and to make mimeograph or microfilm duplicates of theologically significant manuscripts and other archived materials throughout Europe. Thus, the scholarly world would have replacement copies of these documents in the United States, should time or disaster claim the originals.

Nicole was scheduled to make a presentation at the conference on the doctrine of inspiration as found in the Scripture itself. He remembered fondly the occasion this provided for a special meeting:

> That's the place where I first met Jim Packer. I knew of him through the book *"Fundamentalism" and the Word of God* and I had read that with very great interest. Packer was one of the persons who made a presentation. The subject was "The Word of God and the Power of Reason" and he had an extremely effective presentation. After Packer spoke, the floor was open to questions. He had a really fantastic grasp of the questions raised, and his answers were extraordinarily full of insight. He also

demonstrated how a position other than what he held would lead to vagaries. There were some people from Germany there who were a little bit dazzled by the neo-orthodox approach, and so they had some hesitancy about an inspiration that was lodged in the text rather than in the *reader*. So, at that point, Packer was extremely good. It was really one of the most effective question and answer sessions I have ever attended. I was very impressed by it, and I got to know Jim that way.

There were also some discussion groups in which the attendees could participate. From France there was Jean Cadier, who was involved in two evangelical groups, the "Brigade of the Gardonninque" and the "Brigade of the Drôme." They were going into churches and speaking during the evenings. Cadier was surely the most learned person in those groups. He was not the most eloquent, but he was the most effective. He had become a professor in the seminary at Montpellier, and he had also written a book on John Calvin entitled *The Man Whom God Mastered*. Nicole enjoyed the opportunity to discuss theological matters (in French) with so many new and interesting contacts.

There were some quite interesting people from the Netherlands at the conference, although their tendency to "split hairs" became quickly apparent. A question arose about having a worship service that would include the Lord's Supper, but there were some there who could not receive the Lord's Supper in such a mixed company of believers. Nicole reflected, "I am somewhat "low church" rather than "high church," so I have no difficulty having the Lord's Supper with anybody who is a Christian. But they had objections in that way, so in the end we did not have the Lord's Supper." He also commented that there was really no need for the controversy since the conference was not an ecclesial meeting, but merely one of people who shared the Reformed outlook.

The chairman of the conference meetings should have been P. C. Marcel, but he was ill, so Philip Hughes presided in his place. Hughes did very effective work in that respect. It was quite an interesting time of discussion, allowing Nicole to become acquainted with some people that he had heard of or read, but did not know personally. It also allowed others to meet *him*. After the conference,

Nicole and Kik (along with their wives) traveled through various parts of Europe searching for archives. Nicole was granted access to the libraries because he was curator (his title was changed to Curator when accreditation required a person with the degree MLS for librarian) of the library at Gordon-Conwell. Having the title "librarian" and familiarity with libraries gave him an entrée with the head librarians, allowing him to examine any archival material they might have. The couples journeyed to Paris, then to the Netherlands, where there was access to the library of the Free University in Amsterdam. They also visited Utrecht and Groningen. After that they went to Germany, where they witnessed some of the ravages of the war, still apparent sixteen years after the cessation of hostilities. They surveyed significant sites such as Göttingen, Marburg, and Tübingen in order to discover resources that might be available. Next they went to Vienna, Austria and Zurich, Switzerland.

In Zurich, Nicole discovered five thousand letters of the Reformer Heinrich Bullinger that were available in the archive. When he informed the archivist that his party was interested in microfilming this treasure, the man said, "Well, there are *five thousand* letters, and surely you are not planning to microfilm all that!" Nicole noted,

> Zurich is really a more progressive city than others in Switzerland. Yet you have this man in a place of archives, with a lot of very valuable stuff by the immediate follower of Zwingli, and he thought it would be a big job to cover five thousand letters. Mr. Pew was underwriting this project with a *million* dollars available. For him, there was no problem.

In Neuchâtel, the group found some important correspondence of William Farel, who was a companion of John Calvin. The little city of Zofingen contained some theologically significant works of Wolfgang Musculus, who worked in Berne for a time. Richard A. Muller described Musculus as one of the "important second-generation codifiers of the Reformed faith," together with Calvin, Vermigli, and Hyperius (Muller, *Post-Reformation Reformed Dogmatics*, Vol. 1, p. 31). The summer was a memorable one for

Nicole, allowing him to see in person some of the places with which he had been in contact during his research on Moïse Amyraut.

In 1963, Roger and Annette took a trip with his colleague John Nichol and his wife to England, France, Germany, Austria, Switzerland, Ireland, and Scotland. Nichol was doing research on the beginnings of Pentecostalism in Europe. His own theological roots were in Pentecostalism (his father served as a pastor in the Assemblies of God). He met Walter J. Hollenweger, a church historian who wrote his doctoral thesis for the University of Zurich. Hollenweger completed a nine-volume study of Pentecostalism in Europe. Nichol wrote his Ph.D. thesis on the development of Pentecostalism for Boston University. The two professors and their wives enjoyed a good time visiting libraries, bookstores, and other sites of interest in a rented BMW.

Fuller Theological Seminary was coming under increasing suspicion by 1966 for what was perceived to be a weakening on the inspiration of Scripture. Wilbur Smith was just one of several evangelical luminaries who noted this drift. Carl Henry had left Fuller to be the editor of *Christianity Today*. Harold Ockenga had decided to stay at Park Street Church in Boston and serve as president in absentia. E. J. Carnell was appointed as president of Fuller after Dr. Ockenga and served there for about five years. Not too long after Carnell resigned, he died of an overdose of sleeping pills.

To address the concerns about Fuller, a theological consultation was convened in Wenham, Massachusetts, that year. Australia, Netherland, Great Britain, France, and Norway were represented. Delegates from Calvin Seminary, Reformed Seminary (Holland, Michigan), Dallas Theological Seminary, Westminster Seminary, Gordon Divinity School, and Fuller all gathered to consult about inspiration. Bruce Metzger was there from Princeton Theological Seminary, where he was known as a strong advocate of biblical authority, although not to the point of affirming biblical inerrancy. Nicole read a paper that showed how both deduction and induction were necessary in ascertaining the inspired nature of Scripture: one must start with a statement of the Bible, and then determine its precise meaning by analyzing the practice of scriptural authors. Glenn Barker said, "After you did your paper, there was no argument between the deduction and induction proponents." Nicole disagreed with his admired Warfield at this point: "You don't start with induction, the evidences from human experience; you start with deduction, what the Bible actually says." In the end, the consultation drafted a formulation that the Bible is "entirely truthful," but they did not affirm the term inerrancy, which Nicole felt was stronger.

Some said that the Wenham consultation showed that there were clear differences among evangelicals on inspiration. John R. W. Stott (who was not there), for instance, did not like the term inerrancy, though he held a high view of Scripture. President David Hubbard of Fuller was a master of exploiting various positions to show that total unity was not necessary for the evangelical view. He was a diplomat of the first order—"he played hide and seek for Fuller, which vindicated Fuller in part against the claims of Trinity Evangelical Divinity School that they were not doctrinally sound." Gordon's reputation was enhanced because they were shown to have a very sound view of Scripture without lambasting other schools with different formulations than their own. Dr. David Fuller kept pressing his idea of errors in the statement of Jesus about the mustard seed being the smallest and also the order of the temptations in Matthew and Luke. Dr. H. N. Ridderbos was questioning the statement of Jesus about an exorcised demon bringing back seven worse than himself, saying if that was really true there should be concerted prayer for those doing archeological digs! John Warwick Montgomery of Trinity was given to very sweeping statements, such as "If you question anything in the Bible, you are siding with Bultmann!" Robert Preus from Concordia was also there. The meeting was reported in *Christianity Today*, and Harold Lindsell made critical observations. His assessment, Nicole thought, was extreme. He wrote to Lindsell, who was on vacation at the time, and an editor pro tem received Nicole's letter and published it.

Nicole's teaching ministry in Canada was conducted in the context of a rich history. As stated earlier (pages 63,64), in Quebec, up until about 1950, there was a tremendous hold that the Roman Catholic Church had on the whole province, to the point that they controlled the legislative system and the administration of law. People could not bypass what the Catholic Church had determined; it even came to the point where they controlled the post office which would not deliver material that was sent to the people by Protestant organizations. The postmaster would literally dump mail that he deemed religiously inappropriate. So it was exceedingly difficult to penetrate that region with the gospel except by personal contact. But even those personal contacts were frowned upon and would cause difficulty for the people involved. There had been a movement during the nineteenth century in which a woman from Switzerland, Mrs. Feller, had come as an evangelical Christian and had begun bearing witness in the midst of this profoundly Roman Catholic area. This produced some spiritual fruit among the people who gathered together and built up a few churches. They had a movement called the "Grande Ligne," which was markedly evangelical, and in which the gospel was presented in a simple manner so that the folks without much instruction could benefit from it. That was a movement that was blessed by God, and the people who were working in it were largely graduates of Bible institutes. They developed a high school in French for the young people, and they had a church in Montreal, along with several churches in various townships not far from Montreal.

That work prospered to some extent in spite of the Roman Catholic domination. But it was also hampered in many ways and had even begun to decline by the time of Nicole's arrival. There were annual meetings for the people in the Grande Ligne, where folks of various churches had fellowship with each other, but it was basically a situation of diminishing returns. Three people of considerable significance, graduates of McMaster Seminary, Nelson Thompson, John Gilmour, and Richard Foster, really had a vision for the French work. These had a complete dedication to the French-speaking people. Thompson understood clearly that it just was not enough to reach people when they were older. He was very qualified to lead in this movement; in fact, he eventually earned a doctorate for his excellent studies on Calvin and his preaching. There needed to be a way in which their French culture and understanding could be maintained for these Canadians, by people who would preach in their native language. The idea was that there should be an approach to them that would affect the whole family, and particularly through the school. So there was a much more comprehensive gospel approach to the whole of life, rather than just church attendance on

Sunday morning. They had a very fine vision there, and Nicole had close contact with Nelson Thompson, who taught him a lot in this respect. Thompson raised questions that Nicole had never considered, but which would be truly relevant from a missions standpoint. Thompson helped him to understand that the situation was not merely a matter of transferring an Anglo-Saxon culture, but what was needed was to get at the root of the French culture, so that those people would not feel that they were becoming strangers in their own country.

In the 1950's, there were people in Toronto who believed that it was the responsibility of English-speaking people to bring the gospel effectually to French Canada. They started another movement, independent of the older one, in which they held evangelistic services. The new group was very suspicious of the Baptist Union, which the Feller movement had joined. They were disciples of T. T. Shields. They organized a fellowship of Baptist churches, distinct from the Union.

In the 1960s, the whole country began awakening to the damaging effects of the Roman Catholic hegemony in Canada. And there was a terrific revulsion that occurred in Quebec. The populace became disaffected, and there were more people of intelligence who realized they had not received the kind of academic training that should have been available. For instance, in their universities they trained physicians, lawyers, and pastors, but did not give attention to other areas in which people could prosper (such as agriculture). So whenever there was a big undertaking, naturally, there were people who were not French speaking who became the head of it. So the people felt oppressed by the Anglo-Saxon power in Canada generally, and by the Roman Catholic power and domination in Quebec specifically. There was a double reaction: a negative reaction politically to the rest of Canada was manifested in the *Québec Libre* movement, where they wanted to become separate altogether and not belong to a federation in which they were a minority; and then there was the religious reaction against the oppression of the Catholic Church. The people felt that they had been betrayed by the church, and that the way in which the church had functioned seemed to relate to the church's interest in maintaining its hold *on* the people, rather than an interest *for* the people, to provide for them the most desirable situation. They felt that they had been held down, both by the Anglo-Saxon majority who had power and money, and by the church, which was the center of the life of the country.

As a result of that, there arose an increasing movement of people who had private Bible study meetings in various places, and rather than go to the Catholic Church, they would meet together. There would be people who had a little more biblical knowledge than others, and naturally they rose to a position of some leadership within these circles. Soon it became apparent, both to the folks of the old Mrs. Feller approach, and to the other group of the Fellowship, that the time had come to prepare people for the service of God, so that they would have a mature body of pastors they could trust who could offer leadership and ministry within Quebec. That developed tremendously during the 1970s and following. Both groups established a forum of preparation for people who already had some position of leadership in the Bible circles, and who might become leaders in the formation of churches throughout the region. And that is precisely what happened! Some of the leaders, being more capable than their flock, yet having only a little knowledge of the Bible, would be aware of their limitations. They understood that they could not just repeat over and over the provided study material. They sensed the need for increased study.

The Fellowship was the first group to organize some actual work, in which the Bible leaders would have opportunity to prepare themselves as if in a seminary, and without having necessarily the academic prerequisites that established seminaries would demand. They would be strengthened for more effective ministry. The goal was to help them have a more thorough knowledge, both of the needs of ministry and the methods of biblical study, as well as the nature of the Scripture and scriptural doctrine. That was a matter of very considerable concern, so both of these groups decided to organize each its own seminary. The Fellowship called theirs SEMBEQ (Séminaire Baptiste Évangélique du Québec), and the Union, under the leadership of a very good executive secretary, Rev. Boillat decided to have a school that would be connected with a Canadian university. This would give them some freedom to express themselves as they desired theologically, but being connected with the university would also give some supervision to the work and credibility, since they would be receiving university diplomas. This would be important for people who already had a college preparation. The Union of Baptists called their school CETE, for Center of Evangelical Theological Studies (Centre d' Etudes de Théologie Evangélique).

Nicole was the person they invited to speak first at SEMBEQ, during a three day series of meetings. A number of their own people presented messages relating to the substance of Christian doctrine. Nicole spoke on the atonement of Christ in that particular meeting. During the summers, they would have sessions for two to four weeks where students could come and learn. This was done in rented facilities, and the classes would be between forty and fifty students in size. They would have it every year, and gradually they began to offer credits for the courses. This had a tightening effect in academic ways that really gave credibility to what they were doing. Nicole was a professor to whom they had recourse repeatedly. So for twenty-five years, he was going to Canada every year in the summer to teach in the SEMBEQ and later on in the CETE. It was very advantageous for them to have a person like him involved in this project because he had academic credibility, with doctorates from Gordon and Harvard. And his ability to speak French was unquestioned. So they knew they were going to have a French teacher with a French outlook in a sense that also would establish a kind of academic basis that other people might recognize. Nicole had a very happy relationship with them.

SEMBEQ had one person of note who had actually been born within that outlook, D. A. Carson of Trinity Evangelical Divinity School. He was the son of a pastor in Ottawa who belonged to the Fellowship. Of course D. A. Carson is thoroughly bilingual. He was raised in a French Canadian context, and he had his studies in French as well as English. He had some doctrinal emphasis that was apparently controversial, and somebody said that they wished Carson would not accentuate that point. So the president, Jacques Alexanian, approached Carson on behalf of the study committee and requested that he not emphasize this in his teaching. Carson ceased collaborating with them at that point. This was unfortunate because he was teaching New Testament and theology, doing a tremendous job. Carson is a formidable and well-known theologian. Then they approached Nicole in a similar manner regarding his egalitarian view of women in the church. They said, "This approach really doesn't work here." And they asked him not to press that point. When they said that, he responded, "God has not sent me to secure a proper place for women all over the world. God has sent me to preach the gospel, and I have here an opportunity to help prepare people to preach the gospel. I am perfectly willing to conform to what the people desire here." Nicole believed it was not up to him to decide at every point what he should teach, so he was willing to submit to the desires of the school in that area.

This pleased the director, Rev. Jacques Alexanian very much. It was he who told Nicole how they had lost the contribution of Dr. Carson, and he said they were very glad not to be losing Nicole, too. They seemed genuinely grateful that he was willing to adapt himself in relationship to what they sensed was needed. They surely did not muzzle him on this, but they asked him not to make egalitarianism a key point. He was careful to say, "Let us be sure women have a proper place of service where God has put them." He did not say, "Let them be ordained ministers."

Both of those bodies developed, and they, together with the Pentecostals, were some of the only Christian groups who had the foresight to participate in this enormous harvest, to try to gather disciples for Christ. This was a time of revival in Quebec; in fact, there were places that had never heard about the true biblical gospel, and the people were ready to receive it. The Presbyterians were in the region for a long time ("I think Mrs. Feller was originally a Presbyterian and then became a Baptist," Nicole noted), but the Presbyterians did very little except to establish in the 1980's in Quebec City Farel Seminary, named after Guillaume Farel, the friend of Calvin. One of their key leaders was a candidate for the doctorate in the Swiss university, a man who served as a pastor there in Quebec. The Christian Reformed Church also supported this work very substantially. They appealed to Nicole to teach in that connection. This he did several times for them, for about three weeks in the summer.

The Baptists had vision for theological education earlier and fuller, and ultimately had a work that developed with substantial numbers. SEMBEQ had the larger number of people. The CETE had the connection to a Canadian university that gave credibility in the larger Canadian society. Nicole felt that God had put him in the position where he might be able to prepare for a later union of those two bodies, because their differences were not severe anymore. The Fellowship had to fight against some liberalism, but those three men who came over were thoroughly evangelical, even though they graduated from McMaster Seminary. There was a potential for getting together Baptists of various types, on an evangelical basis, which would reinforce the work. They would not be rivals to each other any longer, and the Baptist alliance as a whole would have more respect because of the increased number of people.

Nicole was training the future pastors of both Baptist groups, so he was doing everything he could to encourage the principle of fellowship with other evangelical Christians. He reasoned that when some of the older people died who had lived in the time of the separation, the new group of pastors would be folks more amenable to a union. He encouraged them to check on each other's libraries, so they would know where each other were in terms of shared resources. At one point he even wondered whether he should go to Canada permanently. But he soon realized that if he were there permanently, he would have to be associated with *one* of the two groups, and then he would be "out" with the other. If he remained where he was, he could be accessible to both, and this was especially valuable.

Canada was a delightful aspect of his ministry, which he believed God graciously gave to him. He was able to minister in his own language, to French-speaking people, and in a land that had been dominated by an approach that was failing to represent much of the evangelical truth. Interestingly, he had an amicable contact with some Roman Catholic priests and leaders in the area, who also had become open to a broader view. Some of the priests had suffered under the prevailing system. They had seen what the leaders were doing, and they had seen mishandling of problems in a similar way, Nicole noted, to how the Catholic bishops have handled pedophile priests in recent years. How sad that for the sake of the church, instead of dismissing them, they moved those errant priests around, thinking that this was the only way of preserving the reputation and the authority of the Catholic Church! They did *not* think sufficiently of the sacrifice they were making of those victimized children, a shameful sacrifice to the libidinous instincts of a relatively small group of priests. In Quebec it was not as prevalent as in the United States, but the church was dominating the situation, and was attempting to use it for their own purposes, to the detriment of people.

A significant event occurred in the 1950s, near Sherbrooke, which is one of the larger cities in French Quebec, very much in the center of the French-speaking area. Montreal has a medley of languages, but Sherbrooke is very pure French, just like Quebec City itself. There was a physician at Sherbrooke who was doing his work, caring for his family and living in peace when a group of thugs (with the knowledge of the priest, and perhaps at his direction) kidnapped him, dragged him into the train station, and put him on the train to Montreal, saying, "You are going out, and if you come back, we are going to do the same thing to your family." The man was an evangelical, and what happened to him was not an atypical response by the Catholic authorities at the time. The mistake they made in this instance was that in doing this, they moved into the station that belonged to the Canadian National Railway, so this was not something that was subject to the jurisdiction of the province; it was a federal crime. The perpetrators were caught, and they were tried for kidnapping and for crossing the lines into a federal station with a kidnap victim, a Plymouth Brethren medical doctor who returned to Sherbrooke and continued practicing medicine there. The Catholic hierarchy assured that everything would be "sealed up."

There was another man who had been a senator, and who was won to faith in Christ through the ministry of a little church pastored by Nelson Thompson. When this man died, the Catholic Church produced phony evidence that there had been a special abjuration meeting at his home, and that he had abjured the Protestant faith and had rejoined the Catholic Church. They "trumped up" his will. None of that could be challenged in any way, because all the way through the system the judges would say, "Protestants are out!" That was the situation in the 1940's, but with the revulsion of the people the Catholic Church received diminishing support and exercised less and less influence. A time of revival had come, and many people were coming to the Lord and to the gospel. As a result, today there is a very significant body of Protestant folks in Quebec, particularly Baptists. This was similar to what happened in the United States, where the Baptists and the Methodists had the most vision beyond the original states, and where they were promoting the gospel, particularly among black persons. As a result, Baptists and Methodists have gained a footing in the black community. This sort of situation was repeated in the United States, when a large number of people came to New England from Quebec.

As noted earlier, these transplanted Canadians found themselves estranged from the church, and the Baptists and the Methodists arranged for French-speaking churches in New England in order to meet the needs of those people. In 1920, there were twenty-five such Baptist churches in New England, and Nicole later served as pastor of two of them! Baptists, with a proper sense of mission, sensed that much work had to be done. In spite of the leadership of a very autocratic man named T. T. Shields and of the church he pastored, Jarvis Street Baptist Church, they made a splendid effort in Quebec.

By 1970, they already had about forty churches, while the Union may have had only seven or eight very small and dwindling congregations. All of this partly explains Nicole's very special interest in Canada. He had a special opportunity to work not only for the present but also to ameliorate the possibility for a future cooperation, or even union, between those two Baptist bodies. The petty differences and distinctions between the Fellowship and the Union, in a Catholic-dominated land, really were scandalous! One of the critiques that the Catholic Church regularly levied was that while *they* were united within one single church, the Protestant people were very much divided, and the Baptists were even split in two! They could rightly ask, "What is the matter?" The division was not due to basic differences in doctrine or polity. Instead, it was mainly the result of a particular orientation of some leaders, and at that point the Catholics were right, that *is* a scandal!

Nicole hoped in some way to function for unity among his Baptist brethren and sisters. He was probably the one thoroughly trained person theologically that could be available to them with French as a basic language. Again, Thompson was the one who helped him understand that more than just giving them the gospel was required; Nicole had to think about the situation in terms of the larger picture: how their work would affect the whole Canadian society; the impact it would have on the children; and how the results of their labors could be conserved with respect to future work. One result of this episode in Canadian history was that a lot of people left. In New England there are two million descendants of French Canadian people—a significant number! Quebec, with barely six million people, lost 1/3 of its population, a terrific loss. Some of the more open-minded people would be among those, so Quebec was losing some of its best representatives, going to the United States. Nicole further observed,

> In a sense that is what has happened in the United States in general: we have attracted all kinds of people from various countries who came here to form part of the total medley. We have sucked in some of the benefits that came from these people, and in some cases a few of the defects, like the Italian Mafia. All the elements were not a help, but in many cases they were a tremendous help. The greatness of our nation is due in part to this very exceptional mixture that we have, much greater than other countries, who are more homogeneous. This is also the case in Canada, and I found myself deeply involved in what God was doing there. That is why in our will, one third of our estate is going to Canada for Baptist work, in both the CETE (Union of Baptists) and SEMBEQ (Fellowship of Baptists). The movement I described occurred mainly in the decade 1970-1980, the time when spiritually the people were most buoyant. After that, the revival movement that we had witnessed tended to wind down. Revival is like that, it seems; you cannot keep "reviving" all the time. Instead, you have periods of burning flames and then you have a period of consolidation, in which the presence of the fire is not manifest in the same way. I continued the work there in Canada until 1996. So for twenty-five years, I was there in Quebec every year, mostly in the summers and on special occasions, to the extent that my work elsewhere permitted.

Nicole played a role in the founding of the NAE (National Association of Evangelicals), "a very fine institution." He was part of that from its inception, along with President Nathan Wood of Gordon and Harold John Ockenga. Ockenga was the first president of the NAE. He was also president of Gordon Divinity School and College in the 1970s, during which time the school became Gordon-Conwell Theological Seminary. Dr. Ockenga had an extremely wide range of contacts, and was a key leader in the evangelical movement. The principle for membership in the NAE was simply to agree with the expression of faith of the body without dealing with matters of ecclesiastical relationships. This was in clear contrast to the American Council of Christian Churches (ACCC) in which the emphasis was that, in order to become a member there, one had to renounce any kind of affiliation to any organization connected to the National Council of Churches or the World Council of Churches. So the difference between these two was mainly the question, "Does membership demand such an allegiance that you must cut any relation with anybody who has, in your judgment, an improper approach to the faith, or do you allow anybody who has the right approach to join *you*, irrespective of contacts they may have elsewhere?"

Nicole was a member of the American Baptist Churches (he was actually considered a missionary of theirs, because they had French Baptist missions in Worcester and Manchaug that he had served). During his time there, in the 1950s, he worked with them to establish those congregations, not as missions, but as churches, because they really were churches, functioning as such, and he felt they should have their own constitutions. So that was accomplished with the blessing of the American Baptist churches. Meanwhile, the financial contribution of Nicole's churches to the larger body was strictly designated to people who, in their judgment, were carrying out an evangelical ministry. It was a very small donation, because they were very small churches and very limited financially. What little they gave went to the work of Mr. and Mrs. Bixler-Davis in India, who were recommended to Nicole by the official representative of the American Baptist Churches. He was assured that these were missionaries that the churches could in good conscience support, because they were in agreement with the churches' theological views. The missionaries belonged to their denominational body, and their support had not been already subscribed for them in full. So Nicole and his churches were assured that their contributing to these people would not be a way of liberating some money to go to liberals. Their relationship to the Federal Council was minimal, even though the American Baptists were members of that group.

This Federal Council was absorbed in 1950 by a larger body, the National Council of Churches of Christ. Then it was the World Council. Both of those bodies seemed to Nicole to be very lax in some respects, and very stiff in others. For example, their faith was not sufficiently strong to emphasize the Virgin Birth of Christ uniformly, but on the other hand many had a view of the Lord's Supper that would be strictly sacramental. The irony in this was that they could never celebrate the Lord's Supper in the Federal Council, or the National Council, or the World Council because they were differing too much on that ordinance! Yet evangelicals could have meetings like at Lausanne in 1974, and they could have the Lord's Supper together. In a real way, evangelicals had realized among themselves the ideal that was at the stated center of the World Council movement—getting the people together—and they did it around the Lord's Table. It was ironic that evangelicals who were supposed to be *separatists* were the ones who could get together at the Lord's Table, and the people who were *unionists* just could not do it, because they had the Greek Orthodox among them and others with too much division on the nature of Holy Communion.

Nicole believed Dr. Ockenga was a great leader in that regard. He commanded a tremendous respect among evangelicals as the pastor of Park Street Church in Boston, but also as a person of exceptional insight and influence. He was probably recognized as the number one representative of evangelical people, and one thing he did that would have wide-ranging implications was to support Billy Graham very strongly, at a time when Billy Graham was not yet well known. In the presidency at Gordon Dr. Ockenga exercised a very significant influence that transformed the reputation of the school from that of a provincial institution into being a much more widely recognized seminary.

Ockenga was also a leading figure in the union of Gordon Divinity School and Conwell Theological Seminary in Philadelphia. That was a very important development because Gordon had by that time (1970) achieved in the Divinity School a very remarkable transition. No longer were they just a small institution with faculty who did not have sufficient academic presentation for credibility with the larger educational world; no longer did they just serve mainly to train further into the ministry people who had already been in a Bible college such as Gordon College itself, or Wheaton College, or a Bible institute like the Providence Bible Institute.

At the start, when Nicole graduated for instance, there was no one in the faculty who had an earned doctorate degree from a recognizable institution. When he had his doctoral examination, none of those examining him was a Doctor of Theology himself. Surely, they were men who were admirably equipped for what they were doing, and he never had a feeling of having inadequate teachers at the main level. Among these was Merrill Tenney, who was really a very significant figure in terms of scholarship. Another was President Nathan Wood, who was "a giant" in some respects in the realm of thought, although he had to devote a good deal of his energies to administrative functions in relationship to the outside. Then there was Professor Palmer, who was a graduate of Southern Baptist Theological Seminary and a favorite of A. T. Robertson and John Sampey. He was a very capable scholar. Palmer was Nicole's professor of Hebrew, but he also was a teacher of philosophy, psychology, and New Testament. For one term, Professor Clarence Bouma of Calvin Theological Seminary in Grand Rapids came to Gordon and was very influential in "rounding up" Nicole's Calvinism. Another teacher was Edwin Gedney, an Advent Christian, who was a scientist, a geologist, but also had a very deep and mature approach to the faith, a man who served for forty years in the college with tremendous influence. Recalling fondly the memory of his instructors and early colleagues, Nicole commented,

> Gedney served in many capacities, including dean, and he taught some classes at the Divinity School, though I never had him personally as my teacher. The oldest professor, Edwin H. Byington, was a graduate of Roberts College in Constantinople

(Istanbul), and he had an amazing range of interests in practical theology. He wrote books and was an exceptionally interesting man. All of those people, though, were short of the earned doctorate. When I came in as professor, I had a doctorate, and then there were people who were with me on the faculty who were working toward a doctorate. The dean was Goddard, who had a doctorate from Harvard in Old Testament, and then Edward Dalglish and George Ladd were working toward their doctorates. And so we eventually had folks at Gordon who had sound academic accreditation, and Goddard felt that we had attained a tremendous unity, a kind of co-belligerency so to speak, which really made it a specially well-organized work in educational ministry. We provided very good training for the people that graduated in that period from 1950 to 1970. These students were in required classes for one hundred ninety two hours of exposure in Christian doctrine. I believe that at that time I did some of my best teaching work: if you have too large a group you cannot reach them in the proper way. Some of the older alumni still get in touch with me when they have questions.

There was a kind of mentorship involved at Gordon that is often absent at other schools. Dr. Ockenga took over the helm after a time in which the school had suffered under the presidency of Dr. James Forrester. Forrester had attempted to divide internally the Divinity School, the faculty believed, because he felt that their unity (along with Nicole's seniority and growing prominence as a theologian) was a threat to him as president. He also had various problems that were manifested in many ways in his ministry. Nicole stated that his pastorate in one of the interim church situations was more fruitful at the time than his ministry at the school because of his difficulties with President Forrester. He had an inferiority complex toward the Divinity School and its unity, he obviously favored the College, and Nicole described Forrester's tenure at the school as "seven lean years." He recalled the ultimate departure of Forrester as president:

> Forrester resigned as a result of the clumsiness of his public relations director, a friend he appointed who had been with him in World War II at Okinawa. The man's name was Hagopian. For instance, he thought that a major project of the school should be to collect crutches and wheelchairs for the disabled.

Gordon students should also be out on the highways as good Samaritans, looking for accident victims to assist. On the 22nd of December one year, he wanted to have a celebration of the birthday of General Patton at the school. General Patton's daughter lived in Hamilton, but Hagopian did not even approach the family about this! A big choir of soldiers from Camp Dever was to come. More people were actually on the podium than in the audience on the day of the festival! Hagopian also wanted to restore the buffalo back to the eastern United States, so he was writing to the Secretary of the Interior to get buffalo. His firing led to Forrester's departure.

After 1975, Nicole was not as involved in interim pastorates (he was more involved as a *member* in his church), and he did more traveling to itinerant ministry opportunities. The school was in an unstable situation in many respects, and they found in Dr. Ockenga a leader that they readily could follow. He also had a level of confidence in the faculty that they had not seen in Dr. Forrester, who wanted very autocratically to direct things. Nicole thought, "I might as well stay while the storm was going on, and then be available when the thing would come to a better stage." In his estimation that happened with the coming of Dr. Ockenga. Nicole noted,

By 1969, Gordon Divinity School had maybe 120-150 students. Then we had the union of Gordon-Conwell, with the appropriation of substantial money, and a change of campus altogether. Dr. Ockenga came to be president, so the school grew to about 250 by 1980. Enrollment was up to 750 or so by 1990; now it is about 2000. In my judgment, this figure is not the ideal. Professors have a much better opportunity to invest themselves in the life of the students in a smaller school, though a big school does feed more people into the work. Ockenga was a very spiritual man, given to much prayer. He was not at all "stuck-up"; rather, he was very kind to people not as gifted as he. He set an example of faithful chapel attendance at the school. He loved to have fun. I remember one occasion when a man who had been invited to speak at the chapel used a profane word in the pulpit. Ockenga remonstrated with him, "You'll have to clean up your language or you will be shown to the door!" "Who are you?" the speaker said. Ockenga replied, "I am the president of this institution!" The fellow couldn't say anything with clarity after that, like a chicken with his head cut off.

They had "a very fine time" with Ockenga, who served from 1969-1980. He provided excellent leadership during those ten years.

The union of Gordon Divinity School and Conwell School of Theology accomplished under Ockenga was a tremendous boon, because now the Divinity School had a level of training and of production that would enable it inevitably to be a full member of the Association of Theological Schools. This could not have happened otherwise because they were tied to Gordon College, a school that was not accredited by the association. And ATS would not grant accreditation to a seminary that was affiliated with a college that was not accredited. Conwell School of Theology was the theology school of Temple University. Temple had been founded to provide evangelical instruction, and that was done in 1886 by Russell Conwell, who was quite famous as pastor of a Baptist church in Philadelphia. He had preached a single message some 10,000 times, called "An Acre of Diamonds."

Conwell Seminary had had its accreditation removed, though it had a remarkable history. They had the advantage of securing some professors who had resigned from other institutions because of age, men who had reached the age of sixty-five and faced mandatory retirement. So Conwell was able to get people like Henry Joel Cadbury from Harvard, Richard Kroner from Union, Andrew Blackwood from Princeton, and Eric Lewis from Drew University. These very well known scholars had reached an age where their original institutions had to retire them. So in terms of the reputation of its faculty Conwell was doing very well.

When it was decided that Conwell be removed from accredited status, the school inevitably lost Episcopalian and Methodist students. At that point, it was recognized that this institution could be taken over by evangelicals and developed into an unmistakably evangelical institution, in connection with a fairly important university.

J. Howard Pew of Sunoco had decided to invest rather heavily in Conwell as an evangelical institution. Pew wanted a school in which evangelical Presbyterian students could be trained as ministers of the PCUSA. His thought was that, if there was a seminary that kept feeding sound people into the church, it would eventually turn the denomination away from liberalism. Conwell's dean was Stuart Barton Babbage from Australia. Glenn Barker from Gordon was considered for teaching New Testament, and he was also asked to give some direction to the formation of the faculty, for it was thought that the approach at Gordon Divinity School had been a particularly effective one.

Barker got the idea that perhaps there could be a joint approach there; instead of being two separate institutions there could be work under one head to the benefit of both. It turned out Conwell had money but was strangle-held by administrative constraints. There was money to construct a building but the city of Philadelphia would not let them build it within city limits. Gordon, on the other hand, had great limitations with respect to money, but they had a faculty that was considered so good that they wanted to reproduce it at Conwell. So it was said, "Let the two unite. Let all the professors who are at Conwell, who want to come, join the faculty of Gordon Divinity School, and we will have one institution." By a vote of the two Boards of Trustees (1969), Conwell Theological Seminary and Gordon Divinity School were severed from the institutions to which they had been heretofore united and were joined as one institution named Gordon-Conwell Theological Seminary. It was also decided that the consecration of an existing educational building especially for black students would continue the Conwell influence in Philadelphia.

The International Council on Biblical Inerrancy started in 1977 and continued until 1988. Nicole was privileged to have very close contact with its direction. He became a member of the council itself, not merely of the people assembled there for observation. As a result he had a significant role in discussing the statements that would be produced, the Chicago Statement (1978) on Biblical Inerrancy; later the Chicago Statement on Hermeneutics (1983); and then the Chicago Statement on Application (1987). The most significant in its formulation was the first, according to Nicole, because it sought to define the inspiration of Scripture and the doctrine of inerrancy in a way that would dispel some misunderstandings that were frequently encountered. That particular statement has been recognized as being a standard point of reference for inerrantists. There were people from Switzerland, Germany, France, England, and Australia involved in it, so the representation was very diverse.

Other drafters of the Chicago Statement on Biblical Inerrancy, besides Nicole, included J. I. Packer, Robert Preus, Harold Hoehner, Norman Geisler, Edmund Clowney, and James M. Boice for part of the time. R. C. Sproul prepared a first draft. The last night of that particular meeting the committee worked around the clock to finally forge the statement that now exists. They took notice of all the comments that had been made, though they did not embody them all. They had a very good working team. Packer, Preus, and Nicole were the ones who had been instructors in dogmatics, rather than other disciplines. Geisler was strong in apologetics and Hoehner in New Testament studies, so there were people with that kind of technical specialty involved. Nicole noted humbly,

> I hope I am not overly self-assertive in putting myself in there, but we were the ones with background in creeds and doctrinal formulations. Packer, I would say, would be the most incisive of the three, and he was very helpful in his recommendations. He has a tremendous control of the English language, in his ability to express things, and he had a great mastery of the problems of modern theology. So, in light of this, Packer was the one who was asked to write the introduction and a concluding statement. Sproul then prepared a brief commentary which I edited for printing.

In the ICBI, Nicole had contact with several leaders in the Evangelical movement. The person who was doing the basic administrative work for the project was Dr. James Montgomery Boice of Philadelphia, "an excellent organizer." The meetings were quite impressive in the number of people that were assembled, particularly since there was no subsidy, Nicole recalled, that could be given to anyone for being present. The participants were supported either by the schools they represented or by their own funds. It is really remarkable how many people were present and participated in the deliberations and the work that was done. In addition to those three "summit meetings" as they were called, there were two "congresses" established to promote the model among laypeople. One of these was arranged in San Diego (1982) and another was convened in Washington, D. C. (1987).

Nicole did not think the Washington meeting had the kind of impact that the others had, though some folks at that congress did help out with a Habitat for Humanity project. Charles Colson was involved in that in an interesting way. His organization, Prison Fellowship, had secured a liberty for some of the convicts to come and do some of the construction work. There were some folks in the churches who came to be working side-by-side with convicted criminals, convicts who had been reached by the evangelistic work of Colson. The Congress presented certificates to those convicts for contributing to the work of God, and Nicole "never saw people more happy at receiving a certificate than those convicts. It was beautiful to see the joy of those prisoners in getting a certificate from society, men who had been condemned to prison away from society; it was marvelous to behold." That part of the congress was very impressive. But other than that episode, he did not remember anything that really made a profound impact on evangelicalism generally or on the city specifically.

There was a female participant, Rebecca Manly Pippert, who was one of the most articulate women in the evangelical movement. She was the wife of a man involved in journalism, and she had been quite active in public speaking even before her marriage. Pippert made a presentation that was quite stunning, and in particular she had an illustration about two young people who had been quite active evangelistically in a church, leading many young people to Christ. This young couple had a dynamic witness together, and ultimately they got married, but before marriage they were involved sexually and she became pregnant. Ironically, they feared that this would be discovered and ruin their testimony, so she decided to have an abortion. Afterwards she had enormous pangs of conscience about that, and Pippert, this articulate and godly lady, met her at this point. The girl was despondent and tending toward suicide, saying, "God will never forgive me because I killed my baby." And so this was the state of mind the girl was in, and nothing Pippert could say about forgiveness in Christ could seem to reach through to her. Finally Pippert said, "Did you ever think that this was really not your first murder?" The girl was astonished and said, "What do you mean? I have never committed another murder than this!" "Well," Pippert said, "why do you think Jesus died? Was it not your sins that put Him to death?" A flood of light came into this girl's soul. She realized how great was the forgiveness of God, and even though she had participated in this abortion, and was in fact very guilty, she was not beyond the range of divine forgiveness. Pippert told that story in a very stunning manner, making a very strong impression. So, in Nicole's opinion, she was the highlight of that evening.

Outstanding scholars were invited to Gordon for the McIlvain Lectureships (McIlvain had been an early professor under A. J. Gordon), persons who had been leaders in the evangelical movement. These included F. F. Bruce, A. W. Blackwood and Leon Morris (whose lectures for Gordon were later published as *The Cross in the New Testament*). Morris had already published *The Apostolic Preaching of the Cross*. According to Nicole, Evangelicals have been guilty of a less than well-rounded presentation of the work of Christ because they focus on one or two aspects, rather than presenting the full range of truth that the New Testament does about Christ's work of redemption. Morris gave a good model for the full-orbed approach in *The Cross in the New Testament*. They also had Donald Grey Barnhouse from Tenth Presbyterian in Philadelphia. He presented a defense of dispensationalism versus the non-dispensationalist view, which was presented by Albertus Pieters, a former missionary in Japan. Pieters did a really fine job showing some of the weaknesses of the dispensational approach. He had written a book called *The Children of Abraham*, in which he emphasized the *unity* of the covenant of grace and in which he gave a thorough discussion emphasizing the paedobaptist position. Another speaker that came to Gordon on occasion was J. I. Packer; who made "always an excellent presentation."

Nicole took a particular interest in Pentecostals throughout his teaching career. His goal was to establish them with more "theological iron" because the tendency in Pentecostal circles was to manifest "the foam rather than the beer." This was seen in the theological slippage that occurred in Methodism, and rather than abandon a significantly large denomination, he endeavored to ground such students in the sovereignty of God. One of his students in the 1950s, Russell P. Spittler, observed, "Roger is the typical ideal professor. He did not demand concurrence, and he was fair with those he opposed." This was a lesson learned, in part, from one of Nicole's favorite theologians, Herman Bavinck. He noted that Bavinck's confidence in his position, and the ability to defend it, allowed him to be gracious and irenic: "Polemical theology does not demonstrate the serenity that comes from the confidence of a theology well-grounded." Students should be able to make their argument prevail in a debate, though with an overtly gracious tone.

Between 1972 and 1973, Nicole took a teaching tour of the world for eight months. That school year was a sabbatical for him, and Annette accompanied him on the journey. He recalled that the trip "was oriented to enable us to perceive more clearly what is *essential* and what is merely *cultural* in our understanding and practice of the Christian faith." His experiences in Switzerland, France and the United States had enabled him to recognize differences in the attitudes of evangelical Christians, and in their conception of what constituted acceptable or non-acceptable behavior and practice. Obviously, the Bible delineates certain universal truths and duties that would be acknowledged by all sincere evangelical people. But in some matters of detail, considerable differences could be observed when passing from one country or circle of influence to another.

For example, in the 1930s in Switzerland, it was quite common among evangelicals to refrain from even the moderate use of alcoholic beverages. Nicole's parents, although not utterly restrictive in this respect, were using wine very rarely at the table. Drunkenness was a very serious problem in Switzerland, and many Christians believed that they should renounce the use of any alcohol as a protest and as an example to those thus tempted. An association called the "Blue Cross" was formed to denounce the use of any alcohol except for religious or medical purposes. In France, however, the attitude was very different. In some areas the use of water as a beverage was not safe, and the culture encouraged the use of some wine with every major meal. Nicole noted,

> Dr. Saillens, the most spiritual man I ever knew, had a little glass
> of wine at dinner every day. Ephesians 5:18 was, of course, an

acceptable restriction, but the wedding feast of Cana (John 2) and I Timothy 5:13 made it clear that complete abstinence was not an essential Christian virtue. When I arrived in the United States, the 18th Amendment to the Constitution, barring alcoholic beverages in 1920, was cancelled by the 21st Amendment in 1933. Many evangelicals were perplexed. The use of alcohol was forbidden on the premises of Gordon College and Divinity School, as well as many other evangelical institutions.

Storytelling

In Nicole's teaching ministry, both in the pulpit and in the classroom, he observed that illustrations and anecdotes from real life seemed to be more effective than reasoning from "cold logic." This was perhaps most evident in his French Canadian audiences, where hardly anyone was university trained. He also noticed this tendency among students from Asia and Africa as compared with those from Western cultures. He was aware that "a certain criticism of the enterprise of missions was offered, to the point that missionaries had not simply brought the gospel to those who had not been reached before, but they imposed an acceptance of Western culture and practices to the detriment of the indigenous cultures." This also involved elements that did not need to be abandoned or even criticized. If this were true, he theorized, then two very significant difficulties would obtain for missions.

First, by requiring people to renounce the culture in which they were born and reared, the missionaries made a demand that went beyond the requirements for change contained in the gospel itself. Furthermore, an acceptance of a Western ethos would in many cases deserve itself to be criticized in terms of a biblical outlook. Also, this tended to encourage people in foreign lands to think of missions as "a kin and a help" to colonialism. Of course, colonialism is interested in selfish aims, while missions should always be altruistic, with a desire to help and serve those who are addressed.

Second, by expecting converts to model their lives and practices in terms of a foreign culture, one would cause them to be different from their own people, not merely in religious and ethical matters, but in their whole outlook on life. They would therefore stand out as "sitting ducks" to be victimized if persecution or hostility to the Christian faith should arise. This would provide a very regrettable assistance to people and governments with a hostile stance toward Christianity.

During the sabbatical year, Nicole planned to learn more about the relationship of culture to the Christian outlook. He hoped to grasp more clearly what is really *cultural* rather than *essential* in Western Christianity. His goal was to be more sensitive with respect to inadequacies and distortions that characterized his perspective. He wanted to become more understanding and generous to certain aspects of diverse cultures with which he was insufficiently acquainted. Thus he planned to achieve a more comprehensive and winsome view of the faith, in which no cultural defect would be *admitted* if in conflict with the essence, and in which no acceptable difference would be *ruled out* that was not in fact proved to be contrary.

To this effect, he planned a journey with stays varying from one to nine weeks in different places. He intended to relate to existing evangelical seminaries where he could teach and/or lecture "to earn my keep," while having the liberty to ask questions from mature believers who would not be scandalized by his inquiries. With the help of foreign students past and present at Gordon-Conwell, Roger and Annette embarked on an adventure with the following schedule:

> Hawaii – 2 weeks
> Japan – 3 weeks
> Taiwan – 9 weeks
> Hong Kong – 1 week
> Singapore – 8 weeks
> India – 1 week
> Pakistan – 1 week
> Egypt, Athens, Istanbul, Belgrade, Rome, Lausanne–
> a few days each
> France – 3 weeks
> Britain – 1 week

In each place, their plan was to consider how the missionary effort related to the culture or cultures in place. They also discussed how the cultural outlook was embodied in non-Christian religions in ways that would suggest effective witnessing strategies. Those who understood it heard Nicole's teaching in English, and it was translated in the native tongue for others.

The trip was very stimulating to both Roger and Annette. He reached certain basic conclusions that have characterized his outlook on missions since 1973. First, every human culture has certain elements that are positive and helpful to those who live in it. This is due to the gift of God's common grace in the world that restricts the development of evil. Every human culture, by virtue of the corruption of sin and the hardness of the natural human heart, also has damaging elements that the spread of the gospel should address and curb. This would not of necessity curtail the good elements.

Second, it is extremely difficult for people who are steeped in one culture to achieve a level of impartiality that would entitle them to offer a proper evaluation of another culture. Obviously there are elements that are so bad that an exposure to the gospel would necessarily cancel them (e.g., offering human sacrifices or sacred prostitution). But how to remedy certain problems would surely need at least a substantial participation of those who live in that culture (e.g., the problems raised by polygamy or how the choice for a marriage partner should be determined). Regulations drafted by a mission board that is foreign to a country should probably not be put in force without an influential participation of indigenous people.

Third, the Jewish faith is distinguished from other non-Christian faiths by the fact that it possessed the "oracles of God" (Acts 7:38; Romans 3:2; Hebrews 5:12; I Peter 4:11). This insured their truthfulness. Nevertheless, some of the precepts of God in Judaism were given in view of human hardness of heart (Matthew 19:8). Jewish faith bears witness to the unity and uniqueness of God, and in this respect it criticizes and rejects any polytheism.

Fourth, the whole canonical Scripture is the standard by which any religious claim must be tested (I Thessalonians 5:21). It includes the mystery that the First Advent of Jesus Christ set to light (Romans 16:25; Ephesians 3:3-5), to wit, that the call of the gospel is universally addressed to the whole human race. This involves for the church a universal mandate of missions (Matthew 28:19; Acts 1:8).

Fifth, it is quite evident that in many cases missionaries have exported more than the gospel. In Hawaii, many of the ancient church buildings look as if they were produced in New England. In Japan, many of the hymns sung in church are simply translations of English hymns with Western melodies, which in no way resemble

Japanese music. Nicole observed in several places a certain reluctance to entrust positions of considerable significance to indigenous leaders, "quite contrary to the practice of St. Paul." The result was that Christianity appeared to many as a foreign product, perhaps designed to keep the nationals in a dependent position.

It is, of course, true that many missionaries have manifested such love and concern that their work has produced good results in spite of these obstacles. It is also true that many missionary societies have now been alerted to these dangers and have taken steps to realign their aims in a more central evangelistic way. Hudson Taylor, who insisted that China Inland Missionaries should attempt to conform their manner of living to Chinese ways, surely had a wise insight. The missionary should not be required to deny the value of his/her own cultural background, but should aim to be, so to speak, incarnated in the new milieu. This, Nicole believed, was implied in Jesus' statement, "As the Father sent me, I am sending you" (John 20:21).

Sixth, during this sabbatical year, in his contact with a wide range of cultures, Nicole realized more than ever before "how very Western I am." He continued,

> This affects my way of thinking, talking and relating to others and to myself. I do not have to, nor am able to, dissociate myself from this background. But I learned to be more appreciative of efforts and of people who are different. In preparing students for ministry, I must strive to help them to relate not only to other "Western" people, but also to the people who share a common culture with them. I must try to evaluate their performance in papers and examinations in terms that are wider than my own experience and training.

Finally, he learned that the ultimate problem of discerning what is good or bad in any culture was so complex "as to defy my ability to write a book on this subject." He recognized that his own cultural background inevitably prevented him from being sufficiently impartial to qualify as a judge. As a result of his sabbatical journey, he gained many insights not possessed by those without the benefit of such travel, but he also learned to appreciate more fully the great principle of Jesus, "Do not judge, or you will be judged" (Matthew 7:1).

CHAPTER 7

1980-2001
Closing Years of Teaching

Nicole retired from Gordon-Conwell Theological Seminary in the year 1986. They had a rule there that a professor would cease to be a regular member of the faculty in the school year in which he reached his seventieth birthday. That would be the last year in which he would teach as a regular member of the faculty with the kind of benefits that seniority would involve. He reached that age in 1986. He was seventy on December 10, 1985, and so the academic year 1985-86 was the last one he taught at Gordon. Gordon had a ruling that a professor who reached that point in service could be retained for at most two courses in a year, if the division in which he had taught asked him to do so. This had to be approved by the school's faculty senate, which was in charge of promotions and retentions and, to some extent, calls addressed to new people. The senate had to approve this, and then the faculty as a whole had to approve it by a three-fourths vote. This rather complicated arrangement was designed to ensure that a person would not be asked to continue teaching beyond the time where his teaching was a real asset for the students.

Some of Nicole's colleagues and he had been exposed to what might be called senile professors, who would occupy an important place and draw a substantial amount of money from the institution without providing the kind of challenge which people who are preparing for the ministry ought to receive. The school ensured that it would not be just a question of personal friendships, or respect for a past career, that would rivet on the institution a professor who had actually done his task with usefulness, but had now ceased to be a useful element in the total teaching body. The rule was originally that age sixty-five was when a professor should retire. When Nicole reached that age, in the 1980-81 academic year, there was a crisis faced by the trustees where a portion of the school, according to reports received by the trustees, was not as thoroughly committed to the inerrancy of Scripture as was desired. This crisis was of course also felt very strongly within the faculty and established some difficulty at that point. The trustees were eager to maintain some of the older professors who had been there for a long time and could be very strongly trusted for their commitment to inerrancy. Nicole was one of the professors the trustees desired to retain for this reason. They were concerned not to expose the school to people who were less committed to inspiration, or committed in a different way, who could possibly change the atmosphere of the whole faculty.

They had considerable problems in the area of New Testament. There were people with very solid acceptance of New Testament truth as the Word of God, but who seemed to have followed an interest in form criticism or redaction criticism which attempted to go *behind* the written Gospels to discover how the historical facts related to the biblical presentation. There were students in the school who were questioning the reliability of some of the things that the Gospels said. One professor held that the discourses of Jesus in the Gospel of John were not statements that he made during the days of his flesh, but they were revelations that were given to the Apostle John after Christ's ascension. John supposedly put that down as being indeed the Word of God, but not in fact tied up to the actual events of Jesus' earthly life. This would particularly apply to John 6, where there are a number of statements about eating the flesh and drinking the blood of the Son. The aforementioned professor felt that such would be out of keeping with the situation prior to the death and resurrection of Jesus. So he deduced that this was not a commentary made after the feeding of the five thousand in a concrete locale as it is found in John 6. One problem with this was John 6:59, "Jesus said these things in the synagogue, as he taught at Capernaum." That certainly does not fit with the idea that it was a post-ascension revelation of Jesus, like the Apocalypse. In effect, a student said at one point, "I can preach from the epistles because I think I know what Paul taught, but I don't dare preach on the

Gospels because I don't really know what were Jesus' words and what were not." Nicole recalled of this time at Gordon,

> With that kind of result from the education students received at Gordon, we were working at cross-purposes, and it would be better for people not to come to the school at all if that persisted. We had really the major treasure of the church, the Word of God, which was now in the ministry of such students subject to severe problems of trust. What we desired instead was the development of a total confidence in the Bible that would encourage these people to preach Scripture with great freedom, irrespective of critical remarks they might hear from various quarters. So the trustees were extremely displeased with that.

He believed that by the grace of God, without having a terrific blow to the school, the professors who were oriented in that direction all left, with the exception of Professor J. Ramsay Michaels. A resignation was actually requested from Michaels because of some of the things he had published in *Jesus: Master and Servant*. This book had several statements that seemed to be inconsistent with the inerrancy of Scripture. It was the servanthood of Christ that he emphasized, and that is indeed scriptural, but some other emphases were clearly detrimental to the biblical outlook the school tried to impart to its students. Michaels was really a very sound person in many ways, particularly on the doctrine of inspiration. But he felt strongly that the evangelical case before other people was weakened by the fundamental assumption, "This is God's Word, so we are not going to discuss 'if' or 'but' questions." He felt that the case for inerrancy was so strong that it could be presented in a factual manner that would bypass any attacks and secure confidence in the Gospels, despite the redaction or form criticism that the Gospels might have employed. His book was addressed not really so much to evangelicals as to liberals who were criticizing the evangelicals for just having the basic assumption of inerrancy but not attempting to investigate the facts with a reasonable attitude.

But in the process Michaels made some statements that really were not compatible with the doctrine of inerrancy. For instance, in dealing with one subject he said that Mark "wrote it as he saw it and he was *probably* right." To say that it was *probably* right suggests that it was not certain. And if one affirms inerrancy, it was *certainly* right! One could possibly say, holding to inerrancy, that Mark did not at this point follow the chronological order to which he was not committed, but instead presented the matter in a way which was effective for the reader. A believer in inerrancy is definitely not obliged to think that everything presented in Scripture is now in chronological order. In fact, the Gospels do shift that way. There is no need to deny those shifts. Specifically, in the temptation of Jesus, the order of Matthew and of Luke is different. That is no problem, because neither of the two has said, "I am going to tell you this in a strict chronological order."

Furthermore, as Bruce Metzger once remarked, "These three temptations may not have been just one episode of temptation, but they may have been a recurring theme, and therefore they would intersect in different ways depending on what the writer wanted to develop in the whole scope of temptation." So there is the possibility of repetition of certain events, and there is no commitment to a chronological order that would cause people to have difficulty in recognizing the validity of something that was not chronological. The trustees decided that, in order to safeguard the school, and to keep some of the professors who were reaching age sixty-five (Nicole was the first one in that category), they would extend the time until the seventieth year.

At that point, David Wells had come to be a professor at Gordon. He left a very desirable position as professor of church history at Trinity Evangelical Divinity School near Chicago, and he had an outstanding reputation. He was invited to Gordon-Conwell at the level of full professorship, with some understanding that in view of Nicole's age, Wells would soon come to be the key professor in theology. Also, he would presumably occupy the Andrew Mutch Chair of Historical and Systematic Theology, the one endowed chair the school possessed at the time, in which Nicole was the first occupant. Here suddenly, instead of having the succession secured within two years or so, there was another five years added, postponing the professorship of Wells in that respect. Nicole felt that Professor Wells was in some way set back because of the decision by the trustees to extend his tenure. What the school had led Wells to expect, although not promised in writing, was really not held out for him. On that account, Nicole personally approached both the president and the dean with the suggestion that before he reached the age of retirement, the Mutch Chair should be given to Professor Wells as being the key person in theology. He assured them that he would not feel that he was being slighted in his seniority by such a move. Annette, however, was quite opposed to this, feeling that Roger did not show sufficient gratitude for the honor that had been bestowed on him, to be the one professor who had an endowed chair, and that he was "viewing as a trifle something that was really a major benefit that the trustees had conferred on me."

But Nicole saw that as a matter of institutional integrity, and as a matter that in his judgment was important for the psychological attitude of Professor Wells, and therefore he felt that this would do no harm to anybody. Since it did not come from *Wells*, but rather from *Nicole*, he was confident that the trustees would accept this. And indeed, when the matter was actually transacted, they had a special ceremony at the school. Nicole was asked to speak, and he did, saying, "This is not a situation in which suddenly my career was interrupted, but it was like a relay race in the Olympic games, where you have a baton that is passed from one runner to the other on the team, and there is a point where both are running for a time together, and then the baton is passed and the next runner continues the race." He felt that was really an appropriate illustration, and that it showed how such a transition could be accomplished. It also showed how someone who had an advantage could, at times, care for the interests of a brother, beyond those concerns that were purely personal. In his esteem for Professor Wells, and in his desire to see this come out for him in the appropriate manner, Nicole moved in that direction. By 1986, however, he reached the seventieth year, the age of retirement that the trustees had set, so he then retired.

If deemed necessary, he could still teach as many as two courses a year at Gordon in the major program, but that had to come as a request from the division of Christian Thought, including Church History and Theology. As it turned out, the school at that point did not need that, so the division did not request that Nicole should teach there. There was another professor, Richard Lints, who had been called to the school by the proper approach, with a search and with the recommendation of the Christian Thought division. There was also a considerable interview with the senate and the faculty, and Lints received a positive vote by the senate and faculty without dissent. With his arrival, the division was, as it were, complete. Nicole's departure as a professor was counteracted by the arrival of another professor with an appropriate doctorate from Notre Dame University. This was good for Gordon because Lints had an interest in philosophical theology, which is one line of approach that is closely related to systematic theology. Systematics can proceed either with a special commitment to exegesis and biblical study, as was surely the case with Professor John Murray at Westminster, or else it may be conducted with a particular interest in the history of dogma. This latter approach is also concerned with the way in which mature doctrinal formulation is developed as time goes by, and in the warding off of heretical positions. Such heresies might at first seem to have some right to being part of the conversation, but in the process of church history are eventually eliminated by the wisdom of people who give close examination to the issues.

Nicole's great interests were in both the biblical foundation, which he felt was absolutely basic for any study of theology, and the history of dogma. His work at Harvard for the Ph.D. had been carried out in church history, rather than theology, because in that way he felt he did not place himself in direct opposition to prevailing Harvard thought. Thus, he had a harmonious course of study at Harvard, in spite of the fact that his basic position on the Scriptures was radically different. Before Lints, there was no professor at Gordon who specialized in the *philosophical* approach to theology. David Wells, in particular, seemed to be interested in some of the sociological impact of an evangelical position, along with its influence in the total structure, not only of theology, but also of the church. In his books, he has attempted to assess the significance and the permanency of the evangelical movement, which was growing so marvelously well by 1986. The addition of Lints to the faculty complemented what David Wells and John Jefferson Davis could provide (Davis being interested in ethics), and so there was a refreshing new variety with his arrival.

Since the division did not ask him to teach in the first two years after his retirement, Nicole continued various forms of ministry elsewhere, particularly in Canada, and also by invitations that would be addressed to him from other schools for special lectureships.

During that time the faculty of Reformed Theological Seminary in Jackson, Mississippi, asked him to come to their campus and teach some brief courses. His relationship to that institution was very friendly from the beginning. In spite of his age, a call was addressed to him, unofficially, to join the faculty of RTS in Jackson. He did not feel called for this by the Lord, and definitely Annette did not feel at all any interest in leaving Massachusetts to go to Mississippi! In his view of the relationship of men and women, he believed a decision of that importance had to be shared by the wife, and that she should not just follow the husband's approach. The wife is involved with him at an equal level, and it would not be right for him to accept an invitation that Annette felt disinclined to accept. He remarked, "This was not a situation in which I was swayed away from a form of service that God opened for me; I just did not feel called at that point. I simply had no desire to go to Mississippi, in spite of the very happy relationship I had with RTS and specifically with Dr. Luder Whitlock as president of the institution."

After his retirement from Gordon, from 1986-1989, Nicole taught as a visiting professor in Canada, Maine, and Pittsburgh. The riches of his experience in theological reflection were invested in many students, though he was for a time not teaching in the classroom on a regular basis. Later on, however, in 1989—three years after his retirement from Gordon—RTS decided to open up in Orlando an additional branch of the school that would take advantage of the opportunities that were present in Florida. Florida was the fourth largest state in the United States and there was no theological faculty that was accredited by the Association of Theological Schools. It was thought that opening a branch there in Orlando would be a very useful way of providing training for ministers who had a footing in Florida and elsewhere, but were not inclined to go to Mississippi. The desire of President Whitlock for some time had been to move the Mississippi school to Florida, judging that this would be a more strategic place for exercising the ministry than what they had. It was also thought that this would enlarge their support and their range of usefulness beyond the fairly narrow confines that might be associated with Mississippi. This particular vision on the part of Dr. Whitlock was presented to the trustees and received some attention, but it did not get their endorsement as a desirable move from the location in Mississippi.

Many of the trustees had a close attachment to Mississippi; it was "their baby" and they did not like the thought of its being moved out of state. Also, they had constructed quite a lot of buildings for the institution that would have to be abandoned or sold. Some of the original givers, who had invested large sums for the campus in Mississippi, would be not pleased with the way their gift was now abandoned in order to go to another place.

The trustees would not validate the propriety of moving the school to Florida; however, they were conscious of the potential of an institution in Orlando. They thought that this would really extend in a remarkable way the total input of a sound theological institution within the Presbyterian Church in America. This was at a time of very considerable conflict within the Presbyterian church of the South, where there was disaffection from the major running of the denomination. A number of conservative churches would likely support an institution particularly related to them. There was fairly soon the possibility of having Covenant College and Seminary become *the* school of preference for the PCA, but these trustees of RTS had another vision. They hoped that Reformed Theological Seminary, being an institution from the South, could become that school for Southern people desiring theological training. In 1989 they agreed to the opening of the branch in Orlando, and one of their key professors at Jackson, Dr. Richard Pratt, was committed to move to Orlando. There were other people who were thought of who would be an asset to the Orlando branch from the beginning. There was no knowledge of the way in which this would develop, no buildings available that the school would possess, but they had an arrangement on a particular building that could be rented for five years. This facility came with an option to buy at the end of two years for a certain sum that was stipulated. The trustees proceeded with considerable care; they said, "We're not just going to open this—let's try it, let's rent the building, let's have an opportunity to fix the matter more strongly after two years if it succeeds as we hope. At the same time, let us not commit ourselves to being there permanently, so that if there is a question about the adequacy of what we are doing, we may reverse without a black mark on the institution."

So in 1989 Dr. Whitlock approached Nicole and wanted to know whether he would be willing to serve in that branch from the beginning. At that point he had been for three years in the vicinity of Gordon and had not taught there. He was very challenged with the kind of institution he knew Luder Whitlock was presiding over. His attitude as a president appeared to Nicole particularly fortunate, and when he approached Annette about it, she immediately was greatly attracted and said, "When do we move?" In this matter also, the school acted in a very careful and appropriate manner. They decided to give Annette and Roger a weeklong trip to Orlando in order to see what the situation was, and in order to see whether he would respond positively to a call to become professor there. Another person who was committed to this was R. C. Sproul, who was teaching at the Jackson campus of RTS, but who had to come for brief periods from Orlando where Ligonier Ministries was located. This was a difficulty for him because he did not want to travel by airplane, and so he had to drive back and forth that long distance in order to teach in Mississippi. So the thought of having a branch in Orlando and getting somebody else in Mississippi to teach systematic theology was tempting to the folks at the Jackson campus also. Sproul was one of the early professors and so was Pratt, who was highly esteemed and very colorful as a professor of Old Testament.

When Annette and Roger came to Orlando, during that exploratory visit, the arrangements had been admirably prepared. A team of two very knowledgeable ladies in real estate had prepared a whole list of places that they wanted to show the visitors, one of which presumably they might buy. Special arrangement was made for them to stay in the Quality Inn, in the southern part of the city, and they had all that was necessary for lodging and meals. So in a variety of ways people prepared their visit so that Orlando would appear to them in the most favorable manner—and it was done very well. They examined the housing situation with those ladies, and were led in that process to ask God to provide a sign that they might trust that it was indeed His will that they should relocate. What they asked of the Lord was in connection with one home that seemed to be particularly desirable in Apopka, and which was offered for $169,000. They intended to make an offer at $160,000. Their thought was this: if the Lord really wants us in Orlando, would it be proper that we might take as a sign the acceptance of our offer without a whole lot of negotiating? They first approached their real estate agents asking whether or not this offer was appropriate; they did not wish to be offensive. The agents assured the Nicoles that it was quite appropriate, and that they need not feel fearful that they might somehow antagonize the seller. When the offer was given, at first the husband was not in favor of it, but his wife persuaded him to accept the offer without any further ado! The Nicoles did not know anything about this—the real estate agents said, "Your offer of $160,000 dollars has been accepted." They concluded in this that God had answered their prayer, and that they should have a sense of His blessing on this particular situation. Nicole explained,

> Now there are some people who would raise questions about the propriety of asking signs—the "Gideon Way"—of the Lord, and putting a fleece out, so to speak, as Gideon did (Judges 6:37-40). I don't encourage people to make a habit of that by any means, but I do feel that there may be circumstances where it is not inappropriate for people who are presented with something that seems attractive, and they do not fully trust their own judgment, to have something of a divine manifestation which gives them confidence they are going in the right direction. That surely would be so for missionary vocations; they need to know where they will go and with whom, and these are difficult decisions. That gave Annette and me great assurance as we came here that this was in fact God's will for us. As a result, these have been some of the happiest years of our lives in the ministry that was accomplished there at RTS. I called up Dr. Whitlock in Jackson, and said, "We have examined the Orlando opportunity, we have put our name in for a house, we accept the invitation to teach, and we will be glad to serve under you in this opportunity." Whitlock said, "Well, you have made my day!" I don't want to encourage a rash asking of signs. I think that was the only time in my life where I did ask God for such a sign, and I do feel that God blessed the whole matter. My wife and I were united in having this as a sign for us. There is the example of Gideon, and of the apostles in the upper room casting lots (Acts 1:26), and also there are instances of God giving negative signs, as in the case of the Apostle Paul and his trip to Europe (Acts 16:6,7). Paul was blunted at several points when he thought he should go to one place, yet God prevented him from going there. The *lack* of

divine blessing is often easier to discern as a means of guidance than is the receiving of a *positive* sign to proceed.

One caution that should be mentioned is that this seeking for a sign may actually be an indication of not trusting God's guidance day by day. I am concerned about those who abuse this way of seeking God's direction. One group that I know had great soundness in the faith in most areas, but proceeded very consistently, asking for signs one way or the other. This was very strongly the approach in the so-called Oxford Movement, a movement where people were asking God's guidance at all kinds of moments. I know of one man who was the pastor of a church, and he had some chickens, and his wife sent him to the barn in order to feed the chickens. Two hours later he had not yet returned, so she went out there, and he was in the barn asking God to give him a sign regarding which bag of seed he should use to feed the chickens! He was wasting two hours of his "pastor time" asking for a sign on something that really was ridiculous. So, there are excesses in that practice, and I don't want to encourage any excesses of that kind. On the other hand, I think people who examine the matter may say, "You were not doing the right thing, but God blessed you in spite of it." And of course, there are blessings that God gives to his people in spite of the fact that they were not doing the proper thing. I would not want to encourage people to be "sign-asking," and on the other hand, I do not want to discard the possibility that God in his guidance may use particular signs and help us to have assurance of his work.

I don't believe there has been a cessation of God's guidance to his people from the time of the apostles till now. The cessation of the charismata is a big issue in theology. But God does give signs, and I don't think you can say that his method has definitely changed from biblical times, and that the only way of finding the will of God now is to read the Word and then make your decision from what you see in terms of principles found there. You should do that in any case. But to say that is the *exclusive* way in which the will of God is shown is not my belief. In that sense, I fit better with the Baptists than I do with some rather extreme Reformed people, who say that the charismata have ceased, so people can't expect healing by faith, or to speak in tongues nowadays, and so on—and they can't expect that God will answer their request for a sign to tell them what to do. It is risky, I admit. I even had some qualms about this, whether it was the right thing, and yet I felt sufficient confidence so that when the matter came out as we had asked (about the house), I did feel strongly confirmed. Then my experience of the years that followed, I think, proved that it was not a faulty step. For very important decisions like marriage or vocation, it is not inappropriate to gain a kind of assurance from divine guidance that one is going in the right way. There have been people who were fairly sure of the guidance of God, but it didn't pan out that way. That was true of David Livingstone, who was planning to go to China, but there were such storms in the Indian Ocean that he stopped at the "Cape of Storms" (later renamed the Cape of Good Hope), and then he became a missionary to Africa. So there you have a countermanding sign of God, where people in good faith thought this is what they should do, and God closed the door. But with respect to open doors, somehow it seems to me there may be ways in which God as a *Person* communicates with a believer or believers as persons, in ways that seal up confidence so that the right decision is made (Psalm 32:8,9).

Nicole had a very happy time from the start at RTS. He was very well received by the students, faculty, and administration. He was, in a sense, delivered from a burden that he had wrongly carried for a long time when he was at Gordon. Somehow, because of his long association with that school, he felt himself enormously involved in any decisions that were made. That made matters difficult when the decisions taken were not in line with what he thought was desirable or even essential. Thus he carried there a burden which would probably have been appropriate for a president, but which was not necessary for a professor. And when he moved to Orlando, suddenly he found the burden was lifted. "I actually saw that Gordon was getting along well without me," he said.

When he came to RTS, he figured he was something of a latecomer. Both Pratt and Sproul were there longer than he. There were people there who were Presbyterians, engaged in ministry toward Presbyterians and the PCA, and they had a denominational commitment that was not his. So he felt very free to discuss with them in faculty meetings projects that might come before them, but he was not committed to any of it to the degree that he would be disappointed if things did not go the way he thought was most appropriate. Things developed very well at RTS Orlando; within three years they were the major branch. They had more students, more professors with appropriate credentials, and so on. Everything seemed to be giving the "yes" to the Orlando line of approach. The trustees, Nicole opined, were wise to maintain the Mississippi school, which had also been very successful in its own right.

Because of his long experience in teaching, and the range that he covered, Nicole was used to do things that other professors would not do or would not be trusted to do. One example was the course in apologetics, a course that the faculty insisted should be offered. Available to teach apologetics were Pratt, who was Van Tillian, and Sproul, who was of the John Gerstner/Evangelical Rationalist school. Either of these very capable men was willing to offer the course in apologetics, but in that case the other man would surely object to it. RTS had at the time a very limited choice of professors. To resolve the matter, Nicole was asked, as a professor not thoroughly committed to either apologetic approach, to teach the course. Both Pratt and Sproul were satisfied with this arrangement. Nicole admitted that the course was not one of his best. He stated that he was not sufficiently knowledgeable in the literature of the subject or in the argumentation at some points to cover even the basics. Apologetics is very broad, because it has to vindicate the Christian view against all kinds of attacks. This vindication must be accomplished in such a way as to confirm the people who are *within* that this is the right place to be, rather than just to win over the opponents.

Because of the division that existed between presuppositionalists and rationalists on campus, Nicole felt it was very important that both of those positions should be presented to the students. He requested both Pratt and Sproul to come in to the classroom (he had a whole morning for the course) and have two hours each to make a presentation of his basic approach. Then there would be one hour after chapel where they would expose themselves to questions from the students or from Nicole. Each of the two accepted this invitation, so the students saw that this was an "in-house" difference, though each was very convinced that he was going the right way. Nicole opted somewhat toward the presuppositionalist argument, preferring not to approach the Bible apologetically to start with, get the conviction that this must be the Word of God, and then proceed to develop a theology of apologetics. He believed that experientially apologetics did not develop that way:

> That is not the way it occurs! The way it works is, that when you come into the church upon conversion, they *give* you the Bible! You have made no special effort, no investigation of other religious books like the Koran or the Vedas, you know nothing about that—you just go, and there is the Bread! And you don't need to taste all kinds of food before you know that Bread is good! My approach was simple: the Bible claims to be the Word of God, so that is the starting point. This same idea was outlined by Graham Scroggie of London, who had a little book about the Bible, divided into three parts. First, the Bible *claims* to be the Word of God. Second, it *seems* to be the Word of God. Third, it *proves* to be the Word of God. That is the way, I think, psychologically things work. It gives a privileged approach to the Bible, but not an approach that would be irresistible to anybody who had a careful inspection and was not in their mind and heart convinced.
>
> This is the uncritical way in which Muslims accept the Koran, though I don't think they are hopelessly tied to that book, so that nothing will be able to shake their confidence in it. I think there are good arguments that show the Koran not to be the Word of God. I am anxious about a presuppositionalism in which people, by presupposition, opt for something that is wrong. I think the wrongness of anything can be proved. But the rightness of the Bible doesn't have to be proved by a scientific method before you can begin to understand what it says and apply it. Of course it has to be the Holy Spirit who attests to the Bible that it is the Word of God. That is what the Westminster Confession of Faith says, that it is not external signs that convince us, as great as these may be, but it is the Holy Spirit bearing witness with our spirit that this is the Word of God (WCF, I, 5). That is exactly what happened in my own Christian experience: I took some bread and found it to be bread! I feel I had a more neutral position myself. B. B. Warfield's approach was apologetic theology, then biblical theology, then historical theology, then systematic theology, and then finally practical theology. He had a division of five parts in the theological encyclopedia. And the first was apologetic, where

154 The Life and Legacy of Roger Nicole

one must prove there is a religion that is right, the Christian one is the right one, and it has a revelation that has to be accepted. And all of these have to be proved by reason, by logical argument. Then one can say that now the Bible is the Word of God and it has been proved to be so. But really, in Christian experience, we are going with the Bible *long* before we have argued about it! One very good point is this: suppose a person dies while making the investigation! That is something I would use in a debate. Somehow, it has to be God's work with me, not my own mind's work, but *God's work*.

He had to do a course at RTS called "Preparation for Ministry," showing the importance of theological studies for somebody who was going to be a minister. There was a fellow, a very sharp student, who said, "What are your qualifications for teaching this course?" And happily he could say, "Well, I have majored in professorship, but I was pastor of two churches for 16 years, so I have some idea of the situations that a pastor may encounter." He believed that a professor had to expect students to be a bit brash at times, and that the teachers should not just say, "I am a person of significance. You better deal with me in a proper way." The best thing to do is to seem to be totally unfazed by the brash approach, and give a response to the issue that is raised, irrespective of the way it is presented.

He had a course that was given within the scope of one week, with a very intensive approach, entitled "The Five Points of Calvinism." This was in a Presbyterian institution, Reformed Theological Seminary, and so more than he used to have at Gordon, where he was eager to safeguard some standing for the Arminians, he had great freedom to show the significant strength of the Reformed position "without having to bend down in order to see what Arminians might be thinking." There was a fairly thorough Arminian student, but one of no great learning, and he would raise questions that after a while began to irritate the class. Either the questions had already been answered, or they were things that Nicole would probably deal with at some point in the presentation. His handling of the situation was typical of his approach,

> In my judgment as a teacher, I did not want to say, "I will be talking about that in the right order, so why don't you wait until I come to it?" When the question comes, I think that is the time to

answer! It may disrupt the class notes a little bit, but when you have a class you have to deal with *people*, and you have to deal with the consciousness that they have about the subject. And if there is a problem, and it is raised, then you better deal with it then. I surprised the class by not getting flustered at all, and by permitting this fellow again and again to raise his hand and to ask his questions. Of course the questions he raised were right down my alley! They were not producing difficulties like, "Hey, I hadn't thought about that one!" I knew exactly in what way to respond. I also knew how to preserve for the Arminian some standing within the evangelical position, while showing that a consistent Arminian does not really need to say what he said. The situation became exactly reversed in the class: ordinarily, the class as a whole tries to support the student who is challenging the professor. A legitimate part of instruction is this challenge of whether or not the professor can adequately respond, or is there a way for the student to get him off the platform. That is part of the game. In Europe, unfortunately, that seems to be almost the *whole* game, and there you have a risk that is inappropriate.

But in the United States, people are human also, and if somebody is smart enough to raise a question that seems to stump the professor, it resonates with the class. After a while, the class was more impatient with this fellow than I was. The class became so satisfied with the answer that I gave that some people who were really indecisive said, "I guess this Reformed position can really be defended! This is remarkable. This is biblical!" They were getting impatient with the *student*, not with me. And that of course is the ideal situation for the professor. One student told me, "The way in which you dealt with this fellow was the thing that persuaded me, that somehow there wasn't much to the other student's strength and you had him at every turn." Sadly, I don't think the Arminian challenger himself changed. That was almost getting into the debate situation, where I had to take care of the *class as a whole*, and not especially that one student. But I wanted to take care of him, too, as much as I could. I wanted also not to permit Calvinists to make brash accusations that simply don't prove true in relationship to true evangelical Arminians. They sometimes want to tell you that Arminians are not Christians. They will be surprised in heaven to find quite a number there! Although, at that point, they will not be Arminians anymore. Before the throne of God, there cannot be very many Arminians!

Very shortly, the faculty at RTS was complete, and Nicole was assigned only courses that were "right smack within my own range." They had used him "to plug some holes" in the curriculum during the early period. He learned very practically that one can be helpful, even in areas where there is not a mastery of the subject. In theology, he wanted to be a master of the subject, but in other subjects he was willing to confess uncertainty at some points:

> I am very willing to say, for instance, that the thought of hell does not give me any pleasure. There are some folks who say, "Isn't that good, that the reprobate are going to be punished for all eternity?" I take no joy in that, but the Bible teaches it, and therefore I can't get away from it. That is why I don't believe in annihilation or conditional immortality. I don't believe that they can be harmonized with Scripture. I was very interested in teaching at a school that was denominationally oriented and supported. At RTS the Reformed position had a right to be defended and represented in the most positive manner. Gordon was a more general evangelical school, and there was no doctrinal position that deserved to be defended in an exclusive manner. As a Baptist, for instance, I did give lectures on baptism, but I was careful to give a good presentation of baptism as an expression of the covenant relationship, which is developed not only with individuals, but also with families. My goal was for the students not to know at the outset which view I preferred, paedobaptism or credobaptism. I tried to be even-handed, so that the Baptists would understand what the others are doing, and the others would understand what the Baptists are doing. Here I favor the *dedication* of infants, which has all the truth that is in infant baptism and none of the problems!

Toward the latter part of his service at RTS, from 1995 on, the classes he had were seminars. There he could best present something about his convictions in what seemed to him to be the most effective context for teaching. The students brought out the major substance of the topic through the oral presentation of papers. This conformed to his conviction that the seminary's type of instruction, and what involves the passing of courses, is so dominated by *writing* that it does not fairly represent the responsibilities of an ordinary minister. In the pastoral ministry, ninety percent of what one is called to do is oral: sermons, counseling, and catechizing, where the truth is put at the level of the parishioners—all of that is oral. If one is bound to a manuscript, the presentation loses a lot of its savor. Sermons read from a manuscript, Nicole believed, are seldom really very effective. It would almost be better to have sermons memorized by rote, where one is not attached to a *manuscript*, but rather attached to an *audience*. There may be ten percent writing: putting an announcement in the paper, preparing something for a wedding, or preparing prayers in which exact expression is desirable. One who writes his sermons will be an *accurate* preacher, but not necessarily an *effective* preacher. A person who delivers his sermon with the proper preparation, where the categories of thought are carefully organized in a way that can be perceived by the audience, is more likely to be an effective preacher.

Nicole felt that in the seminary, ninety percent was written and ten percent was oral, but in the ministry ten percent is written and ninety percent is oral. That just did not make good sense to him. He liked to have, rather than just papers, oral presentations made by the students. That meant that he had to be able to correct erroneous elements in the presentation without being a violent critic of the student. Next, he had to supplement elements of the truth that were lacking. Finally, he needed to make some developments especially in the relationship of one doctrine to the others, so that they would see that this is not one single piece, but it is a piece of a larger puzzle and has to get in its right place in order to bear its full impact. He let them have twenty minutes for a presentation, and then he took ten minutes for his remarks. He often took much more than his allotted ten minutes, because he needed that to supplement and extend what was done. If he detected a deficiency in emphasis or a wrong date, he would correct that.

Then he would give an oral exam at the end of the course, and that was very threatening to the students. They felt they were not ready to present the matter before somebody they viewed as an expert, and for that reason he put on the desk a cartoon of himself, with an alpenstock and a copy of Calvin under his arm—"I have some stationery with that cartoon." He had that as a painting on the desk, to show the spirit that was to prevail in the exam. He was not there as a critic to try to find fault with them; he was interested in supporting them. The desire was for the students to do the very best job they could, and so they ought to feel Nicole was their friend here, not their adversary. He was interested to show them, if they were lacking, not just where they were lacking in truth, but also in effectiveness of presentation. He would discuss things with them like speaking louder, or articulating more fully, and things of that kind. At that point, being somewhat deaf himself was a help, because he would tell them that they were going to have partially deaf people in their churches, and they have to make sure they can hear the sermon!

At Gordon, he was very unpopular in the registry office, in terms of delivering the final marks to the registrar, in courses where he had a lot of papers to grade. When it came to correcting papers he *hated* the task, and he "was slow like all get out in it." The problem was that he was very detailed in his corrections; he wanted the student to have the full benefit of his careful examination. After he gave the oral exams, he could come in very soon with the list of grades to the registrar. He gave himself the appellation "Lightening Fast Nicole!" At Gordon, he was a source of very great concern to the registrar, who was hampered in his/her work because of him, and he "felt unhappy when he had to go to the president about my turning in grades so late." He recalled a professor who once said, "That is what I get paid for, grading papers; teaching I do because I love it." Nicole gave seminars at Gordon, and some of them were large in terms of attendance. After a sabbatical one time, he gave a seminar on the person of Christ, and he had more than forty students. "That was not a good situation," he remarked, "an ideal number is between eight and ten."

There were definite concessions that were asked of Nicole when he came to RTS regarding his egalitarianism. The year in which he came to the seminary, 1989, was also the year in which the first international meeting of Christians for Biblical Equality took place in St. Paul, Minnesota. He was asked to present an address in the absence due to illness of Ms. Storkey from London. At this convocation a statement was presented entitled "Men, Women, and Biblical Equality" which detailed the biblical basis for their position and some of its implementation in the church. Nicole was joined in this effort by co-authors Gilbert Bilezikian, W. Ward Gasque, Stanley Gundry, Gretchen Gaebelein Hull, Catherine Clark Kroeger, and Jo Anne Lyon. This event naturally was reported in *Christianity Today*. It was stated that Nicole had given the "keynote address" of the egalitarians in St. Paul. This appeared in that periodical about two weeks after he had informed Luder Whitlock that he would be coming to RTS Orlando! Some pastor apparently saw that article, and the matter was referred to the trustees.

Mr. Cannada, father of the current chancellor of RTS, was the chairman of the board of trustees at the time, and he deemed it necessary to have a meeting with Nicole. Whitlock was extremely embarrassed by this because he thought that it would cause disruption before he even started teaching. Whitlock invited Mr. Cannada and Nicole for a luncheon meeting about this matter. Nicole assured Whitlock that he should not be embarrassed in any way, for it is an appropriate concern for trustees, who are charged with supervising the school, to ensure that professors coming in have proper views. He was also assured that, though Nicole was convinced of the propriety of the egalitarian outlook, it was only one part of his work, and he felt that he could do his work at RTS without "making waves." At the luncheon meeting, before any questions were posed, Nicole asked to be allowed to make a statement. He said that he did believe in the equality of women and that God does not forbid them to exercise the ministry but,

> I know the position of the Presbyterian Church in America, which has been wary of the example of the PCUSA that has forced almost an eclipse of males in the pastorate. I am not coming to RTS to vindicate the equality of women. I will commit myself, before any public appearance, to check in advance with President Whitlock so that he might approve the content of my presentation. Mr. Cannada surely could not say at that point, "Well, we do not want the president to be the arbiter on this." So the matter was settled quite amiably. As a result, the women who were in the M.Div. program were assigned to me, that I might serve as their advisor. This was done since the administration knew that I could best counsel them and that I could help them not to cause a ruckus! I told them that God had not called them to make a ruckus. I *do* believe that God called them, but God called

them to perform their service in a way that would cause advance and not quarrels. They were able to see in me an example that actually worked: here I was an egalitarian teaching at a non-egalitarian school. I would not have had that position, where I was specifically able to help women in ministry, if I had insisted on making egalitarianism a main emphasis.

This biography's author, as director of the Orlando Center of New Orleans Baptist Theological Seminary, first became acquainted with Roger Nicole during this period. It was his privilege to drive the theologian to the facilities of Orlando's First Baptist Church for classes each Monday evening during the fall and spring semesters of the 1997-98 academic year. Nicole taught from 6 p.m. until 10 p.m., with a twenty minute break (during which he slept on the floor of an office adjacent to the classroom, with a rolled up blanket as a pillow). He awakened himself without assistance and finished teaching the class. Teaching without notes, his only props were a Greek New Testament and an NIV Study Bible. Nicole recalled the experience:

> The New Orleans Baptist Theological Seminary, in a desire to make it easier to prospective pastors to receive instruction without moving to driving distance of New Orleans, invited me to give a course in theology to students who would come to Orlando on Mondays, have two four-hour classes in the facilities of the First Baptist Church of Orlando, and return home that same evening. In this way I met with some thirty students from 6-10 p.m. Most of these did not have regular access to a theological library, and since Grudem's *Systematic Theology* was not yet in print, I used Berkhof as my textbook and loaned a number of relevant volumes from my library to students who needed them to fulfill my outside reading requirement. There was no appropriate desk, so I sat on a large table and delivered the course that way. Many of the students had not had a course in theology before, and were tired at the end of the day and eager to leave for home. Nevertheless it was an interesting experience for me. Some of the participants manifested a lively interest in this way of approaching the Bible by subjects rather than by a study of individual books of the Old and New Testaments. Dr. David Bailey was in charge for New Orleans Seminary and I was very happy to make acquaintance with him.

God's sovereignty, biblical inspiration and substitutionary atonement have been three major focuses of Nicole's teaching and lecturing ministry. His mid-year lectureship in Portland, Oregon (1953), was centered in the atonement, and his Payton Lectureship at Fuller Seminary in Pasadena, California (1959), dealt with a history of definite atonement in Christian theology. His critique of C. H. Dodd originated in the Portland lectureship in connection with a study of Vincent Taylor's volumes on the atonement.

One thing that has not been fully covered in this biography is the importance for Nicole's life and development of his close relationship with his colleagues and students at both Gordon Divinity School (Gordon-Conwell Theological Seminary) and Reformed Theological Seminary. His contact with other scholars in the Evangelical Theological Society, the International Council on Biblical Inerrancy, the Philadelphia Conferences on Reformed Theology, and the Boston Theological Society greatly enlarged his vision. This is not a place for "dropping names" but it is good to remember some colleagues at Gordon with whom he was closely allied for 15 to 40 years: Glenn Barker, Robert Fillinger, Burton Goddard, Lloyd Kalland, David Kerr, William Kerr, Meredith Kline, T. L. Lewis, Charles Schauffele, Elmer Smick, Gwyn Walters.

Twice colleagues issued a *Festschrift* (a book of essays by different authors) in Nicole's honor:

David F. Wells, editor. *Reformed Theolgy in America. A History of its Modern Development.* Grand Rapids: Eerdmans, 1985. xvi, 317 Pp. This covered five areas, each by 3 essays: Princeton Theology, Westminster School, Dutch Schools, Southern Tradition and Neo-Orthodoxy.

Charles E. Hill and Frank A. James III, eds. *The Glory of the Atonement.* Downers Grove: InterVarsity, 2004. 495 Pp. This included 20 essays about the atonement in various books of Scripture, in Church History and in the Life of the Christian and the Church, by some of the leading contemporary evangelical scholars, including Nicole's nephew Dean Emile Nicole of Vaux-sur-Seine.

Nicole also stated regarding collegial influences, "Ever since 1945, I was in frequent contact with Carl F. H. Henry, who did much to encourage me to write. Since 1961, I was privileged to relate to James I. Packer, with whom I, though a Baptist, have a maximum of agreement." He noted concerning several students,

> It would have been pleasant to list here the names of some people, women and men, who studied with brilliance in my classes and went on to distinguish themselves in God's service. The list would be too long and the memory of a nonagenarian too fragile to undertake this. If this were done there would undoubtedly be regrets for omitting some names that should be included.

> One of the notable cases is that of Dr. Chang Lit-Sen, an important member of the Chinese government until 1949 and former university president in China, who was converted in the early 1950's. He graduated from Gordon in 1959 and devoted himself tirelessly to write an apologetic (4 volumes) and theological (8 volumes) presentation of Christianity for educated Chinese people. I was proud that Dr. Chang called me "my professor."

> Some students, particularly from foreign countries, were so affectionately related to Annette and me that they came to know them as "Mama" and "Papa" Nicole. It was an adoption of parents rather than of children:

> Dr. Eleftheria Sideropoulou (Greece)
> President Takeo and Kimiyo Miyamura (Japan)
> Rev. Daniel Shen (Taiwan)
> Dr. Claude and Anne-Marie Decrevel (Switzerland)
> Dr. George and Barbara Stulac (U.S.A.)
> Dr. Betta and Sophia Mengistu (Ethiopia)
> Dr. Ronald and Sally Gleason (Southern U.S.A.)
> Daniel and Lynne Wright (Canada)

CHAPTER 8

Ministry in Retirement

During one of the interviews for this biography, the author asked Nicole, "How would you describe your ministry now that you are no longer in the classroom fulltime?" Nicole responded, "I don't walk as fast and I tire more easily. This is definitely a time of retrenchment." Judging from his continued literary output, his chaplain-like ministry to his community, and his ongoing evangelical statesmanship, one would be hard-pressed to find corroborating evidence for his claim!

In the decade between 1994 and 2004 the Evangelical Theological Society was confronted with a movement called by its own supporters "open theism." They claimed that the "classical" view of God as immutable and possessed of a complete foreknowledge of all future events is not an adequate representation of the biblical view of God, but owes its origin to Greek philosophy, particularly as mediated through Augustine (354-430).

The opening salvo was a symposium entitled *The Openness of God* in which five authors dealt respectively with the biblical, historical, systematic, philosophical and practical avenues of research (Intervarsity Press, 1994). Strong objections were recorded in some reviews of the book. Two members of ETS published more extensive works on this theme: John Sanders (*The God Who Risks*, IVP, 1988) and Clark H. Pinnock (*Most Moved Mover: A Theology of God's Openness*, Baker, 2001). To these fairly heavy volumes was added a book intended to popularize the whole position, that of Gregory Boyd (*God of the Possible*, Baker, 2000).

Several books and symposia were published to criticize this approach. What was of particular concern to ETS members was the view that God does not know in advance what the decisions of free agents will be and that prophecies that are related to such agents may not eventuate as originally expressed. The prophecies of the pending destruction of Nineveh (Jonah 2) and of the early decease of Hezekiah (II Kings 20) are advanced as a proof that God may change his mind and void a prophecy, even though a condition for its fulfillment had not been expressed. Some went so far as to claim that future events are not objects of knowledge, although it is surely evident that the stating of a prophecy puts them in that category.

On August 7, 2000, as a founding member of ETS, Nicole took the initiative of sending a letter to the eleven surviving charter members (out of the 121 charter members from 1949-50), asking whether they agreed with him that to deny that God has knowledge of the future decisions of free agents is incompatible with the inerrancy of Scripture. He sought consensus from the founders that those who hold such a view should be asked at an annual meeting to resign from membership in ETS. The letter never reached Kenneth Kantzer, who was too ill at the time to respond. All the ten others responded in agreement on incompatibility, but three indicated doubt that such a vote would resolve the problem.

On November 9, 2000, Nicole approached the Executive Committee of the Society, giving them full details of this correspondence. It was too late to do anything at the annual meeting that year, but at the 2001 annual meeting in Colorado Springs, with the theme "Defining Evangelical Boundaries," there were no less than 31 papers dealing with open theism. There were two plenary sessions by John Sanders and Bruce Ware, respectively, in support and criticism of the subject. A majority vote was taken by the full membership of the Society that declared, "We believe the Bible clearly teaches that God has complete, accurate, and infallible knowledge of all events past, present, and future, including all future decisions and actions of free moral agents." Nicole presented a paper on "Why I Am Comfortable with Inerrancy," meant to confront difficulties alleged against the doctrine and to reassert the evangelical propriety of supporting it.[8]

At the ETS annual meeting in 2002, convened in Toronto, Ontario, the Executive Committee gave Nicole an opportunity to present very briefly his concern about open theism. After a special plenary discussion session, it was voted by a majority that the cases of both Clark Pinnock and John Sanders be considered by the Executive Committee so as to present at the next annual meeting recommendations regarding their memberships in the Society. Nicole had written a brief paper of nine pages summarizing the contrast between the "open view" and the biblical affirmation of the truthfulness of God, entitled "'Open Theism' is Incompatible with Inerrancy."[9]

President David M. Howard requested Nicole to present to him by May 1, 2003, a formal indictment of each of the men. He was permitted to and did use the contributions of a committee of scholars: Bruce Ware, John Frame, Kenneth Barker, Simon Kistemaker and Robert Picirilli. Two indictments of twenty pages each, along with eight supporting documents, were forwarded in time and shared with Pinnock and Sanders for their written reply. Howard called a meeting of the full Executive Committee to meet with Pinnock and Sanders, as well as with Bruce Ware and Nicole, on October 2-4 of that same year. Discussion was organized between members of the Committee and the indicters (Nicole and Ware) and between the Committee and the indictees.

Pinnock recognized that he had used language that needed to be corrected, both in *Most Moved Mover* and in *The Scripture Principle*. He submitted voluntarily a corrected form of note 66 in *Most Moved Mover*, which in its original wording denied the fulfillment of some prophecies. He also provided an additional explanation of his revised form, eliminating the idea that any prophecy might be non-fulfilled.

---

[8] "Why I am Comfortable with Inerrancy." In Kent Matthews, editor, *Not Omitting the Weightier Matters: Festschrift for Dr. Robert Rodgers.* Belfast and Greenville, SC: Ambassador Publications, 2002. Pp. 52-64. See Bibliography B41 and D76.

[9] See Bibliography D77

In view of his positive statements and his willingness to acknowledge that some of his earlier statements had been misleading, the Committee voted unanimously to recommend to the Society at its 2003 annual meeting that the charges against Pinnock not be sustained. The Society's vote was 432 in his favor and 212 against him. His membership was thus maintained.

In the case of John Sanders, he acknowledged from the start that he had wrongly stated that God could be mistaken (*The God Who Risks*, pp. 132, 205). He wished to withdraw these statements without canceling the position that had led him to make them. Through a very intense questioning by the Committee he remained adamant that some divine prophecies relate to probabilities and not to certainty concerning the future. The Committee voted 7-2 to recommend to the Society that his membership be terminated. Both negative votes arose from the view that "inerrant" in the ETS statement of faith had not been sufficiently defined to warrant an actual cancellation of membership. It was conceded, however, that the founders of the Society and the majority of the members had not considered inerrancy a deficient term. The two dissenting members asserted that their own view was the same as that of the founders.

When the recommendation was presented to the annual meeting, the vote was 432 to sustain the charge and 231 to uphold Sanders' membership, or 62.7% to 37.3%. Since a 2/3 majority is required for cancellation, the charge, while valid, did not lead to Sanders' expulsion. Before the meeting was adjourned, a resolution was offered by Dr. L. Russ Bush including the statement, "The case for biblical inerrancy rests on the absolute trustworthiness of God and Scripture's testimony to itself. A proper understanding of inerrancy takes into account the language, genres, and intent of Scripture. We reject approaches to Scripture that deny that biblical truth is grounded in reality." This resolution was adopted by a vote of 234 in favor and 58 opposed (a majority of 80.1%) at the 2004 annual meeting.

In 2003, Nicole presented a paper entitled "Open Theism: Whence? Where? Whither?" which has not been published. For the 2004 annual meeting he presented the paper "Inerrancy and Truth." He explored the historical meaning of the word inerrancy and the inappropriate erosion of this meaning in the last century. The original intent as expressed by the founders implied the absence of any error, that is, violation of truth.

Regarding the open theism challenge in the Evangelical Theological Society, Nicole chose not to resign from ETS, though he was "disappointed that there was not a more formal reaffirmation of the proper meaning of 'inerrant.'" He gave three reasons for his decision to stay in the Society. First, Clark Pinnock especially, but even to some extent John Sanders, retracted some very bad points, retractions which most likely would not have happened without Nicole's indictment. Second, Pinnock and Sanders will surely be more careful about clarity in the future as a result of the controversy. Third, the whole process showed that the Society is capable of disciplining itself, can be fair in the method, and is well balanced with real accountability.

He described a further action the Society should have taken but did not: "When Drs. Pinnock and Sanders accepted to cancel some expressions they had used, it was not sufficiently explored why they would write incorrectly in the first place and whether such expression was the natural way to expound their views! If that be the case, it was not enough to cancel some improper words, but to renounce the views that had led to their use." He hopes that the ultimate outcome will be an unambiguous statement on inerrancy for the Society.

This period of Nicole's life also saw the publication of his major works in two volumes: *Standing Forth* and *Our Sovereign Saviour*. He was asked, "What, in your opinion, are the most significant works you have published?" Five were mentioned, and all are included in the published collection. He listed "C. H. Dodd and the Doctrine of Propitiation"; "The Nature of Redemption"; "The Nature of Inerrancy"; "Polemic Theology – How to Deal With Those Who Differ From Us"; and "Calvinism: The Five Points."[10] Of these five, the work on Dodd was the *most* profound in Nicole's estimation. He described the article,

> I made a complete coverage of all the words related to propitiation in Hebrew, along with their translations in the

---

[10] See Bibliography: B4, 15; D2, 15, 46-48.

Septuagint, and then the usage of the New Testament. In this I made a refutation of Dodd, who wanted to exclude the idea of propitiation from the language of Scripture. The article was a forty-page survey, with a table showing the full range of usage, in Hebrew, in the Septuagint, and in New Testament Greek. Incidentally, the work I was doing in Hebrew I reviewed with E. J. Young of Westminster, during a summer school we taught together at Winona Lake School of Theology in 1954. We actually shared a cabin during that course, and so while I am not strong in Semitics, Young was able to validate thoroughly the Hebrew part of my study. That article is actually indexed in *BAGD* (*A Greek-English Lexicon of the New Testament and Other Early Christian Literature*) under the entry for *hilaskomai* and also in Colin Brown's *New International Dictionary of New Testament Theology*. My friend Allen Mahwhinney thinks that this article is the only thing by a thoroughly conservative person that is indexed in *BAGD*! And Leon Morris, in later editions of *The Apostolic Preaching of the Cross*, began referring to my work, which he called "irrefutable." Glenn Barker showed the article to Krister Stendahl at Harvard, whose response was "Dodd will have to watch himself!"

Well, I spent a whole summer on that, poring over the concordance of the Septuagint, and I found almost thirty inconsistencies in Dodd's work. I concluded that if the words do not mean propitiation, but rather expiation, then we have to ask the question, "*Who* requires expiation, and for what purpose?" If the answer is that *God* requires it, because his righteousness demands a solution for the problem of sin, then we go right back to the meaning of propitiation! If the answer is that the *sinner* requires expiation, because he needs some kind of positive expression of God's forgiveness, then we have a point of view that is so different from what we have actually in the Scripture that it becomes almost ridiculous. I was able to exploit some concessions that Vincent Taylor made about the language of propitiation. He said at one point that Paul had come within a "hair breadth" of penal substitution; well I showed that it was not even a hair away, he was fully endorsing it!

Nicole serves as a Bible study teacher for Village on the Green, and he ministers as the unofficial chaplain for the community, doing hospital visitation and other forms of outreach. In 2003, the Nicole

Scholars Program was established at RTS, providing select foreign students a full semester with their families at the seminary. His library will be made perpetually available for the study of Reformed thought in the Orlando area. Nicole was once asked, "What one piece of advice would you give to a pastor/theologian desiring to give glory to God in his life and ministry?" His answer was telling, both in regards to his personal discipleship and also to his humility: "Give yourself to personal Bible study and prayer; have a disciplined approach to it—more disciplined than mine. Be proactive in your relationship to God rather than reactive." He often worshipped when driving alone in his car, meditating on Scripture and praying rather than listening to the radio.

One of the author's great delights in the preparation of this biography has been his acquaintance with Annette Nicole. Genteel, kind, hospitable, godly, prayerful, energetic, generous—these adjectives only begin to describe the life partner of Roger Nicole. Nicole noted,

> Annette has flourished at Village on the Green. She had relatively good contacts as a professor's wife, but here she has dinner with the people, and she has an outgoing personality and spirit that is extremely beneficial. She is very much better at reaching out to people in social settings than I am. My ministry here in the community is greatly enhanced by the contacts she has with people. I have often wondered, since her health has not been that good, whether she might have died had we not been here. But she has a brand new zest for life since we have been here, where her own personality and gifts have come to expression beyond anything that was possible before. I definitely feel that God has put us here for a *job*, and not just for pampering our old age. When someone that we both know asks a question about general knowledge or about the faith, then I am able to answer it in the context of ground that has already been prepared through Annette's ministry. Like the parable of the sower, it is the same seed, but in some places it does not come to fruition. When the ground is prepared, that is part of what God is doing to work toward harvest. That is why I go and visit people at hospitals; that is the time when God is harrowing the ground. That develops the kind of contact that nothing else could ever replace. We need that here at Village on the Green because we

live among successful people, and successful people do not have that sense of need as acute as people who are not successful. I'll be honest with you. I am not so concerned about jewels in my crown when I get to heaven; I am interested in the joy that will be mine in just being there at all!

We experienced in 2004 a major problem in Annette's health. In 1991, it was found that her left carotid artery was 99% choked by cholesterol and that she needed immediately to have an operation in which a temporary bypass was established, so a section of the carotid might be cut, cleared and reinstalled in its place. This involving a major artery was a delicate surgical intervention, from which Annette recovered well in the succeeding months. Unfortunately she was then diagnosed as having a 69% stenosis in the right carotid, which required a similar operation, yet with less urgency. This was done with such skill that she did not even have a scar in her neck as a result.

Since she continued to have a higher blood pressure than normal, it appeared necessary to clear a better passage in both renal arteries. This fortunately could be accomplished by a new process by which a tube was inserted in the femoral artery and run through to the renal artery's clogging, where a balloon would enlarge the passage and a metal stent be inserted that made the clearance more permanent. This was done in the same year for both renal arteries so that the major problem of cholesterol blocking would be solved for some years.

Unfortunately in 2004 it was discovered that there was significant obstruction in two coronary arteries that supply the blood to the heart itself. This cannot be remedied by a stent, for the artery is as thin as the lead in a lead pencil! What is needed then is to provide a supplemental channel to the original artery with access above the blocking and reentrance below it. This is known as a bypass. Since this operation cannot be performed when the heart is "beating," it is necessary to supply a temporary replacement of the heart and lungs, so as to provide the indispensable immobility of the heart. In order to do that one has to split the sternum to open up the thoracic cage and permit the insertion of the substitute respiratory and circulatory system and provide access to the heart itself. In this way Annette received a triple bypass on June 14. This operation was conducted with splendid skill and provided and immense help to the coronaries.

Two complications, however, developed in the lung area. First, a portion of the right lung collapsed. Second, after this was remedied, some fluid accumulated in the lung. These conditions required two additional surgical interventions with anesthesia and consequent weakening.

By God's mercy, however, and in response to many prayers, her life was safeguarded, but she had to remain four weeks in intensive care in the hospital and six more weeks in the Health Center of our retirement place of Village-on-the-Green. She finally returned home at the beginning of September. She still needed special attention and a great deal of rest, but I am happy to state that by September 2005 she had recovered, as far as I can judge. We are immensely grateful to the Lord and to the many people who supported us in their prayers, visits, cards and good wishes. We are particularly thankful to Lynne and Daniel Wright who have adopted us as their parents and who have been special comforts to us during the whole year. Lynne visited Annette in the health center practically every day. They were for us "angels without knowing it" (Heb 13:2).

I naturally made frequent visits at the hospital, located 12 miles from our home. During this period of tension I had two automobile accidents: one in late June, in which I lost control in a left turn near the hospital and crashed head-on against a cement pylon; the other in late July, when another car hit mine on the right hand front door. In both cases my car was judged beyond repairs, but I am happy to state that in neither case was there any significant personal damage. Some people who know me have an opinion that my driving habits were bound to have such results. By the grace of God, however, I have driven close to one million miles on the roads of the United States and Canada without having any accident on account of which anybody was hospitalized. Repairs to my car in fender-benders were always very limited before the two accidents of 2004. Naturally, I am redoubling my care in driving, because the authorities are quick to suspend the driver's licenses of superannuated persons. Annette believes that God has sent a guardian angel to protect me from serious accidents over the years. Whether this is the case or not, I discern a footstep of our Lord in the watch-care I received on these two occasions.

Conclusion

Nicole's mastery of the biblical text, every area of theology, and church history made him uniquely qualified to answer a bevy of occasional questions from pastors, former students, and academic colleagues. His gracious spirit was always evident in his willingness to provide answers. One representative query was put to him, and the answer that follows is typical both in its clarity and in its thoroughness. He was asked, "How would you help someone who is trying to understand the differences between covenantalism and dispensationalism?"

> Robert Saucy has a book on modified dispensationalism, called *The Case for Progressive Dispensationalism*, in which you have an elimination of some of the defects of dispensationalism as it is often expressed. There have been some hopeful changes within dispensationalism, and already a noteworthy scholar like Charles Ryrie had differed from Lewis Sperry Chafer in a number of ways, so it is not a monolithic movement. I have a reference from something that happened in my life related to this. The 1974 annual meeting of ETS was in Dallas, and the subject for that year was interpretation. I offered a paper on "Dispensationalist Interpretation of Scripture Versus Other Types of Interpretation," and the people thought that since I was covenant-inclined, I would make a wholesale attack on dispensationalism. Now this meeting was not only in Dallas, but at Dallas Theological Seminary. I was scheduled for the paper and Ryrie was to be the respondent. People thought that there would be a bloodbath there! This was not a plenary paper, it was just one of the sections, but there were a tremendous lot of people who came to the presentation, thinking this was going to be a wholesale attack. I failed my brother Ryrie in not giving

him an advance copy so that he might know what I was doing. I started by saying, "I have decided to come not with my boxing gloves, which I left in Boston, but with a palm leaf instead."

The goal was not to discard one system of interpretation and to show that another will do the job, but to consider some advantages of dispensationalism and of covenant theology. I desired as well to show some of the difficulties that may arise from each, and to demonstrate errors into which they may slip unknowingly. So I did point to a number of difficulties in dispensationalism, and the major one is that it tends to subdivide into morsels a redemptive plan that is unified from Genesis to Revelation. There is a unity of the plan of redemption, with one divine purpose, one saving of a group of people, and one ultimate union with Christ that I find especially entrancing in Scripture. That could possibly be damaged in dispensationalism, particularly since the divisions presented are not always as clear as they think. In fact, they would not even agree among themselves what were the dispensations and how many there were, although many like the number seven. Especially questionable, as I saw it, was the idea that God was testing humanity under several different approaches, and they failed in everything. That seemed to me a strange approach: God having different tests and humanity always failing, rather than God having a redemptive purpose that dominates the whole history of mankind.

But then also I said there are some problems with covenant theology. One such problem would be that it failed to articulate a very great difference made by the coming of Christ and by the coming of the Holy Spirit at Pentecost. They seem to represent the Old Testament as being just a New Testament with a rather thin coating. They should see that the New Testament was a very powerfully articulated development, for which indeed some of the principal sources were found already in Old Testament Scripture, but in which very definitely a difference of implementation was manifest. In the New Testament, the abundance and power of the grace of God was made superlatively manifest with a special relationship of the Holy Spirit to God's people that was not present in the Old Testament. Covenantalism might tend to minimize the importance of

Christmas, Good Friday, Easter and Pentecost if people don't see that there is something really radically new there. That to my way of thinking is not proper hermeneutics.

Well, there was hardly anything that was negative for Ryrie to respond to, so he was cast in a rather unfavorable role. He came ready with boxing gloves and I came with the gracious approach and monopolized it so to speak. The people who strongly supported the covenant doctrine never strongly disagreed with me on that, so I had nobody that came to me saying, "You dirty scoundrel! You gave up the play to people that we really shouldn't favor!" I felt that this was really an in-house contestation and that we had to learn from each other. If you were dispensationalist, I hoped for you to see something of the unity of the redemptive purpose. And if you were a covenant theologian, I hoped you would see the approach God himself has taken and sanctioned in Scripture, but that you would realize that there are different forms of application, and that there was a wealth of development with the coming of the New Testament. Moses represented something of God's purpose, then the prophets represented something more, then Jesus represented superlatively more than anything that preceded him. You have an unfolding in the revelatory nature of the redemptive purpose, and you need to see that God demonstrated this in an increasing manner as time went on. This came to a supreme revelation in Christ, with no further revelation needed. Hebrews makes this plain: "Now we've got it!" Vern Poythress has a more recent book dealing with the subject entitled *Understanding Dispensationalists.*

I think there has been unnecessary hostility between the two groups. Meredith Kline was very hostile to dispensationalism, and we had a lot of students who were dispensationalists when they came to Gordon. I did not consider myself hostile to dispensationalism, but I thought these students needed to be put on a more solid foundation than this. You have a very serious difficulty, in the book of Revelation for instance, if you analyze it from a dispensationalist point of view. In this approach, you have two chapters for the history of the church, chapters 2-3, and after that you have sixteen chapters for the Tribulation, and then another three verses for the Millennium. So you have a period of at least two thousand years that is covered in chapters 2-3. Then there are seven years during which the Church is not even present. Sixteen chapters go seal by seal, trumpet by trumpet and vial by vial, but the church isn't even there. Then when the church comes back there are only three verses for the Millennium, another one thousand years with nothing much said, while the church is supposed to be reigning there with Christ, and this is *what the Spirit says to the churches!* That is not a message to the Jews but to the *churches*, and it gives us such great detail about a thing in which the church is supposedly not even present. To my way of thinking that is almost absurd, so I have problems interpreting the Apocalypse, but I think I can see clearly enough that *dispensationalism doesn't cut it!* What is mentioned *after* the Millennium, where you have the fight with Gog and Magog, are words that are found in the Old Testament, but they are found *before* the Tribulation in Ezekiel. So the Millennium may be found in Ezekiel 40-48, but Gog and Magog come in *before* that, so this is exactly the wrong place as far as Revelation is concerned. Then of course the kind of geopolitics that the dispensationalists were pushing were things like *rosh* being equivalent to Russia and Gomer or To-garmah to Germany (Ezekiel 38:2-6). This came to be so unrealistic that I just don't see how people could actually think that this is what prophecy really means. I find great difficulty in a consistent dispensational interpretation. I feel that it skews the Scripture by putting it in a framework that the Scripture cannot accept. Covenant theology may get into the same kind of difficulty by pressing biblical truth into a systematic approach. In doing that you need great care, because you are engaged in a *human* activity in relation to Scripture, and in that we can easily go astray. We desperately need humility! I may see it this way, but there are other factors to be taken into consideration, and I may not have the ultimate harmony. So that is what my life has been, searching for that harmony. In many areas I think I can see that harmony, where other people see a jumble of difficulties, but that does not mean that I am free of difficulties. I think there *is* a coherence to truth, and that therefore one who is searching for the truth is going to move in the direction of getting into that total coherent system.

Another "occasional student" of Roger Nicole wrote of his experience of on-the-spot instruction from this remarkable teacher. The following account was discovered in a review of *Dictionary of Scottish Church History & Theology* written by David J. MacLeod:

> I first met Dr. Roger Nicole, evangelical elder statesman and theologian, at a meeting of the Evangelical Theological Society on the campus of Gordon-Conwell Divinity School. He saw the word "Emmaus" on my nametag and commented that he knew Brethren in Europe and knew Emmaus Bible School in Switzerland. The next time we met he commented on the Midwest. We met again in November 1994, at the E.T.S. meeting in Chicago, and he noted that my name was Scottish. "The Scots have produced a number of great theologians," he observed, "particularly between 1830 and 1880." He singled out "James Buchanan, James Bannerman, George Smeaton, and William Cunningham." I responded, "Don't forget James Denney." "No," said Dr. Nicole, "he wasn't so good. That's why I said '1880' Denney came after 1880!" I must confess that one of the first things I did when I received this splendid new dictionary was to look up "James Denney." In a fine little piece the author mentions Denney's famous works on the atonement, but he adds that Denney "scorned the idea of the verbal inerrancy of Scripture." This, I am sure, is the aspect of Denney's theology that bothered Dr. Nicole, himself a staunch defender of the doctrine of inerrancy.

Those in ministry must be willing to answer questions from those they serve, whether in the classroom or in the pastorate. Sometimes ministers will say that the questioner is asking the wrong question, but in Nicole's view there *are* no wrong questions! You cannot blame people for asking a question. So if somebody asked, "What did God do before he created the world?" he would not rebuke them for asking the wrong question! There was a man who answered that particular question, raised by his daughter, "God was preparing switches to punish little girls who ask wrong questions." That is entirely the wrong answer. The answer is not true in fact, because God was not preparing switches prior to creation. And it is false psychologically. One might reply that while this is a valid question, it is a subject upon which we cannot give a complete answer. Or, for that specific question you might say with confidence that God was surely resting in the sufficiency of his own being as the Triune God. Nicole noted further,

A pastor must try to win people over in his preaching with the truth that has won *him* over. He must not try to mow down people with the truth; this is usually what happens with a pastor who does not visit. He gets to know his own office very well, but not the people. You've got to endear yourself to them as the presenter before you can really let go with all the power that the truth may have. In this way humor can be helpful, though you must be careful because it can be misused. If people are willing to laugh with you, they may be willing to weep with you as well. Sometimes you feel as though in preaching that you "laid an egg," but then someone comes up to you and tells you afterwards how much the sermon really meant to them. At other times, you feel as though you really understood the text, and really carried the day, but no one was moved. But maybe *you* were the one who needed that message that day! I am always surprised by the intangible element of truth's impact on people.

Dr. Saillens once related to me that one time when he was preaching, during his reading of Scripture, he turned one page extra by mistake and started reading at the top on the next page. When he realized that this was not right, he went back and read the right thing. After the message, there was somebody who responded to an appeal that was given. He asked the person what it was about the service that really made an impression on him spiritually. This fellow mentioned the Scripture reading that was made by mistake. That was the moment when God touched him!

When there are persons who are not happy at a church, there are two possibilities. First, you might be able to win them over. Endeavor to do that. But don't automatically take the blame on yourself for the strife. Recognize that the other possibility might happen, and that is that they would be happier somewhere else. Then we have to say (I am quoting the man I view as the most challenging Christian mind that I have known in the evangelical world: Gordon Clark) with Luther, "Let goods and kindred go . . . some memberships also!"

It has been my desire to emphasize the fullness of the work of salvation as the answer to the human predicament. This presentation takes into account man's *standing* with God and the guilt that he necessarily carries because of sin as well as man's *condition* that is one of corruption in his body, soul, and mind. The gospel responds to those two very grievous defects with justification and sanctification. Personally, I sense the presence of God most immediately when God punishes me in some way or other. I am very far from perfectionism, because it involves either a lowering of God's standard so that humans can actually reach it, or else it involves a refusal to acknowledge that the standard is really what God has established, claiming for oneself something that is very unrealistic. In that sense I am not a Methodist. It is one thing for a man to say he is perfect; it is another thing for his *wife* to say he is perfect, or his employer, or his employees!

In God's final judgment there will be no way of escaping the presence of the court, there will be no defaulting. There will be no lawyer presenting the case, because the case is already fully known by God himself. There will be no technicalities offered, because God knows all the truth. There will be no jury, because God is the only one capable of making the right decision. There will be no appeal, no special plea, no parole, and no pardon (except for those for whom Christ has borne the punishment). There will be a perfect and complete finality to it. Any limitations of human justice normally encountered in the courts will be superseded. Therefore, the best hope, even for sinful people, is in the final judgment of God, even though they may be condemned. It is better for them there than in any other court. Nobody will get away with anything, and nobody will face injustice at the final judgment.

Though Nicole is not as widely known as some of his contemporaries in theology, his colleagues, students, and friends were enthusiastic in their assessment of his impact on their lives. Freeman Barton, Head Librarian at Gordon-Conwell Theological Seminary, wrote this biography's author, "I'm delighted a biography is being written. Although many others know Roger Nicole much better, I've known and respected him all my life. He was first a friend of my father. But I pity the poor biographer who must try to read his handwriting!" Fortunately, the fact that Nicole was alive and able to clarify challenging manuscripts made the work much easier.

Nicole's literary production was ample, especially considering his numerous other commitments (itinerant teaching, local church ministry, seminary instruction, and evangelical statesmanship). His writings span the gamut of biblical, systematic, and practical theology, demonstrating Nicole's passion for the text of Scripture, its orderly presentation, and its obedient application.

Biblical inerrancy was for Roger Nicole "a hill on which to die." The subject was no esoteric concept for idle contemplation or sectarian debates; instead, it was a presupposition that he accepted intuitively and defended with all of the resources of his ample intellect. His article "The Nature of Inerrancy" was a concise summary of his careful thought on the matter.

Christian believers of a Reformed theological persuasion owe a tremendous (if largely unrecognized) debt to Roger Nicole. His contributions have been numerous and weighty, but they have seldom been in the limelight. As a theology professor for over fifty years, Nicole shaped and clarified the doctrinal framework of several generations of pastors, teachers, writing scholars, and missionaries. He similarly influenced the parishioners at the churches he served as pastor (though in the fortunate experience of those congregants, Nicole's *personal example of godliness* was perhaps more readily observable than in the classroom). Nicole published extensively, and his thought is readily accessible to most Reformed pastors and students through theological dictionary and encyclopedia entries, and in the many compendia and journals in which his essays are included. When asked why he was not included in Walter A. Elwell's *Handbook of Evangelical Theologians*, Nicole replied,

> Well, there were quite a number of other people that were not included. So I did get in touch with the publisher, Baker, and I said, "This is a very fine book. I am presenting J. I. Packer in this. But I notice the absence of some people whom I think you might be interested to have included." And so I gave them a list

of as many more theologians as they had already. And I included my name in it, just mentioning it with the others. I remarked, "I do not include my name because I think obviously you should have me, but because I am afraid you might *forget* it!" But they said they were aware of the fact that there were many omissions of some great theological thinkers. I just felt that it would have been nice to have another book about that size, perhaps a two-volume set.

To "forget" Roger Nicole would be a formidable task for anyone at all acquainted with him. The intent of this biography has been to trace the sovereign influence of God in the life of one man, a man wholly devoted to Christ and His kingdom. Hopefully the reader has been challenged and encouraged to employ every advantage and opportunity for service to the Lord Jesus. It has been the inestimable privilege of this book's author to work with Roger Nicole and to call him not only *teacher*, but also *friend*.

"for God is not unrighteous to forget your work
and the love which ye showed toward his name,
in that ye ministered unto the saints, and still do minister"
Hebrews 6:10

Appendices,

Bibliography

and Indices

Appendix A

How to Deal with Those Who Differ from Us

The following article, so typical of the life and legacy of Roger Nicole, had its origin in a class he taught with students for whom definite atonement was a novel doctrine, even irksome. One fellow, a graduate of Cornell University who later went on the mission field, found the course content very offensive. Rather than becoming defensive himself, Nicole reflected, "How can I properly deal with these people?" He knew he had to start where they were, putting himself "in their shoes." It was not enough that he had proved the reasonableness of definite atonement to his own satisfaction—how did *the students* look at it? He determined not to press so hard, not to make it as important as, say, justification by faith alone. He reorganized the syllabus to consider the reception of these truths by the students. They had thought that he was coming to passages like I John 2 with a fixed notion and artificially interpreting it. Two or three years afterward, at his 25th anniversary at Gordon, they asked him to give an address. The substance of that message became the article *How to Deal with Those Who Differ from Us*.

Part 1: What Do I Owe to the Person Who Differs From Me?

We are called upon by the Lord to contend earnestly for the faith. (Jude 3) That does not necessarily involve being contentious; but it involves avoiding compromise, standing forth for what we believe, standing forth for the truth of God-without welching at any particular moment. Thus, we are bound to meet, at various points and various levels, people with whom we disagree. We disagree in some areas of Christian doctrine. We disagree as to some details of church administration. We disagree as to the way in which certain tasks of the church should be pursued. And, in fact, if we are careful to observe the principles that I would like to expound for you, I would suggest that they may be valuable also in disagreements that are not in the religious field. They also would apply to disagreements in politics or difficulties with people in your job or friction within the family or contentions between husband and wife or between parents and children. Who does not encounter from time to time people who are not in complete agreement; therefore it is good to seek to discover certain basic principles whereby we may relate to those who differ from us.

It seems strange that one should desire to speak at all about Polemic Theology since we are now in an age when folks are more interested in ecumenism and irenics than in polemics. Furthermore, Polemic Theology appears to have been often rather ineffective. Christians have not managed in many cases to win over their opponents. They have shown themselves to be ornery; they have bypassed some fairly important prescriptions of Scripture; and in the end, they have not convinced very many people. Sometimes they have not even managed to convince themselves! Under those circumstances, one perhaps might desire to bypass a subject like this altogether.

In order to approach this subject, there are three major questions that we must ask; and I would like to emphasize very strongly that, in my judgment, we need to ask them precisely in the right order: (1) What do I *owe* the person who differs from me? (2) What can I *learn* from the person who differs from me? (3) How can I *cope* with the person who differs from me?

Many people overlook the first two questions and jump right away to: "How can I cope with this? How can I bash this person right down into the ground in order to annihilate objections and differences?" Obviously, if we jump to the third question from the start, it is not very likely that we will be very successful in winning over dissenters. So I suggest, first of all, that we need to face squarely the matter of our duties. *We have obligations to people who differ from us.* This does not involve agreeing with them. We have an obligation to the truth that has a priority over agreement with any particular person; if someone is not in the truth, we have no right to agree. We have no right even to minimize the importance of the difference; and therefore, we do not owe consent, and we do not owe indifference. But what we owe that person who differs from us, whoever that may be, is what we owe every human being-*we owe them to love them.* And we owe them to deal with them as we ourselves would like to be dealt with or treated (Matthew 7:12).

And how then do we desire to be treated? Well, the first thing that we notice here is that we want people to know what we are saying or meaning. There is, therefore, an obligation if we are going to voice differences to make a serious effort to know the person with whom we differ. That person may have published books or articles. Then we have an obligation to be acquainted with those writings. It is not appropriate for us to voice sharp differences if we have neglected to read what is available. The person who differs from us should have evidence that we read carefully what has been written and that we have attempted to understand its meaning. In the case of an oral exchange where we don't have the writing, we owe the person who differs from us to listen carefully to what he or she says. Rather than preparing ourselves to pounce on that person the moment he or she stops talking, we should concentrate on apprehending precisely what the other person holds.

In this respect, I say that Dr. Cornelius Van Til has given us a splendid example. As you may know, he expressed very strong objections to the theology of Karl Barth. This was so strong that Barth claimed that Van Til simply did not understand him. It has been my privilege to be at Dr. Van Til's office and to see with my own eyes the bulky tomes of Barth's, *Kirchliche Dogmatik* (Incidentally, these volumes were the original German text, not an English translation). As I leafed through these, I bear witness that I did not see one page that was not constellated with underlining, double-underlining, marginal annotations, exclamation points, and question marks galore. So here is someone who certainly did not say, "I know Karl Barth well; I understand his stance; I don't need to read anymore of this; I can move on with what I have." Every one of the volumes, including the latest ones that were then in existence, gave evidence of very, very careful scrutiny. So when we intend to take issue with somebody, we need to do the job that is necessary to know that person so that we are not voicing our criticism in the absence of knowledge but that we are proceeding from the vantage point of real acquaintance.

Even that is not enough. Beyond what a person says or writes, we must *attempt to understand what a person means*. Now it is true that there are what are called "Freudian slips," that is there are people who do not express themselves exactly the way it should be done; but in the process somehow they give an insight into a tendency that is there in them all along and which leads them to express themselves in an infelicitous but revealing manner. So it is appropriate, I suppose, to note this as a personal footnote, so to speak, in order possibly to make use of it at some time in the discussion. But if somebody fails to express himself or herself accurately, there is no great point in pressing the very language that is used. We ought to try to understand what is the meaning that this language is intended to convey. In some cases, we may provide an opportunity for an opponent to speak more accurately.

I have experienced this in my own home. I have noticed that my wife sometimes says things like this: "You never empty the wastebasket." Now as a matter of fact, on January 12, 1984, I did empty the wastebasket. Therefore, the word *never* is inappropriate! This tends to weaken the force of my wife's reproach. Well, I've learned that I don't get anywhere by pressing this point. This kind of reaction is not providing dividends of joy and peace in my home. I've learned, therefore, to interpret that when my wife says "never" she means "rarely" or "not as often as should be." When she says "always," she means "frequently" or "more often than should be." Instead of quibbling as to the words *never* and *always*, I would do well to pay attention to what she finds objectionable. And indeed, I should be emptying the wastebasket. That is a regular part of a male role in the home, isn't it? Feminist or not feminist, a husband and father should empty the wastebasket; and therefore, if I fail to do this, even only once, there is good reason to complain. Nothing is gained by quibbling about how often this happens. I ought to recognize this and be more diligent with it.

Similarly, in dealing with those who differ, we ought not to quibble about language just in order to pounce on our opponent because he or she has not used accurate wording. It is more effective to seek to apprehend what is meant and then to relate ourselves to the person's meaning. If we don't do that, of course, there is no encounter because this person speaks at one level and we are taking the language at another level; and so the two do not meet, and the result is bound to be frustrating. So if we really want to meet, we might as well try to figure out the meaning rather than to quibble on wording.

Moreover, I would suggest that we owe to people who differ from us to *seek to understand their aims*. What is it that they are looking for? What is it that makes them tick? What is it that they are recoiling against? What are the experiences, perhaps tragic experiences, that have steeled them into a particular stance? What are the things that they fear and the things that they yearn for? Is there not something that I fear as well or yearn for in the same way? Is there not a possibility here to find a point of contact at the very start rather than to move on with an entirely defensive or hostile mood?

As an example, it may be observed that in the fourth century Arius, and undoubtedly many of his supporters, were especially leery of modalism, a serious error in the conception of the Trinity whereby the Godhead manifested Himself in three successive forms or modes as Father, Son and the Holy Spirit rather than to exist eternally as Three Who have interpersonal relations with each other. From Arius' vantage point, the orthodox doctrine of the full deity of the Son and the Holy Spirit did of necessity imply a modalistic view. It did not help that one of his very vocal opponents Marcellus of Ancyra did, in fact, border dangerously on modalism. Arguments designed to show the biblical and logical strengths of the doctrine of the Son's full deity or vice versa the weakness of Arius's subordinationism would not be likely to be effective unless the instinctive fear of an implied modalism were addressed and shown to be without solid foundation. With all due respect to the soundness, courage, and perseverance of those like Athanasius and Hilary who consistently resisted Arianism, one may yet wonder if a more effective method of dealing with this error might not have been to allay the fear that orthodoxy inevitably would lead to modalism.

In the controversy between Calvinism and Arminianism, it must be perceived that the fact that many Arminians (possibly almost all of them) conceive to affirm the complete sovereignty of God inevitably implies a rejection of any free will, power of decision, and even responsibility on the part of created rational beings, angelic or human. Their attachment to those features naturally leads them to oppose Calvinism as they understand it. It is imperative for the Calvinist controversialist to affirm and to prove that he or she does not, in fact, deny or reject these modalities of the actions and decisions of moral agents but that he or she undertakes to retain these—even though their logical relation to divine sovereignty remains shrouded in a mystery that transcends finite, human logic.

Similarly, the Calvinist should not glibly conclude that evangelical Arminians are abandoning the notion of divine sovereignty because they assert the freedom of the human will. It is plainly obvious that

Arminians pray for the conversion of those yet unbelievers and that they desire to recognize the Lordship of God. The Arminian will do well to emphasize this in discussion with Calvinists so as to provide a clearer perception of the actual stance of both parties. It is remarkable that committed Calvinists can sing without reservation many of the hymns of Charles and John Wesley, and vice versa that most Arminians do not feel they need to object to those of Isaac Watts or Augustus Toplady.

In summary, I would say we owe our opponents to deal with them in such a way that they may sense that we have a real interest in them as persons, that we are not simply trying to win an argument or show how smart we are, but that we are deeply interested in them-and are eager to learn from them as well as to help them.

One method that I have found helpful in making sure that I have dealt fairly with a position that I could not espouse was to assume that a person endorsing that view was present in my audience (or was reading what I had written). Then my aim was to represent the view faithfully and fully without mingling the criticism with factual statements; in fact, so faithfully and fully that an adherent to that position might comment, "This man certainly does understand our view!" It would be a special boon if one could say, "I never heard it stated better!" This then could earn me the right to criticize. But before I proceed to do this, it is only proper that I should have demonstrated that I have a correct understanding of the position I desire to evaluate.

Part 2: What Can I Learn from Those Who Differ From Me?

In the last section, we discussed the answer to the question, "What do I *owe* the person who differs from me?" It is very important throughout that one should remain keenly aware of such obligation, for otherwise any discussion is doomed to remain unproductive. The truth that I believe I have grasped must be presented in a spirit of love and winsomeness. To do otherwise is to dispute truth itself, for it is more naturally allied to love than to hostility or sarcasm (Ephesians 4:15). These may, in fact, reflect a certain insecurity that is not warranted when one is really under the sway of truth. It may well be that God's servant may be moved to righteous indignation in the presence of those "who suppress the truth by their wickedness" (Romans 1:18). This explains the outbursts of the Old Testament prophets, of our Lord in His denunciation of the Pharisees and of the apostles in dealing with various heresies and hypocrisies in the early church. These severe judgments were ordinarily aimed at warning members of the flock rather than winning over some people who had distanced themselves from the truth of God to a point which left no room for hope of recovery (Psalm 139:19-22; Isaiah 5:8-25; Daniel 5:26-30; Matthew 12:30-32; Acts 7:51-53; Galatians 5:12; Revelation 22:15). But when dealing with those we have a desire to influence for the good, we need imperatively to remain outgoing and gracious.

When we are sure that our *outward* approach is proper, we need secondly to safeguard the *inward* benefits of courtesy. We need to ask the question, "What can I *learn* from those who differ from me?" It is not censurable selfishness to seek to gain maximum benefits from any situation that we encounter. It is truly a pity if we fail to take advantage of opportunities to learn and develop what almost any controversy affords us.

Could I be Wrong?

The first thing that I should be prepared to learn is that I am wrong and the other person is right. Obviously, this does not apply to certain basic truths of the faith like the Deity of Christ or salvation by grace. The whole structure of the Christian faith is at stake here and it would be instability rather than broad-mindedness to allow these to be eroded by doubts. Yet, apart from issues where God Himself has spoken so that doubt and hesitancy are really not permissible there are numerous areas where we are temperamentally inclined to be very assertive and in which we can quite possibly be in error. When we are unwilling to acknowledge our fallibility, we reveal that we are more interested in winning a discussion and safeguarding our reputation than in the discovery and triumph of truth. A person who corrects our misapprehensions is truly our helper rather than our adversary, and we should be grateful for this service rather than resentful of the correction. As far as our reputation is concerned, we should seek to be known for an unfailing attachment to the truth and not appear to pretend to a kind of infallibility that we are ready to criticize when Roman Catholics claim it for their popes!

Our reputation will be better served if we show ourselves ready to be corrected when in error, rather than if we keep obstinately to our viewpoint when the evidence shows it to be wrong. I should welcome the correction. This person is really my friend who renders a signal service to me! I should respond, "I was mistaken in this; I am glad that you straightened me out; Thank you for your help." People who are unwilling to acknowledge their mistakes, by contrast, may be called stubborn and lose their credibility.

What are the Facts?

In the second place we may learn from one who differs that our presentations, while correct as far as it goes, fails to embody the truth in its entirety on the subject in view. Although what we assert is true, there are elements of truth that, in our own clumsy way, we have overlooked. For instance, we may be so concerned to assert the deity of Christ that we may appear to leave no room for His humanity. As a Calvinist, I may so stress the sovereignty of God that the reality of human decision may appear to be ruled out. Here again, I should feel grateful rather than resentful. The adversative situation may well force me to give better attention to the fullness of revelation and preclude an innate one-sidedness which results in a caricature that does disservice to truth no less than the actual error may do. Many of the mainline elements of Christianity are thus, "two-railed," if I may express myself in a metaphor. Unity, yet threeness in God, immanence yet transcendence, sovereignty of God and yet reality of rational decision, body and soul, deity and humanity of the Mediator, justification and sanctification, divine inspiration of Scripture and human authorship, individual and corporate responsibility. One could multiply the examples. When one of the factors is overlooked, one is doing no better than the railroad operator who would attempt to run an ordinary train with only one rail (I do not speak here of monorails!) The person who differs from me may render me great service by compelling me to present the truth in its completeness and thus avoid pitfalls created by under-emphasis, over emphasis and omissions. Thus my account will be "full-orbed" rather than "half-baked!"

What are the Dangers?

I may learn from those who differ from me that I have not sufficiently perceived certain dangers to which my view is exposed and against which I need to be especially on guard. I may find out notably that there are certain weighty objections to which I had not given sufficient attention heretofore. Here again, I must be grateful for a signal service rendered by the objector. Instead of being irked by the opposition, I should rise to the challenge of presenting my view with appropriate safeguards and in such a way as to anticipate objections that are likely to arise.

For example, consider how the Westminster divines were led to express the doctrine of divine decrees (Confession III/I).

> "*God from all eternity did, by the most wise and Holy counsel of His own will, freely and unchangeably ordain whatsoever comes to pass; yet so as thereby neither is God the author of sin, nor is violence offered to the will of the creatures, nor is the liberty or contingency of second causes taken away, but rather established.*"

The three clauses following "yet so as thereby" are specifically designed to ward off misunderstanding and to meet objections commonly raised by Arminians or Arminianizing divines. The peculiar wisdom of setting up these safeguards in the first article of that chapter is the fruit of the bitter experiences made in more than half a century of controversy issuing in rich balanced and nuanced expression of truth in the Westminster standards.

In France, certain barriers placed on bridges, terraces or quays are called "*garde-fous*", that is to say "safeguards for the crazy." They provide a fence to prevent those who are careless from falling off the edge. Those who disagree with us provide us with an opportunity to ascertain areas of danger in our view and to build "garde-fous" there. It would be a pity if we failed to take advantage of such an opportunity.

What about Ambiguities?

We may learn from those who object that we are not communicating as we should and that they have not rightly understood what we wanted to say. In this we can be benefited also, for the whole purpose of speaking (or writing) is to communicate. If we don't communicate, we might as well remain silent. And if we don't manage to communicate properly what we think, we have to learn to speak better. If ambiguities remain, and it is apparent from the way in which the other person reacts that ambiguities do remain, then we are challenged to make a presentation that is clearer, more complete, more wholesome, and one that will communicate better.

We have Biblical precedents for this. The apostle Paul, for instance, anticipated objections which arise from misunderstanding of his doctrine. In Romans 6:1 he writes "What shall we say then? Shall we go on sinning so that grace may increase? By no means!" This objection provides a launching pad to articulate more fully his thoughts so that readers will not be permitted to wander away, but will gain a proper understanding of the truth. There are many other examples of this approach in the Pauline writings (Romans 3:3; 6:15, 19; 7:7, 13; Galatians 2:17, 19 etc.). Even our Lord took pains to rephrase or amplify some of His statements that the hearer had not rightly understood at first (Matthew 13:18-23; 37-43; John 11:12-14, etc.).

The effort made to clarify our thought for others will often result in clarifying it also for ourselves. We may thus secure a firmer hold upon the truth, a better grasp of its implications, and relationship to other truths, a more effective way to articulate and illustrate it. These are boons for which we may be grateful to those who differ from us.

When we give due attention to what we owe those who differ and what we can learn from them, we may be less inclined to proceed in a hostile manner. Our hand will not so readily contract into a boxing fist, but will be extended as an instrument of friendship and help; our feet will not be used to bludgeon another, but will bring us closer to those who stand afar; our tongue will not lash out in bitterness and sarcasm, but will speak words of wisdom, grace and healing (Proverbs 10:20, 21; 13:14; 15:1; 24; 26; 25:11; James 3).

Part 3 How Can I Cope with Those Who Differ from Me?

In the previous two sections, we sought to explore how to derive the maximum benefit from controversy both as to those who differ by being sure that we do not fail in our duty toward them, and as to ourselves in welcoming an opportunity to learn as well as an occasion to vindicate our position. Now after having given due attention to the questions, "What do I owe?" and "What can I learn?" it is certainly proper to raise the query, "*How can I cope with those who differ from me?*"

Now "coping" involves naturally two aspects known as "defensive" and "offensive." Unfortunately, these terms are borrowed from the military vocabulary and tend to reflect a pugnacious attitude which injects bitterness into controversies. We should make a conscious effort to resist that trend. Furthermore "offensive" is often understood as meaning "giving offence" or "repulsive" rather than simply "passing to the attack." It may therefore be better to use the adjectives "protective" and "constructive" to characterize these two approaches.

I. Biblical Arguments

In evangelical circles obviously this type of evidence carries a maximum of weight if properly handled, for it invokes the authority of God Himself in support of a position. This is what Luther so eloquently asserted at the Diet of Worms, and what the Westminster Confession also bears witness to in these words:

> "*God alone is Lord of the conscience, and hath left it free from the doctrines and commandments of men which are in any way contrary to His Word, or beside it in matters of faith or worship*" (WCF 20:2).

We need here to be careful to make a reverent use of Scripture, quoting every reference in a way that is consistent with its context. This will protect our approach against the legitimate criticisms levied against "proof-texting," a method that lifts scriptural statements from their environment, and marshals them as if they were isolated pronouncements vested with divine authority without regard to the way in which they are introduced in Holy Writ. A notable example of this wrong approach would be to claim that God sanctions the statement, "There is no God" because it is found in Psalm 14:1 and 53:1.

We must therefore, be careful to use the Scripture in such a way that an examination of the context will strengthen, not weaken the argument. Very few things are as damaging to a position as a claim to be grounded in the authority of God's Word, only to find that a more careful examination of the text in its context cancels out the support it was presumed to give. An argument of this type, like the house built on sand, "... falls with a great crash" (Matthew 7:27).

Likewise, a well-advised person will be careful to avoid passages that "boomerang,"- passages that are used as proof, but turn out to be more decisive against the view advanced. For example, some people quote Philippians 2:12, "Work out your own salvation with fear and trembling" and forget that Paul continues, "For it is God who works in you to will and to act...."

All this demands that we should know the Word of God. God entrusted the sacred Scriptures to His people in order that they may search it diligently (John 5:39) and make it the object of their daily meditation (Psalm 119). To be acquainted with the whole counsel of God (Acts 20:27) must be the aim not only of professionals like pastors and professors, but of everyone who wants to be known as a Christian. To be sound in the interpretation, correlation and application of the Scriptures is the way "to be approved, a workman who does not need to be ashamed" (2 Timothy 2:15) and every child of God ought to aspire to that.

Defensively we may be aware of passages that are often quoted to invalidate a stance which we find scriptural. Sometimes we may anticipate this objection even before it is raised and be prepared to show how it does not undercut our view. If we have a particularly strong refutation, we may at times wait until the person who differs quotes the passage. In this was we may score the psychological advantage of destroying an argument thought valid. Even this however, must remain within the framework of "speaking the truth in love" (Ephesians 4:15).

In some cases it may be possible to show that the interpretation which would see in a particular passage an objection to the scriptural truth we are undertaking to advocate is simply improper and indefensible because it sets this Scripture in conflict with its context, or at least with the larger context of the unity of divine revelation. In other cases, it may be sufficient to show that there are one or several plausible alternative explanations of this text that do not precipitate the alleged conflict. Since we are obliged to seek the unity of the truth, a plausible interpretation that averts a conflict deserves the preference.

To sum up, we must ever strive to take account of the fullness of biblical revelation to have the boldness to advance as far as it leads, and the restraint to stop in our speculations where the Bible ceases to provide guidance. Polemic theology in this respect is simply biblical light focused in such a way as to assist those who appear yet caught in some darkness.

II. General Arguments

These arguments direct their appeal to something other than the actual text of Scripture, namely to logic, history and tradition. While the authority involved is not on the same level as the Bible, the Word of God, it has a bearing on the discussions and must be considered by those who wish to make a strong case.

Appeal to Reason. Human reason, especially when not guided by divine revelation, is apt to go astray either in being unduly influenced by prejudice (what we call "rationalizing") or when reason forgets its proper limits and attempts to apply to the infinite what is valid only for finite categories. Nevertheless, reason is a divine gift to humankind, indispensable to the process of receiving, applying and communicating revelation. (Cf. J.I. Packer, *"Fundamentalism" and the Word of God*, pages 128-137.) It is a part and parcel of God's image in humanity. To fly in the face of logic is to court self-destruction, for logic has a way to beat its own path in the process of history. Rational arguments may therefore be presented with propriety, and those advanced by people who differ from us must be addressed.

1. *Positively*, it behooves me to show that my view is in keeping with the totality of revealed truth, with the structure of the Christian faith as an organism of truth. I will promote the acceptance of an individual tenet if I can show that it is inescapably related to some other element of the faith on which I and the one who differs from me have agreement. For instance, one who accepts the doctrine of the Trinity is pretty well bound to confess the deity of Christ and *vice versa*.

Specifically, it is in order to make plain the damaging or even disastrous effects that a departure from the position I advocate will logically entail. In doing this, I must carefully distinguish between the view that the other person actually espouses and the implication that I perceive as resulting from it. Failure to make this distinction has resulted in the ineffectiveness of much polemic theology. Christians have wasted a huge amount of ammunition in bombarding areas where their adversaries were not in fact located, but where it was thought they were logically bound to end up. Perhaps God has providentially so ordained in order that polemic theology should not be as destructive as the combatants intended. To struggle with a caricature is not a "big deal." and to knock down a straw man does not entitle one to the Distinguished Service Cross! To be sure, it is a part of the proper strategy to show those who differ that their view involves damaging implications that will be difficult to resist in the course of time, but one must remain aware that it is the present position rather than anticipated developments that must be dealt with.

2. *Negatively*, I need to face the objections that are raised against my view. Some of them are irrelevant because they are based on a misunderstanding of the issues. To deal with these will help me to clarify my position and to reassert it with proper safeguards against one-sidedness, exaggeration or misconceptions. For instance, I may show that definite atonement is not incompatible with a universal offer of salvation in Christ, even though the supporters of universal atonement frequently think it is. Other objections may be shown to be invalid because they apply to the view of those who differ as well as to mine. Still other objections may be recognized as peripheral, that is to say, difficulties that may or may not be resolved rather than considerations that invalidate a position otherwise established. For instance, some alleged contradictions between two passages of Scripture represent a difficulty for the doctrine of inerrancy rather than a discreditation of this otherwise well-established tenet of the faith. Obviously the most advantageous situation is found when an objection can be turned around to become a positive argument in favor of the view objected to. Jesus' treatment of the Old Testament Law in Matthew 5:21-42 is a case in point. It might appear to a superficial reader that in this text Jesus repudiates the authority of the Law, when in fact He confirms it and reinforces it by His spiritual interpretation.

Furthermore, it is sometimes effective to challenge a person who differs from us to press for an alternative approach which we may then proceed to criticize. For instance, a person who denies the deity of Christ may well be pressed to give his or her answer to the question, "Who do say that I am?" (Matthew 16:15). Any answer short of full deity may be shown as deeply unsatisfactory, as leading to some form of polytheism or as failing utterly to account for the facts of the life, death and resurrection of Christ. It may be hoped that those who have unsatisfactory views may then leave the smoldering ruins of their system and take refuge in the solid edifice of the faith "once for all entrusted to the saints" (Jude 3).

Appeal to History and Tradition. The course of history is a remarkable laboratory that permits us to observe the probable developments that issue from the holding of certain tenets. The decisions of councils or the pronouncements of confessions of faith are often geared to guard against erroneous opinions that God's people recognized as dangerous or even fatal to the faith. To neglect this avenue of knowledge is to risk repeating some mistakes of the past that an acquaintance with history might well have enabled us to avoid. The Christological debates of the fourth and fifth centuries should protect us from the twin errors of Arianism and Apollinarianism, of Nestorianism and Monophysitism without our passing through the convolutions that the church of those days experienced. The Reformation of the sixteenth century, similarly, should shield us from repeating some of the mistakes of the Roman Catholic Church.

Positively, it is proper for me to attempt to prove that I am in line with orthodoxy in general and specifically with statements of faith that have received wide acceptance or that are part of the subordinate standards of my church or of the church of the one who differs. This will be especially significant if the formulation was established for the purpose of warding off a position analogous to that of my opponent. Now all manmade statements are subject to revision and correction, but it appears *prima facie* impossible that a view that flatly contradicts the Nicene Creed or even the Westminster Standards should turn out to be right, while these revered creeds, tested as they were through centuries of Christian thinking, should be wrong.

Specifically, the position of the one who differs may so closely approximate a well-known heresy adjudged as heterodox that the course of history may provide a portrayal of what happens to those who entertain it. The disastrous course of Arianism, culminating as it did in the Moslem conquest of North Africa, may be an example. We need, however, to be careful to recognize the importance of weighing all operative factors rather than just some selected ones which seem to suit our purpose. The demise of Christianity in North Africa applied largely to Egypt where a monophysite tendency prevailed, as well as to the lands that had been conquered by the Vandals with their Arian commitment.

Those who would gloat over the increasing heterodoxy of the Arminian movement in the Netherlands should probably be somewhat sobered in thinking of the destiny of Calvinism in New England, which moved from high orthodoxy around 1650 to the rather massive Unitarian and Pelagian defection at the beginning of the nineteenth century. These remarks do not invalidate the value of the lessons of history, but merely admonish to caution in applying them.

Negatively, the course of action would parallel closely what was described above. Objections raised against my view may be shown to be counterproductive, because they support rather than undermine my view; irrelevant, because they fail to address my real position or because they burden equally the objector's view; or inconsequential, because they have only a peripheral bearing on the issues.

III. Christian's Goal

Perhaps the most important consideration for the Christian is to remain aware at all times of the goal to be achieved. It is the consistent perception of this goal that will give a basic orientation to the whole discussion: Are we attempting to win an argument in order to manifest our own superior knowledge and debating ability? Or are we seeking to win another person whom we perceive as enmeshed in error or inadequacy by exposing him or her to the truth and light that God has given to us?

If the former be true, it is not surprising if our efforts are vain: we should be like physicians who take care of patients simply in order to accredit some pet theory. If the latter be true, we will naturally be winsome. This will increase our patience when the force of our arguments does not seem to have an immediate effect. This will challenge us anew to understand those who differ in order to present the arguments that are most likely to be persuasive to them. God has appointed all of us to be witnesses to the truth (John 1:7; Acts 1:8). God is the one who can and will give efficacy to this witness. We should never underestimate His ability to deal even with those who appear most resistant. Who would have thought that Stephen could actually reach the heart and mind of anyone in the lynch mob that put him to death? But his great discourse was actually sowing goads in the very heart and conscience of Saul (Acts 26:14). Acts 7 showed that his argument was sealed by his Christ-like spirit in the face of this atrocious murder (Acts 7:59-60). His witness was used by God to win over perhaps the ablest of his adversaries, who was to be the great apostle Paul!

A Christian in carrying on discussions with those who differ should not be subject to the psychology of the boxing ring where the contestants are bent upon demolishing one another. Rather "The Lord's servant must not quarrel: instead, he must be kind to everyone, able to teach, not resentful. Those who oppose him he must gently instruct, in hope that God will grant them repentance leading them to a knowledge of the truth, and that they will come to their senses..." (2 Timothy 2:24-26).

The above article concerns our relationship to those who differ from us. There are many occasions, however, when we do not meet them singly. Instead, we are facing mixed groups, including some who differ, others who agree, and still others who have not decided conclusively on the issues. This is particularly the case when we participate in an oral debate. Here we have an obligation to provide support and encouragement to those who share our perception of the truth we are called to vindicate. We should also be mindful of those who are yet hesitant and whom we should hope to rally in support. Under those circumstances, we cannot afford to function exclusively in terms of our concern for our opponents: our concern for the truth itself (which here I would presume we represent) and for those who are allies or neutral may demand that we should work toward the discomfiture of the opposition.

A debate consists of a presentation of factors for and against two or more positions on which there is (or may be) disagreement in the audience. The well-known series of books entitled *"Four Views On . . ."* is typical. The weight of the considerations listed should help the members of the audience to make up their minds on the issues.

Below are provided some principles that should continue to regulate our behavior, along with methodological advice that may be helpful.

I.   Regulative principles for an oral debate

A.   A debate involves more than the objective value of the arguments presented by both parties. There are psychological factors that exercise a considerable influence on the audience. It is not wrong for a contender to seek to be as psychologically effective as possible, as long as that impact is not a substitute for argument. Watch for the following:

1.   We must continue to exercise Christian love to our opponents, even though we may thoroughly disagree with their position.

2.   We must remain courteous at all times, especially if our opponents lack courtesy.

3.   We cannot afford to lose our temper. An angry debater has lost the debate.

4.   Do not show discouragement in your attitude or language, even if the audience does not appear responsive.

5.   Be sure that your stability or smiling countenance cannot be interpreted as "patronizing" your opponents.

6.   Watch for the over-kill! You may ruin a deserved victory by over pressing or ridiculing an opponent, for whom the audience may then cheer, as the weaker party.

7.   Don't hesitate to acknowledge a mistake if you made it. That reversal may not lose the debate; to insist on what was wrong might and should!

B. In preparing your argument, observe the following:

1.   We must not be slow to recognize the truth of some of the opponent's contention, if there is truth that we may have appeared to violate or disregard. We cannot afford to be construed as rejecting any truth, but must show our willingness to be subject to truth, whencesoever it comes!

2.   Make sure that the core of your contention is crystal clear to the audience.

3.   In advance of the debate, be careful to express your position in a pithy formulation in which the weight of each word is carefully calculated (as in a creed). Then stick to that language so that you may not open yourself by carelessness to objections you were careful to anticipate.

4.   Be sure to state in your positive presentation an affirmation of what your opponents are likely to say you are disregarding or denying. This will ease your talk at rebuttal time.

5.   Concentrate in the positive presentation of the truth you contend for, and attempt to present it in such a comprehensive way as to show the inappropriateness of some frequent misunderstandings.

6.   Do not fail to show that your position is scriptural. Quote convincing passages to prove it.

7.   Remember that some truths are held in tension with, and not in contradiction to, other scriptural truths. Your faithfulness to the Bible demands that you should not even appear to cancel or misrepresent either truth. Examples would include the sovereignty of God/human responsibility and deity/humanity of Christ incarnate.

8.   Do not permit a misrepresentation to prevail concerning what you claim or said, but correct any such in rebuttal.

9.   Do not fail to explain how Scriptures quoted by your opponents are not violated or by-passed in your view.

10.   Do not advance any argument of which you are doubtful: it may "boomerang" against you.

11.   Do not advance arguments based on passages of Scripture whose interpretation is greatly controverted. Examples would include "baptism for the dead" (I Cor 15:19) and "the spirits in prison" (I Pet 3:19).

12.   Do not allow yourself to be waylaid into a complicated discussion of minor points. Avoid dead-ends. They don't lead anywhere.

13.   Don't call dead-end an objection to which you have a cogent, compact response.

14.   If appropriate, show that historical precedents support your position.

C. In rebuttal, consider the following points:

1.   Do not risk misrepresenting your opponents. Try to use their language about their view, whenever possible.

2.   Show how historically the dangers seen in your view by your opponents failed to materialize. Examples would include "sovereignty of God leads to a failure to accept responsibility" and "forensic justification leads to antinomianism."

3.   Show how your opponent's view appears to violate Scripture.

4.   Show how it has led historically to damaging effect: Arianism, Pelagianism, etc.

5.   Show that logically it leads to unacceptable positions.

6.   Conduct yourself and your argument in such a way that:

(a)   Your supporters will say: "That's the way to contend for the truth" (Jude 3).

(b)   Your opponents will say: "I don't agree with you, but you surely have presented a strong case for your view."

(c)   Those who are hesitant will say: "This was a very meaningful debate; I am (almost) persuaded to accept your view!"

II.   Methodological advice for oral debate

1. Anticipate objections that you expect anyway, but do not use *your* time in stating them.

2. We must not spend our time in answering objections that have not been raised in this debate. Let the opponents spend *their* time in presenting these, if they please. Then we may answer such in rebuttal.

3. If there is an opponent's contention that is likely to "boomerang" against their view, let them raise it. Your answer will score more heavily than if you had raised it first. For example, if someone used Matt 5:21-48 to show that Jesus overruled the Old Testament, you could show that it is inconceivable in this context (Matt 5:17-20) and that in fact Jesus reinforces the Old Testament text in every one of the six cases ("hate your enemy" is NOT an Old Testament quotation!).

4. Keep one or two simple arguments or objections in store for the final submission, so that you have something like "coffee after dinner" to add to your case, rather than saying, "This is my case, there is nothing more to say."

In closing, let me emphasize three things:

1. Insist on the precise scope of the debate, so it will not wander all over creation.

2. Prepare yourself with care by making a written set of notes on:

a. Factors supporting your contention: biblically, historically, logically.

b. Objections presumably to be raised by your opponents, with answers to the same: biblically, historically, logically.

c. Objections that may be raised against your opponents: biblically, historically, logically.

3. Prepare yourself in prayer, so that you surely may appear as wearing "the belt of truth" (Eph 6:14) rather than seeking to accredit yourself in a big show.

I hope to have done this in this article.

Appendix B

Theological Illustrations

A. Temptation can be real without the possibility of falling: Suppose a tightrope walker is crossing a cable stretched between the two towers of the Notre Dame in Paris. Now suppose that an invisible pane of glass is placed just below the cable, providing an invisible barrier between the tightrope walker and a fatal fall. His traversing of the cable would be done with the real thought that he might fall to his death, but there would be no actual possibility of a fatal fall. In a similar way, Jesus was actually tempted in all points as we are, yet without sin or the possibility of sin.

B. Completeness of God's final judgment: God's tapes of our lives will be without the 18 ½ minutes missing!

C. The Trinity: A table with 3 legs is stable, although not always horizontal; one with four legs often limps.

D. Illustration of believers being blessed "in the heavenly places": The "yellow shirt" in the Tour de France.

E. Importance of systematic theology: Individual elements of truth are like the pieces of a picture puzzle—to have a proper picture these have to be assembled in a proper way.

F. Interrelationship of various Christian doctrines: like a wheel with a hub, spokes, and a rim.

G. Petal view of the relationship between divine essence and attributes is false; every attribute is in the essence and the essence is in every attribute (W. G. T. Shedd)

H. Faith like a garden hose: What saves the plant is the water. The garden hose does not save; it only brings the water to the plant. Salvation is of the Lord (Jonah 2:9). Faith is the appropriation, not the saving element.

I. A universal offer of the gospel does not require a coextensive provision: A newspaper advertising for a specific type of washing machine for a stated price does not require the store to have as many such washing machines in storage as there are copies of the newspaper. It is not the business of the customer to ask, "Do you have enough washing machines for everyone who received this advertisement in the newspaper?" It is the business of the customer to go to the store with the right amount of money and purchase; if anyone comes to Jesus Christ in repentance and faith, like the customer, all he can require is that he not get an answer, "Sorry, friend, there has been no preparation made for you!" Jesus has assured in John 6:37 that whenever the terms of the offer are complied with, what has been offered (salvation/washing machine) will be provided. What has God's preparation been for salvation? Not a valid question! The question is, will I receive salvation if I comply with the terms that go along with this universal call of the gospel that I heard? And the answer is an authoritative YES!

J. Trinity: Each Person of the Trinity embraces the whole Godhead. This is similar to the fact that every point in the volume of a box is on a line of the width and of the length and of the height of the box (borrowed from Nathan R. Wood).

K. Trinity: Each Person of the Trinity is essential to the Deity. This is similar to the fact that each dimension of a box is essential for the reality of the box. If one dimension disappears, there is no box (borrowed from Nathan R. Wood, *The Secret of the Universe*)!

L. Diagram showing the relationship between the three major affirmations in the doctrine of the Trinity:

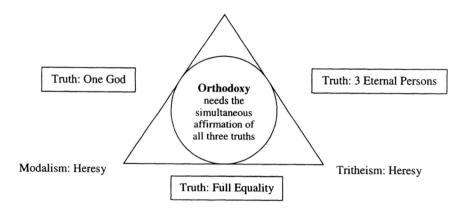

The three major Trinitarian heresies affirm just two sides of the triangle and reject the third. Of course, this is not a diagram of the divine being, but of the relationships in the doctrine of the Trinity.

M. Salvation in various relations:

Humans *sin*, therefore they have *guilt*. This is an offense against the divine perfection of *righteousness*, which relates to human *standing in relationship to God*. Salvation's answer to this predicament is *Christ in the place of His elect*, which yields *justification, adoption*, and *sealing*.

Sin also leads to *pollution* of the sinner. This is an offense against the divine perfection of *holiness*, which relates to the human's *condition, the integrity of his nature*. Salvation's answer to this predicament is the *Holy Spirit in the lives of believers*, which yields *regeneration* and *conversion* (through *repentance* and *faith*, given as gifts from God), *sanctification*, and *glorification* (of both *soul* and *body*).

N. I was dealing with the first chapter of Ephesians, verse 3-14, and I'm addressing a group of women, and here you have quite a number of theological terms in that area, but it is mainly intended to show the wealth of the Christian, and so I suggested to the women that what we have here is a crown that is given to Jesus and on that crown there are some diamonds which make it particularly flashy. The first diamond is election; the second is adoption; the third is redemption. I would have to add now the fourth, revelation. These are blessings that God has provided, and they are like diamonds in the crown of Christ. Here, I think, women are interested in diamonds and that is my point for making the comparison there. We have a majority of women in the Village on the Green Bible Study, and so I want to use illustrations that are of interest to them.

O. Predestination is not a violation of human decision. We are not forced to do certain things by the prior decision of God; this is a wrong outlook. God has a plan, and we have a function in that plan. We make decisions for which we are answerable. God has thought of us long before we came into this world. Women, particularly, can understand that because long before they have a baby, they have that child growing in their own womb, and they are planning for it. We don't have people who deliver a baby, get home, and have no place to put it. They buy a cradle, they buy clothes; Christian women begin to pray for this baby long before the birth. What God is telling us in predestination is that He thought of us long before we came on the scene, from before the foundation of the world. His plan does not come in a haphazard manner. [Here the emphasis is not on the predestination of persons in some abstract way that might just extend the debate, but on the care and personal nature of it as a loving act of God.].

P. The claim is made that John 3:16 teaches a universal love of God that is equal in all cases, for all people, without any preferential approach. They say "God so loved the world" and 'the world' includes all people. I attempt to show how you may have a love for a particular group of people within the designation that already shows an interest in that group. Cecil Rhodes was a very rich person in England, who in disposing of his fortune, decided to provide a tremendous amount of money for the purpose of providing some very capable people in the United States the very best that British education could offer. One would have thought that Rhodes would not provide for those who had been for some time the enemies of his native country, but he really had a care for those who had been enemies to have a sample of the best that Britain could provide, in this case, education. But his provision did not provide for *every* person in America! It provided it for *some* people in America, and it was a demonstration of love oriented toward *America*, made manifest particularly toward *some*, and providing for the improvement of the relationship between America and Britain in a general way. God loved the *world*, the world was at enmity to God, and one could have expected that God's main purpose would be to take vengeance against humanity for its terrible disobedience, and catastrophic separation between humanity and God. And instead of that, on the contrary, God shows a tremendous concern for us to the point of sacrificing good, but sacrificing His own Son. So the love of God is already oriented in the direction of humanity, but that does not mean that God has a saving disposition or intent for every member of the human race. Therefore, it is not an appropriate understanding of the passage to say that God has universality of love without distinction.

Q. A lightning rod takes away the damage of the lightning from the building, in a similar way to the way that the substitution of Christ takes away the wrath of God from the believing sinner.

Appendix C

Musings of a Nonagenarian
by Roger Nicole

Webster's 10th Edition *Collegiate Dictionary* defines to muse, "To become absorbed in thought; *esp*: to turn something over in the mind meditatively and often inconclusively" (p. 763). This is common in humanity at all ages of life. If the definition be accepted, it turns out that many thoughts should be called "musings." The view is often entertained that musing is a practice predominantly found among old people. It is thought that when a person reaches the age of ninety, he/she is pretty much unable to do anything else! Life is then turned into a long process of reminiscing with a futile attempt to reconstruct what could have been, usually inconclusively. Having reached 90, I desire to humor this penchant, and while musing for myself perhaps at times amusing the reader.

A. "I never met a person from whom I could not learn anything." This statement, which parallels the affirmation of Will Rogers "I never met a man I did not like," can be very useful in personal relationships. We ought not to be unwilling to provide teaching for others. My profession as a teacher should certainly not leave me in any hesitation on this point. But the attitude of being willing to learn may become an asset in being able to teach. When I meet someone whom I do not know well, I try to steer the conversation to an area in which he/she knows a lot more than I, and then I profit from her/his knowledge to increase mine.

B. I would like to muse on the question of my ability or ineptitude in driving a car. On this subject some of those whose affection I treasure most highly have made statements with which I differ sharply. Specifically, my dear wife is not hesitant to offer derogatory comments about my driving in general, and when she rides with me, she frequently objects to the speed, the closeness to the side of the road or to other vehicles, my unwillingness to allow other cars to pass me, my preparation or lack of it when intending to take a right or left turn, or what she fears is my lack of awareness of some features that could result in an accident. She happily shares her concerns with several close friends of ours, and encounters there a considerable level of agreement that surprises me and at times irks me.

The facts of the case are as follows, quite irrespective of my opinions here. From 1939 to 2005, I have driven at least 10 different automobiles for a mileage of approximately one million miles on the roads of the United States and Canada. This has occurred in all kinds of weather, including icy or snow-covered roads. While I acknowledge that there have been a few collisions, including three in which my car was totaled, I have never had any accident that caused anyone including myself to be hospitalized. I have never failed in any test given me by the registry.

My wife explains this by assuming that God has always sent a guardian angel to protect me, a blessing for which, if it be true, I would be immensely grateful to God. I realize that danger on the road is not merely due to one's own mistakes, but that other cars can cause havoc on some people who are not at all at fault. God's gracious providence has spared me so far in this respect. Whether my freedom from major accident due to my faulty driving is to be viewed as a fruit of God's general providence or to His special care vouchsafed to the redeemed will remain moot, so all I can do is to "muse" and to make an effort to drive carefully whenever I am behind the wheel.

C.   Don't say, "It's disgusting." I remember rather vividly an incidental event in our family when I was about 7 and my sister 11 years old. I believe that the apportionment of dessert had been somewhat uneven and my sister who felt shortchanged said, "It's disgusting!" Immediately my father rose from his seat, saying, "One does not say, 'It's disgusting.'" He started moving around the table toward my sister who was seated on the other side, intending to give her a slight slap on the face. [This was unusual because father very seldom took part in our punishments, especially physical ones.] My sister, sensing what was coming, rose from her seat to flee. At that point my godmother, who was also seated at the table, rose to intercept Mariella so that Dad, who was nearly blind, could reach her. But my sister, who was but a sliver of a girl, managed to elude her so that the first person father reached was my godmother and blindly he smacked her on the cheek, saying again, "One does not say, 'It's disgusting.'" I was also seated at the table and I was rooting for my sister, although I knew she was wrong. Somehow I did not think how painfully this must have reminded my dad of his handicap, and how embarrassed my godmother must have been!! For the next sixty years, I guess, nobody said, "It's disgusting" in my parents' home!

D.   There is a biblical injunction about musing: Deuteronomy 8:2 – "Remember how the LORD your God led you all the way . . ." More than fifty times in Scripture, we are challenged to remember, perhaps supremely in the Lord's Supper: "in remembrance of Me" (I Cor. 11:24-25). Thus our knowledge of the past must serve us in our decisions in the present. Our experience in the past is an important element in our preparation for the future. It should help us to avoid repeating the mistakes that we made previously. Memory is the bond that unifies the series of experiences and decisions that constitute our life.

E.   In the Village on the Green there was a one hundred year old lady who was still taking dancing lessons. As I was speaking to another elderly lady, I used the centenarian as an example, saying that too often elderly people look backwards to the past, and those who are *seventy* or more should be careful not to weary their listeners by so doing. "Well, I am only 67," she replied with indignation! This closed our conversation for that day. In a sense it may by good that old people are somewhat forgetful, because that tends to abridge sometimes their boring reminiscences! What they *do* remember gives them a better long-range judgment – they grow in wisdom. It is remarkable how much youth seems wasted on young people, who seem unable to appreciate their advantages, and how much wisdom seems wasted on older people to whom others are not prepared to listen.

It is claimed that older folks lose their memory. One of them who wanted to arouse compassion said: "Old people tend to lose three things. First, they lose their hair, and that is obvious. Secondly, they lose their memory. Thirdly . . . I have forgotten." It is of course true that forgetfulness is not exclusively a problem of age. As a teacher I had occasion to notice an amazing degree of it at the time of examination by those who were much younger than I. One of my colleagues, when he was in his fifties, went from Boston to Washington, D.C. to attend a prayer meeting. He took a plane back to Boston, found no one at the airport, and calling his wife on the phone heard the stunning reply, "You *drove* to Washington."

Memory is a strange thing. I know that I have often a hard time to remember where I put my glasses, but at the same time minor events of my youth seem to come to mind with a strange vivacity. For example, while driving, I find myself singing some hymns in French that I have not heard or thought of for decades!

Thinking about the past is surely good to keep one humble. The memory of mistakes and inadequacies do help us "not to think of self more highly than one ought, but to think of self with sober judgment" (Rom 12:3). Surely the advice of Ecclesiastes is good: "Do not say, 'Why were the old days better than these?'"

When I compare my present faith with that of my youth, I find that my evangelical commitment has increased rather than waned. In three areas I do find that I made a significant progress:

> 1.   Until I was 25 I thought of the death of Christ as having a universal intent, but in 1941, having to write a paper on substitution, I saw clearly that it had a particular reference to those who would be saved, thus being *effectual* for those for whom it was intended. I found this to be biblical.

> 2.   In my youth I lived in an atmosphere in which it was thought evident that women should be subordinate in marriage and in the church. With the good example of my brother, and in view of God's manifest concern and love for women in Scripture, I perceived inequality to be a curse (Gen 3:16), and for the last forty years I have been convinced that equality is God's purpose. This view is championed by Christians for Biblical Equality and will be fully realized in heaven (I Pet 2:5, 9; Rev 1:6; 5:10).

> 3.   Up to the age of 15, I had been exposed only to the premillennial, pre-tribulational view of prophecy. As I grew, other positions also claimed my attention. I am attracted now to a view in which one future advent of Jesus marks the climax of all history and is coterminous with final resurrection and judgment. The dispensational view appears to me as fracturing unduly the redemptive purpose of God; the strict covenantal approach tends to an insufficient recognition of the difference between the Old and the New Covenant (Heb 8:8; 12:24): Christmas and Pentecost are immensely significant events!

F.   Even old people are musing about the future, although presumably they will be on earth less time to enjoy it than those who are younger. The desire to know, to influence, and even to control the future is irrepressible in the human breast. This is something that is peculiar to rational creatures: angels and humans. This truth has been effectively expressed in lines from the poem "Napoleon II" by Victor Hugo (translation from French by Roger Nicole) –

> *The future does not belong to any person*
> *The future belongs to God.*
> *Whenever the bell sounds*
> *Everything here below says goodbye.*

The future, the future – mystery.
All earthly things:
Glory, military success,
The shining crowns of the kings
Victory with its flaming wings,
Realized ambitions
Are no more ever settled on us
Than a bird on our roof.

***

Sire, you can, if you please,
Take away Europe from Charlemagne
And Asia from Mohammed.
But you will never take tomorrow from God.

All one can do is muse, and plan, but the fulfillment remains firmly in God's hands.

Even though the time that one is to remain on earth inevitably diminishes as one advances in age, those with great age continue to muse about the future. Instructed by their own experience, they will rely more than before on the promises of God recorded in Scripture. Once in heaven they will no longer be actuated by jealousy that so easily colors our attitudes on earth. They would reflect the kind of humility that characterized George Whitefield, who when asked whether he expected to see John Wesley in heaven, replied: "I fear that Wesley will be so far ahead of me in his closeness to Christ that I shall not be able to see him at that distance."

Muse on, old man or old woman, and count the days, as the riders in the Tour de France bicycle race count every stage as bringing them closer to a triumphal entrance to Paris!

"Now unto him who is able to do immeasurably more
than all we ask or think . . . be glory . . . in Christ Jesus."
Ephesians 3:20, 21

Appendix D

Roger Robert Nicole

Born December 10, 1915, a Swiss citizen, in Charlottenburg (Germany).
Naturalized: U.S.A., 1959
Grandfather: Jules Nicole (1842-1921), professor of Greek in Geneva
University.
Father: Albert Nicole (1873-1966), pastor and lecturer in Switzerland.
Married: To Annette Cyr, June 18, 1946.

A.B., 1935 (Bachelier ès lettres classiques), Gymnase Classique, Lausanne.
M.A., 1937 (Licence d'enseignement ès lettres classiques), Sorbonne, Paris.
Graduate 1938, Institut Biblique, Nogent/Marne, near Paris.
B.D., 1939; S.T.M., 1940; Th.D. (*summa cum laude*), 1943, Gordon
Divinity School.
Ph.D., 1967, Harvard University.
D.D., 1978, Wheaton College, Wheaton, Illinois.
Litt.S.D., 2006, Columbia Evangelical Seminary, Longview, Washington.

Pastor: Worcester and Manchaug French Baptist Churches, 1939-46,
1948-1956.

Instructor and Associate Professor: Languages and Theology, Gordon,
1944-1948.

Professor: Theology, Gordon Divinity School, 1946-1976. Andrew
Mutch Professor of Theology, Gordon-Conwell Theological Seminary,
1976-1985. Professor 1985-86, Emeritus 86 – present

Visiting Professor: Western Baptist Theological Seminary, Summer
School, Portland, Oregon, 1947; Winona Lake School of Theology, 1954;
American Baptist Churches Pastors, China Lake, ME, 1968, 1978, 1989;
China Evangelical Seminary, Taipei, Taiwan, 1972; Discipleship Training
Centre, Singapore, 1973; Faculté Libre de Théologie Evangelique, Vaux-sur-
Seine, near Paris, France, 1973, 1983; Institut Biblique, Sherbrooke, PQ, 1975,
1977, 1979, 1980, 1981, 1983, 1985; Ontario Theological Seminary, Toronto,
1977, 1978, 1979, 1981, 1986, 1987; SEMBEQ, Montréal, 1975, 1978, 1980,
1982, 1984, 1986, 1987, 1988, 1989, 1990, 1993; Andover-Newton, 1980;

Pittsburgh Coalition, 1978, 1981, 1987; Centre Evangélique d'Etudes Théologiques, Montréal, 1984, 1987, 1989, 1990, 1991, 1992, 1994, 1996; Northwest Baptist Theological Seminary, Vancouver, 1984; Farel Institute, Quebec, 1985, 1990; Winnipeg Theological Seminary, 1986; Toronto Baptist Seminary, 1987; Reformed Theological Seminary, Jackson, MS, 1988, 1989, 1990, 1991; Talbot Divinity School, CA, 1990; St. Andrews Presbyterian Church (U.S.A.), CA, 1992; Outreach, MI, 1992; RTS, Vienna, Austria, 1993; New Orleans Baptist Theological Seminary (Orlando Campus), 1998; Visiting Professor of Theology, Reformed Theological Seminary (Orlando), 1989-2000, Emeritus, 2001-present.

Lecturer: Mid-year Lectures at Conservative Baptist Theological Seminary, Portland, Oregon, 1953; Lectures on Christian Thought and Ministry, Denver Conservative Baptist Theological Seminary, Denver, Colorado, 1954; Annual Theological Lecture, Houghton College, Houghton, NY, 1958; Payton Lectureship, Fuller Theological Seminary, Pasadena, California, 1959; Japan Protestant Centennial, 1959 (in Sendai, Tokyo, Nagoya, Kobe, Kyoto and Osaka); International Reformed Congress, Cambridge, England, 1961; Theological Consultation, Wenham, Massachusetts, 1966; Moncton, New Brunswick, 1967, 1971; Commencement, RTS, Jackson, MS, 1969. Annual Lectureship, Japan Bible Seminary, Tokyo, Japan, 1972; Union Bible Seminary, Yeotmal, India, 1973; Lyman Stewart Lectureship, Talbot Theological Seminary, La Mirada, California, 1974; International Congress of World Evangelism, Lausanne, 1974; Philadelphia Conference on Reformed Theology, 1974, 1976, 1978, 1980, 1982, 1983, 1984, 1986, 1993; Reformed Baptist Conference, Detroit, MI, 1974; Denver Theological Seminary, CO, 1974; Westminster Theological Seminary, 1975; Atlantic Christian College, Moncton, New Brunswick, 1977; Theological Institute, Warren, Ohio, 1977; University of Western Kentucky, Bowling Green, KY, 1978; Theological Seminary, Regina, Saskatchewan, 1978; Reformed Fellowship, Pittsburgh, PA, 1979; Reformed Bible College, Grand Rapids, MI, 1979; Rustand Lectureship, Westminster Theological Seminary, 1979; Bethel Bible School, Sherbrooke, PQ, 1979; Reformed Bible College, MI, 1979; Christian Librarian Association, Nyack, NY,1981; Campus Crusade for Christ, Montréal, 1981; Opening Convocation, Farel Theological Seminary, Quebec City, 1982; ICBI Summit II, Chicago, 1982; Founder's Week, Bethel College and Seminary, St. Paul, MN, 1983; InterVarsity Fellowship, Montreal, 1983; Navigators, Montreal, 1984; Soli Deo Gloria, Pittsburgh, PA, 1984, 1991, 1994; Staley Lectureship, Southeastern College, Lakeland, FL, 1985; Conference sur la Bible, Paris, 1985; Reformed Theology Conference, Austin, TX, 1985; 3rd International Baptist Conference, Toronto, 1986; ICBI Summit III, Chicago, 1986; Toronto Baptist Seminary, 1987; Church Conference, New Rochelle, NY, 1988; Conférence sur le Mariage, Montreal, 1989; Evangelical Affirmations Conference, Chicago, 1989; Beeson Divinity School, Birmingham, AL, 1989; Associated in Christian Service, N.J., 1989, 1990, 1991; Annual Gideons' Conference, Montreal, 1991;

Reformed Baptist Conference, Birmingham, AL, 1991; Church Conference, Ithaca, NY, 1992; Delaney Street Baptist Church, Orlando, FL, 1993; Conference of Baptist Evangelicals, Wheaton, IL, 1993; Spurgeon's Conference, Kansas City, MO, 1993; Tennessee Temple, Chattanooga, TN, 1993; Covenant Fellowship, Fayetteville,Arkansas, 1994; John Bunyan's Fellowship, Skippack, PA, 2003; Kistemaker Lectures, Reformed Theological Seminary, Oviedo, FL, 2004.

Church Lectures and Retreats: Convention Chrétienne, Morges, Switzerland, 1957; Convention Chrétienne, Alès, France, 1957; Family Retreat, Pensacola, FL, 1958, 1962; Vermont Congregational Retreat, 1959; Six-Principle Baptists, Annual Meeting, 1960, 1962; Reformation Day, Lawrence, MA, 1960; Retreat, Jackson, MS, 1963; Westminster Theological Seminary Retreat, 1965; Rock Hill Baptist Church Retreat, MA, 1965; Students Retreat, Quebec, PQ, 1969, 1972, 1983; Church Retreat, Burlington, Ontario, 1970; Church Retreat, Lenoxville, PQ, 1970, 1971; Church Lectures, Loudenville, NY, 1971, 1974, 1977, 1978; First Presbyterian Church, Jackson, MS, 1975; IVF, PQ, 1976, 1983; Family Retreat, Alma, MI, 1977; Knox Presbyterian Church, Toronto, 1977, 1979, 1983, 1985-1991; Navigators, Quebec, PQ, 1978, 1984; Bryn Mawr PCA Church, 1978, 1981, 1982, 1987; Presbyterian Church (U.S.A.), Silver Springs, MD, 1979, 1984; Trinity Congregational Church, Wayland, MA, 1978, 1981; First Congregational Church, Boxford, MA, 1979; Baptist Church, Hamilton, Ontario, 1979; Annual Baptist Union, Montreal, PQ, 1980; Campus for Christ, Montreal, 1981; Calvary Temple, Hartford, CT, 1981-1988; Retreat, Montgomery, NY, 1982; Tremont Temple, Boston, MA, 1982; Gordon-Conwell Bermuda Retreat, 1986; Columbia, SC, 1987; PCA Church, Lancaster, PA, 1987, 1991; Church Retreat, Appaloosa, LA, 1987; Church Retreat, Salisbury, NC, 1988; Mt. Vernon, NY, 1988; Swedish Baptists, Minneapolis, MN, 1989; Reformed Retreat, Fayetteville, AR, 1990; Network, NJ, 1990; Church Retreat, Ithaca, NY, 1992; Presbyterian Church, Gainesville, MD, 1992; Christians for Biblical Equality, Tulsa, OK, 1992

Ministerial Institutes: Calvin Theological Seminary, 1954; Calvin Theological Seminary (Atonement), 1959; Berkshire Christian College, 1964; Baptist Ministers, China Lake, WI, 1968; Reformed Baptist Ministers, Detroit, MI, 1974; RTS, Jackson, MS, 1975; Evangelical Pastors, Montreal, PQ, 1983; RTS, Jackson, MS, 1984; Gordon-Conwell Alumni (in 5 locations), 1986; Evangelical Pastors, Montreal, PQ, 1988

Interim Pastorates: French Baptist Church, Woonsocket, RI, 1947; French Baptist Churches, Worcester and Manchaug, MA, 1948-1956; Concord, 1965; Baptist Church, East Rochester, NH, 1965-1966; Baptist Church, Groton, MA, 1966-1967; Baptist Church, North Bellingham, MA, 1967; Merrimac Baptist Church, Manchester, NH, 1968; Conservative Baptist Church, Nashua, NH, 1970-1971; Baptist Church, Exeter, NH, 1972; Belmont

Street Baptist Church, Worcester, MA, 1974; Haverhill Second Baptist Church, 1978-1979; College Church, Northampton, MA, 1979

Trips: Around the world: 1959, 1972-1973; Europe: 1946, 1953, 1957, 1961, 1963, 1966, 1969, 1971, 1974, 1976, 1983, 1985, 1992, 1993, 1997

Memberships: Phi Alpha Chi, 1940-National President, 1943-1945; Evangelical Theological Society, 1949-President, 1956; China Evangelical Literature Committee; American Academy of Religion, 1977-1983, International Council on Biblical Inerrancy, 1980-1987.Assistant Editor: The Gordon Review, 1957-1965. Chairman of the Board, 1959-1965.

Collaborator: NIV

Contributing Editor: Christianity Today, 1956-1980. Corresponding Editor, 1980-present.

Appendix E

List of Byington Fellows in Theology
Assigned to Dr. Nicole at Gordon and Gordon-Conwell

1957-59	Charles Davis
1959-60	Gerald Flokstra
1960-61	Joseph Mortensen
1961-62	Arthur Gay, Jr.
1962-63	Gene Huntzinger
1963-64	Hobart Farrell
1964-65	Lloyd Carr
1965-66	Ed Whitman
1966-68	Tom Finger
1968-70	Robert Godfrey
1970-71	David McDowell
1971-72	Eugene Wright
1972-73	*Sabbatical leave*
1973-75	Ewald Pointner
1975-76	Stuart Boehmig
1976-77	Phillips Long
1977-79	Joel Kruggel
1979-81	Donna Kozarski
1981-82	Scott Hahn
1982-83	George Harper
1983-84	Susan Jaquette
1984-85	Jim Moelk and Mark Bolton

1985-86   Mark Dever (*One of the best students I ever had; he would have fellow students come to his room and he would teach them—they would drink it up like milk—he would make Xerox copies of the Puritans for them to read, and then he would discuss that with them*)

Annotated Bibliography

The selected bibliography (with Nicole's own annotations) that follows is indicative of the scope of Nicole's scholarly and pastoral writing.

A. Books and Pamphlets

1. Inspiration and Barth. Japan Protestant Centennial Movement Memorial Lectures. Mimeographed. Sendai: Seisho Tosho Kankokai, 1960. 21 Pp. *A criticism of the typical Neo-Orthodox view that inspiration has more to do with the reader than the writer..*

2. A Bibliography of Benjamin Breckinridge Warfield, 1851-1921. With John E. Meeter. Nutley, N. J.: Presbyterian and Reformed Publishing Company, 1974. *viii,* 108 Pp. *This covers his published works, his many essays in periodic literature and his book reviews in various journals.*

3. Introduction and Appendices to A. A. Hodge and B. B. Warfield, Inspiration. Grand Rapids: Baker Book House, 1979. Pp. i-xiv, 83-100. *Both the introduction and the appendices are useful in understanding the 83 pages of the original text.* See B13, F5.

4. Inerrancy and Common Sense. Edited with J. Ramsey Michaels. Grand Rapids: Baker Book House, 1980. 203 Pp. *My essay on "The Nature of Inerrancy" is an attempt to define the evangelical stand.*

5. Moyse Amyraut: A Bibliography with Special Reference to the Controversy on Universal Grace. New York and London: Garland Publishing Inc., 1981. *x,* 209 Pp. See G7. *This is both a bibliography and an inventory of the presence of Amyraut's works in almost 200 libraries of the world.*

6. Inerrancy at Gordon-Conwell. Hamilton, MA: Gordon-Conwell Theological Seminary, 1982. 8 Pp. *A mere pamphlet on the subject.*

7. Ma confiance dans la Bible. (Interview of November 1985). Bevaix, Switzerland: Action chrétienne pour la Radio et la Presse, 1987. 14 Pp. *A pamphlet in French.*

8. Standing Forth. Fearn, Scotland: Christian Focus Publications, 2002. xii, 492 Pp. See also B2, 4, 6, 8, 15, 16, 18, 19, 20, 33-35, 38, 39; D2, 15, 30, 38, 45, 46-48, 68, 71, 74. *These are essays of special interest for scholars.*

9. Our Sovereign Saviour. Fearn, Scotland: Christian Focus Publications, 2002, 184 Pp. See also B16, D14, 15, 18, 19, 22, 23, 25, 26, 27, 29, 31, 32, 42. *These are mainly addresses presented to pastors and informed lay people.*

B. Published in Books

1. "Theology." In Carl F. H. Henry, editor, <u>Contemporary Evangelical Thought</u>. Great Neck, N. Y.: Channel Press, 1957. Pp 67-106. *This was a survey of evangelical production from 1900-1950 in English, French, German and Dutch.*

2. "The New Testament Use of the Old Testament." In Carl F. H. Henry, editor, <u>Revelation and the Bible</u>. Grand Rapids: Baker Book House, 1959. Pp. 135-151. Reprinted in R. Youngblood, editor, <u>Evangelicals and Inerrancy</u>. Nashville: Nelson, 1984. Pp 1-12. Reprinted also in G. K. Beale, <u>The Right Doctrine from the Wrong Texts</u>. Grand Rapids: Baker Books, 1994. Pp. 13-28. See D1. Also SF 223-242. *A vindication of inerrancy in the New Testament use of the Old Testament.*

3. "A Postscript on Theology." In Carl F. H. Henry, editor, <u>Basic Christian Doctrines</u>. New York: Holt and Rinehart, 1962. Pp. 297-302. *A very brief statement on the place of "theology" in religious studies.*

4. "The Nature of Redemption." In Carl F. H. Henry, editor, <u>The Christian Faith and Modern Theology</u>. New York: Channel Press, 1964. Pp 191-222. Also SF 244-282. *An emphasis on atonement as central to the Christian faith and substitution as central to the atonement. A review of the relevant work of Vincent Taylor.*

5. "The Theology of Gordon Clark." In Ronald A. Nash, editor, <u>The Philosophy of Gordon Clark</u>. Philadelphia: Presbyterian and Reformed Publishing Company, 1968. Pp. 391-398. An admiring account of Gordon Clark's theology with a reply by Clark himself.

6. "Some Comments on Hebrews 6:4-6 and the Doctrine of the Perseverance of God with the Saints." In Gerald F. Hawthorne, editor, <u>Current Issues in Biblical and Patristic Interpretation</u>. Grand Rapids: Eerdmans, 1975. Pp. 355-364. Also SF 437-451. *An essay presented to my professor Merrill C. Tenney, with a vindication of God's perseverance with the saints.*

7. "Jesus Christ, the Unique Son of God: The Relationship of His Deity and Humanity with Reference to Evangelism." In J. D. Douglas, editor, <u>Let the Earth Hear His Voice</u>. Minneapolis: World Wide Publication, 1975. Pp. 1041-1047. Republished with modifications in "The Savior and His Work" in K. Kantzer, editor, <u>Applying the Scriptures</u>. Grand Rapids: Zondervan, 1987. Pp. 29-35. *A standard presentation of the doctrine of the union of divine and human nature in the Person of Jesus Christ.*

8. "Induction and Deduction with Reference to Inspiration." In R. C. Sproul, editor, <u>Soli Deo Gloria: Festschrift in Honor of John H. Gerstner</u>. Nutley, NJ.: Presbyterian and Reformed Publishing Company, 1976. Pp. 95-102. Also SF 151-158. *A clarification of the kind of reasoning that is involved in determining the nature of inspiration.*

9. "The 'Five Points' and God's Sovereignty," "The Doctrines of Grace in Jesus' Teaching," "Optimism and God's Sovereignty," "<u>Soli Deo Gloria</u>." In James M. Boice, editor, <u>Our Sovereign God</u>. Grand Rapids: Baker, 1977. Pp. 29-36, 37-48, 147-152, 167-175. See F10 *Three addresses in the first Philadelphia Conference on Reformed Theology.*

10. "The Attitude of Jesus Toward Scripture." In Mark H. Tanenbaum, Marvin R. Wilson, and A. James Rudin, editors, Evangelicals and Jews in Conversation on Scripture, Theology and History. Grand Rapids: Baker, 979. Pp. 197-205. *A very brief summary of my B.D. thesis. A fuller summary is found in this biography on pp. 27-35.*

11. "The Relationship Between Biblical Theology and Systematic Theology." In Kenneth S. Kantzer, editor, Evangelical Roots. Nashville: T. Nelson, 1978. Pp. 185-194. *A brief statement about biblical theology that carries out Vos' understanding of it.*

12. "A Call to Biblical Fidelity." In Robert E. Webber and Donald Bloesch, editors, The Orthodox Evangelicals. Nashville: T. Nelson, 1979. Pp. 68-76. *A brief statement on Scripture, seeking to carry the strict doctrine without using the word "inerrant."*

13. "Introduction and Appendices." In A. A. Hodge and B. B. Warfield, Inspiration. Grand Rapids: Baker, 1979. Pp. i-xiv, 83-100. See A3.

14. "The Old Testament in the New Testament." In F. E. Gaebelein, editor, The Expositor's Bible Commentary. Vol. I. Grand Rapids: Zondervan, 1979. Pp. 617-628. See D1 and G2. *Discussion of the quantity of quotations and hermeneutical explanation of some difficult cases.*

15. "The Nature of Inerrancy." In Roger Nicole and J. Ramsey Michaels, editors, Inerrancy and Common Sense. Grand Rapids: Baker, 1980. Pp. 71-95. Reprinted in The Gospel Witness 66/1 (March 1987), 5-13. Also *SF* 27-29. *A plea for the acceptance of inerrancy with a clarification on the definition of error.*

16. "The Meaning of the Trinity." In Peter Toon and James D. Spiceland, editors, One God in Trinity. London: Samuel Bagster, 1980. Pp. 1-10. Also *OSS* 11-19; *SF* 389-396. *A very simple statement showing how orthodoxy differs from the 3 major heresies on the subject.*

17. "Reconciliation and Propitiation," "Particular Redemption." In James M. Boice, editor, Our Savior God. Grand Rapids: Baker, 1980. Pp. 117-124, 165-178. *An affirmation of the Godward aspect of the atonement with a plea for definite, not universal atonement.*

18. "The Biblical Concept of Truth." In D. A. Carson and J. Woodbridge, editors, Scripture and Truth. Grand Rapids: Zondervan, 1983. Pp. 283-298, 410-411. Also *SF* 133-149. *An examination of the Old and New Testament concept, involving correspondence, faithfulness and completeness.*

19. "The Neo-Orthodox Reduction." In Gordon Lewis and Bruce Demarest, editors, Challenges to Inerrancy. Chicago: Moody Press, 1984. Pp. 121-144. Also *SF* 51-77. *A discussion of the inadequacy of Barth's and Brunner's concept of inspiration.*

20. "Patrick Fairbairn and Biblical Hermeneutics as Related to the Quotations of the Old Testament in the New." In Earl Radmacher and Robert Preus, editors, Hermeneutics, Inerrancy and the Bible. Grand Rapids: Zondervan, 1984. Pp.765-776. Also *SF* 79-90. *A call to recognize that the New Testament interpretation of the Old reflects the teaching of Jesus.*

220   *The Life and Legacy of Roger Nicole*

21. "Friedrich Spanheim (1600-1649)." In W. Robert Godfrey and Jesse L. Boyd III, editors, Through Christ's Word: A Festschrift for Philip E. Hughes. Phillipsburg, N J: Presbyterian and Reformed Company, 1985. Pp. 166-179. *A brief study and bibliography of this neglected Reformed theologian.*

22. "Biblical Authority and Feminist Aspirations." In Alvera Mickelsen, editor, Women, Authority and the Bible. Downers Grove, IL: IVP, 1986. Pp. 42-50. *An investigation showing how biblical egalitarians do not need to violate or discard restrictive passages.*

23. "The Savior and His Work." In K. Kantzer, editor, Applying the Scriptures. Grand Rapids: Zondervan, 1987. Pp. 29-35. (Some parts of this article are adapted from B7). *A simple avowal of the orthodox doctrine of the Person of Jesus Christ.*

24. "Benjamin B. Warfield." In John Woodbridge, editor, Great Leaders of the Christian Church. Chicago: Moody, 1988. Pp. 343-346. *A very brief statement about this great Reformed theologian.*

25. "What will happen to those who will not repent?" In David Neff, editor, Tough Questions Christians Ask. Wheaton, IL: Victor Books, 1989. *A very brief statement reaffirming the doctrine of endless conscious punishment.*

26. "Ecclesiology: Reformed and Reforming." In Harvie M. Conn, editor, Practical Theology and the Ministry of the Church: 1952-1984. Phillipsburg, NJ: Presbyterian and Reformed, 1990. Pp. 149-161. *A brief discussion of several concepts of ecclesiastical government.*

27. "John Calvin and Inerrancy." In Richard Gamble, editor, Articles on Calvin and Calvinism. Vol. 6. Calvin and Hermeneutics. NY and London: Garland Publishing Inc., 1992. Pp. 273-90. *A vindication of Calvin's doctrine of inerrancy with an extensive bibliographical appendix.*

28. "John Calvin's View of the Extent of the Atonement." In Richard Gamble, editor, Articles on Calvin and Calvinism. Vol. 8. Elaboration of the Theology of Calvin. NY and London: Garland Publishing Inc., 1992. Pp. 197-225. *A vindication of Calvin's endorsement of definite atonement.*

29. "The Privilege of Assurance." In R. C. Sproul, editor, Doubt and Assurance. Grand Rapids: Baker, 1993. Pp. 55-59. *A very brief exposition of assurance.*

30. "James I. Packer." In W. Elwell, editor, Handbook of Evangelical Theologians. Grand Rapids: Baker, 1993. Pp. 379-387. *A brief exposition of Packer's contribution until 1992.*

31. "Sermon on 2 Timothy 3:16a." In Donald K. McKim, The Bible in Theology and Preaching. Nashville: Abingdon, 1994. Pp. 71-75. *A sermon typifying an evangelical exposition of Scripture.*

32. "The Lordship of Christ as the Taproot of Congregationalism." In Michael Plant and Allan Toyey, editors, Telling Another Generation. Beverly, G. B.: Fellowship of Evangelical Congregational Churches, 1994. Pp. 13-16. *A very brief assertion of the evangelical character of Congregationalism.*

33. "Notes on the Gospel of John." In The New Geneva Study Bible. Nashville: T. Nelson, 1995. Pp. 1658-1707. Also in The Reformation Study Bible.

Orlando: Ligonier Ministries, 2005. Pp. 1508-1555. [Greatly shortened by the editors.] A more complete form appeared in The Spirit of the Reformation Study Bible. Grand Rapids: Zondervan, 2004.

34. "The Problem of Infant Salvation." In J. Sanders, editor, What About Those Who Have Never Heard? Downers Grove, IL: IVP, 1995. Pp. 119, 120, 164. *An argument for a positive view of salvation for all those dying in infancy.*

35. "James I. Packer's Contribution to the Doctrine of the Inerrancy of the Scripture." In Donald Lewis and Alistair McGrath, editors, Doing Theology for the People of God. Downers Grove, IL: IVP, 1996. Pp. 176-189. *A grateful acknowledgement of Packer's considerable contribution.*

36. "Le Canon du Nouveau Testament." Esprit et Vie. Paris, 1997. *See D72. Extremely short vindication of the divine origin of the canon.*

37. "New Dimensions in [the Doctrine of] the Holy Spirit." In David Dockery, editor, New Dimensions in Evangelical Thought: Essays in Honor of Millard J. Erickson. Downers Grove, IL: IVP, 1998. Pp. 330-337. *A recognition of the importance of the work of the Holy Spirit in salvation, by Reformed authors.*

38. "The Wisdom of Marriage." In J. I. Packer and Sven K. Soderlund, editors, The Way of Wisdom: Festschrift for Bruce Waltke. Grand Rapids: Zondervan, 2000. Pp. 280-296. Also *SF* 453-475. *An emphasis on marriage as a foreshadowing of the ultimate consummation of salvation.*

39. "Covenant, Universal Call and Definite Atonement." In Howard Griffith and John R. Muether, editors, Creator, Redeemer, Consummator: A Festschrift for Meredith G. Kline. Jackson, MS: Reformed Academic Press, 2000. Pp.193-201. A reprint of D112. Also *SF* 331-342. *A relation of the universal call of the gospel to definite atonement.*

40. "Grace-Not Race-Counts Here." In Tom J. Nettles and Russell D. Moore, editors, Why I Am A Baptist. Nashville: Broadman & Holman, 2001. Pp. 226-229. *An account of the origin of my Baptist convictions.*

41. "Why I am Comfortable with Inerrancy." In Kent Matthews, editor, Not Omitting the Weightier Matters: Festschrift for Dr. Robert Rodgers. Belfast and Greenville, SC: Ambassador Publications, 2002. Pp. 52-64. *A defense of inerrancy against opposition and misunderstanding.*

42. "The Atonement – I and II." In Thomas Ascol, editor. Reclaiming the Gospel and Reforming Churches. Cape Coral, FL: Founders Press, 2003. Pp 53-94. *A discussion of the centrality of the atonement in theology and of the centralityof substitution in the atonement.*

43. "Biblical Hermeneutics: Basic Principles and Questions." In R. M. Groothuis, Gordon Fee and R. W. Pierce, editors. Discovering Biblical Equality: Complementarity Without Hierarchy. Downers Grove: IVP, 2004. Pp. 355-363. *A discussion of the hermeneutical appropriateness of biblical egalitarians' approach to restrictive passages.*

44. "Postscript on Substitution." In Charles E. Hill and Frank A. James, editors. The Glory of the Atonement. Downers Grove, IL: IVP, 2004. Pp 445-52. *A reaffirmation of substitution as the indispensable element in any view of the atonement that accounts for the immensity of Christ's sufferings.*

C.   Articles in Dictionaries, Encyclopedias, etc.

1-2. "Annihilationism," "Arminianism." In E. F. Harrison, editor, Baker's Dictionary of Theology. Grand Rapids: Baker, 1960. Pp. 43, 44, 64, 65.Reprinted in Walter A. Elwell, editor, Evangelical Dictionary of Theology. Grand Rapids: Baker, 1984. Pp. 50-51.

3.   "Amyraldus, Amyraldianism." In Edwin H. Palmer, editor, The Encyclopedia of Christianity. Vol. I (1964). Pp. 184-193.

4.   "Arminius." In Edwin H. Palmer, editor, The Encyclopedia of Christianity. Vol. I (1964). Pp. 405-411.

5.   "Old Testament Quotations in the New Testament." In Ralph G. Turnbull, editor, Baker's Dictionary of Practical Theology. Grand Rapids: Baker, 1967. Pp. 111-115. Reprinted in Bernard Ramm, editor, Hermeneutics. Grand Rapids: Baker, n.d. (1971?). Pp. 43-53. See D1 and G2.

6-8.   "Authority," "Divorce," "Pelagian Ethics." In Carl F. H. Henry, editor, Baker's Dictionary of Christian Ethics. Grand Rapids: Baker, 1973. Pp. 47f.,189f., 497.

9-12. "Exaltation of Christ," "Maranatha," "Mortal Sin," "Offices of Christ." In Merrill C. Tenney, editor, The Zondervan Pictorial Encyclopedia of the Bible. 5 vols. Grand Rapids: Zondervan, 1975. Vol. II. Pp. 421f., Vol. IV. Pp. 70f., 276, 505-512.

13.   "Woman, Biblical Concept of." In Walter A. Elwell, editor, Evangelical Dictionary of Theology. Grand Rapids: Baker, 1984. Pp. 1175-1180. 2d ed. Grand Rapids: Baker, 2001. Pp. 1281-1286. *This is the first written expression of my egalitarian outlook.*

14-15. "Amyraldism," "Dort." In Sinclair Ferguson, David Wright and J. I. Packer, editors, New Dictionary of Theology. Downers Grove, IL: IVP, 1988. Pp. 16-18, 207-208.

16-17. "Perseverance of the Saints," "B. B. Warfield." In Donald McKim, editor, Encyclopedia of the Reformed Faith. Louisville: Westminster and John Knox Press, 1992. Pp. 275-276, 390-391.

D.   Articles in Periodical Literature [This is selective, not exhaustive.]

1.   "Old Testament Quotations in the New Testament." The Gordon Review, I (1955), 7-12, 63-68. German translation. Fundamentum, 4/2003, 72-84.

2.   "C. H. Dodd and the Doctrine of Propitiation." The Westminster Theological Journal, XVII (May 1955), 117-157. Also *SF* 343-385.

3.   "Some Notes Toward a Bibliography of John Calvin." Summary of Proceedings. 9th Annual Conference. American Theological Library Association, 1955. Pp. 6-19.

4.   "Some Notes Toward a Bibliography of John Calvin." I The Institutes and Commentaries. The Gordon Review V (Winter 1959), 174-181.

5. "Some Notes Toward a Bibliography of John Calvin." II The Sermons. The Gordon Review VI (Sp-Sum 1961), 21-28.

6-7. "A Reply to 'Language and Theology.'" The Gordon Review, I (1955), 143-151. Cf. also The Gordon Review, III (1957), 67f.

8. "Propitiation." Christianity Today, I/14 (April 5, 1957), 7f.

9. "The Punishment of the Wicked." Christianity Today, II/18 (June 9, 1958), 13-15.

10. "The Doctrine of Definite Atonement in the Heidelberg Catechism." The Gordon Review, VII (1964), 138-145. Reprinted in Torch and Trumpet, XIV/6 (July-August 1964), 10-12.

11. "The Inspiration of Scripture: B. B. Warfield and Dr. Dewey M. Beegle." The Gordon Review, VIII (1965), 93-109. See E3.

12. "William Farel." The Watchman-Examiner, LIII/21 (October 21, 1965), 648f.

13. "The Case for Definite Atonement." Bulletin of the Evangelical Theological Society, X (1967), 199-207. Reprinted in Torch and Trumpet, XVIII/10 (December 1968), 20-23. *A very concise statement with a survey of Scriptures advanced by opponents.*

14. "The Doctrines of Grace in the Teaching of Jesus." Tenth, July 1974, 5-15. Also *OSS* 75-89.

15. "Calvinism: The Five Points." Tenth, October 1974, 22-29. *This was first presented at a Westminster Seminary commencement. It was somewhat bold for someone who was quite young to come into a standard seminary, steeped in the Reformed faith, and to say that the language used in the traditional formulation of TULIP is not adequate!* Also *OSS* 47-56; *SF* 429-436.

16. "The Christian's Superlative Optimism." Tenth, April 1975, 2-8.

17. "Adventures and Discoveries of a Book-Rat." Summary of Proceedings. 29th Annual Conference. American Theological Library Association, 1975, 95-100.

18. "Freedom and Law." Tenth, July 1976, 22-29. Also *OSS* 153-162.

19. "Soli Deo Gloria." Tenth, July 1965, 13-21. Also *OSS* 21-31.

20. "'Hilaskesthai' Revisited." The Evangelical Quarterly, XLIX/3 (July-September 1977), 173-177. *A vindication of my article D2 against some criticism.*

21. "Aphorisms on Bible Translations." The New Testament Student, IV. Nutley, NJ: Presbyterian and Reformed, 1977.

22. "Reconciliation and Propitiation." Tenth, 8/3 (July 1978), 17-24. Also *OSS* 91-100.

23. "Particular Redemption." Tenth, 8/3 (July 1978), 60-73. Also *OSS* 57-73.

24. "One Door and Only One." Wherever, 4/3 (Winter 1979), 2-3.

25. "When God Calls." Equipping the Saints, 1979. Also *OSS* 143-151.

26. "Justification: Standing by God's Grace." Tenth, 10/3 (July 1980), 33-43. Also *OSS* 101-114.

27. "Sanctification: Growing unto God." Tenth, 10/3 (July 1980), 53-63. Also *OSS* 115-129.

28. "The Spiritual Dimension of the Librarian's Task." The Christian Librarian, 25/3,4 (May-August 1982), pages 106-114. *When speaking to a group of fellow Christian librarians, I commented: "As custodians of the work of the Holy Spirit we have a task which has spiritual dimensions."*

29. "Prayer: The Prelude to Revival." Tenth, 12/3 (July 1982), 13-21. Also *OSS* 163-174.

30. "John Calvin and Inerrancy." Journal of the Evangelical Theological Society, 25/4 (December 1982), pages 425-442. German Translation, Fundamentum, 1985 (December), 35-52. See B27. Also *SF* 103-132. *A very elaborate survey of previous treatments of Calvin's view of inspiration.*

31. "Predestination and the Divine Decrees." Tenth, 13/3 (July 1983), 17-25. Also *OSS* 33-45.

32. "Predestination and the Great Commission." Tenth, 13/3 (July 1983), 62-70. Also *OSS* 131-142.

33-35. "The Inspiration and Authority of Scripture: J. D. G. Dunn versus B. B. Warfield." Churchman 97/3 (1983), 198-214; 98/1,3 (January, July 1984), 7-27, 198-208, 215, 216. Also *SF* 159-222. *A very elaborate discussion of a critique of inerrancy by a noted New Testament scholar.*

36. "Playing with the Pluperfect?" Reformed Journal, 34 (June 1984), 6.

37. "The Scholarship of Glenn W. Barker." Theology News and Notes. 31/3 (October 1984), 9-10.

38. "John Calvin's View of the Extent of the Atonement." Westminster Theological Journal, 47/2 (Fall 1985), 197-225. German Translation, Fundamentum, 1985 (December), 53-76. See B28. Also *SF* 283-312. *An elaborate discussion of Calvin's statements that could appear to support universal atonement, with 13 reasons for recognizing definiteness in his outlook.*

39. "A Response to John Goldingay." Transformation 2/4 (October-December 1985), 4-5.

40. "La Bible: Manuscrits faillibles, Texte infaillible." Cahiers de l'Institut Biblique, No. 65 (March 1986), 9-16.

41. "Pre-mil, Post-mil, A-mil." J. M. Boice, editor, Our Blessed Hope. Philadelphia: P. C. R. T., 1986, 17-29.

42. "The Final Judgment." J. M. Boice, editor, Our Blessed Hope. Philadelphia: P. C. R. T., 1986, 65-72. Also *OSS* 175-184.

43. "Reconciliation." The Gospel Witness, 65/15 (November 20, 1986), 1-4, 12-15.

44. "Universalism: Will Everyone Be Saved?" Christianity Today, 31/5 (March 20, 1987), 32-39. Also *SF* 477-489. *A paper in support of endless conscious punishment versus universalism, conditional immortality and annhilationism.*

45. "L'Ancien Testament dans le Nouveau." Fac Reflexion, No. 5 (July 1987), 21-27. Italian Translation, Cartezze, pages 7-10.

46-48. "How to Deal with Those Who Differ from Us." The PCA Messenger 11/9 (November 1987), 8-10; 11/10 (December 1987), 12-13; 12/1 (January 1988), 8-10. The Founders Journal, 33 (Summer 1998), 24-35. ABE Journal 6/3 (9, 1998), 19-25; 6/4 (12, 1998), 22-26. The Journal of Biblical Counseling, 10/1 (Fall 200), 5-12. *I am aware that I have better principles than practice in this area.* Emmaus Journal XIV/2. See Appendix A, pp ?? Also *SF* 9-25.

49-50. "Confessions of Faith in Baptist History." Sola, 1/1 (October 1988), 8-10, 1/2 December 1988), 6-10. The Founders Journal, 27 (Winter 1997), 21-30. ABE Journal, 4/2.3 (6, 9/1996), 35-46. *A historical study of the very strong place of creeds and confessions of faith in the Baptist movement.*

51. "Le Mariage dans le Dessein de Dieu." Le Trait d'Union, 20/1-2 (Mars-Juin 1989), 8-17.

52. "The Importance of Transcultural Contextualization in Communicating the Gospel." Interview, I/1 (Fall 1989), 12-18.

53. "Baptism: A Discussion with Roger Nicole and R. C. Sproul." TableTalk, 13/10 (November 1989), 6-10. *This anticipates what I published in B40.*

54. "One Hundred Years: Two Issues." Stillpoint, 5/1 (Fall 1989), 20-21.

55-57. "The Achievement of the Cross." Sola, 2/6 (December 1989), 2-8; 3/1 (February 1990), pages 2-8.

58. "Philip: One-on-One Evangelism at its Best." RTS Ministry, 9/1 (Spring 1990), 12-13.

59. "Why Was God Made Man?" TableTalk, 16/11 (December 1992), 4-6.

60. "The Authority of Scripture." The ABE Journal, 1/1 (June 1993), 8-12.

61. "The History and Theology of Creeds." TableTalk, 17/9 (September 1993), 15-18.

62. "Hermeneutics or Evasion?" The ABE Journal, 1/2 (September 1993), 15-18.

63. "God Glorified in Conversion." Modern Reformation (September-October 1993), 8-10.

64. "The Original Geneva Bible." TableTalk, 19/4 (April 1995).

65. "Calvin and Strasbourg." TableTalk, 19/10 (October 1995), 11-13.

66. "A Letter to the Editor." The ABE Journal, 3/4 (December 1995), 2. Reprinted in 4/1 (March 1996), 2.

67. "Covenant, Universal Call, and Definite Atonement." JETS, 38/3 (9/95), 403- 411. Reprinted in B39. *An emphasis on all three.*

68. Review of Clark Pinnock et al. The Openness of God. Founders Journal 22 (Fall 1995), 26-29. Also *SF* 397-401 and E23.

69. "What Evangelicalism Has Accomplished." Christianity Today, 40/10 (9/16/96), 31-34. See E25.

70. "Unbounded Love or Unbounded License?" The Founders Journal, 20 (Fall 1996), 8-12.

71. "An Open Letter to Dr. Estep." Founders Journal, 29 (Summer 1997), 14-16.

72. "The Canon of the New Testament." JETS, 40/2 (June 1997), 199-206. See B36. Also *SF* 91-101.

73. Review of Iain Murray, Evangelicalism Divided. Founders Journal, 42 (Fall 2000), 7-10. See E19.

74. "A Response to Gregory A. Boyd's God of the Possible." Reformation and Revival, 10/1 (Winter 2001), 231-258. Also *SF* 403-427. See E5.

75. "Inerrancy and Equality." Edited by Carol Thiessen. Priscilla Papers, 15/2 (Spring 2001), 21.

76. "Why I Am Comfortable With Inerrancy." Reformation and Revival. 11/3 (Summer 2002), 112-124. See B41. *This issue also has "Interview with Roger Nicole." Pp. 146-174.*

77. "'Open Theism' is Incompatible with Inerrancy." Founders Journal 52 (Spring 2003), 14-21.

78. Review of Robert E. Picirilli, Grace, Faith, Free Will—Contrasting Views of Salvation: Calvinism & Arminianism. Founders Journal 52 (Spring 2003), 26-29. See E21.

79. "Open Theism: Whence? Where? Whither?" Paper read at 55th ETS Annual Meeting, November 19, 2003. 8 Pp.

80. Review of Richard Muller, Post-Reformation Reformed Dogmatics. Founders Journal 55 (Winter 2004), 28-31. See E18.

81. "Inerrancy and Truth." Paper read at the 56th ETS Annual Meeting, November 18, 2004.

82. "Biblical Egalitarianism and the Inerrancy of Scripture." Priscilla Papers, 20/2 (Spring 2006), 4-9.

E.   Book Reviews (Some important reviews are also listed under D.)

1. Armstrong, Brian. Bibliographia Molinaei. Genève: Droz, 1997. clvii, 564 Pp. The Sixteenth Century Journal xxix/2 (Summer 1998) 554-556.

2. Bavinck, Herman. Reformed Dogmatics. Vol. II. God and Creation. Grand Rapids: Baker, 2004. 697 Pp. The Founders Journal. 62 (Fall 2005) 30, 31.

3. Beegle, Dewey M. The Inspiration of Scripture. Philadelphia: Westminster, 1963. 223 Pp. The Gordon Review VIII (1965) 101-109. See D11.

4. Berkouwer, Gerrit C. The Triumph of Grace in the Theology of Karl Barth. Grand Rapids: Eerdmans, 1956. 414 Pp. The Gordon Review III (1957) 33-35.

5. Boyd, Gregory A. God of the Possible. Grand Rapids: Baker, 2000. 175 Pp. Reformation and Revival. 10/1 (Winter 2001) 231-258. See SF, 403-427 and D5.

6. Broomall, Wick. Biblical Criticism. Grand Rapids: Zondervan, 1957. 320 Pp. The Gordon Review III (1957) 172.

7. Cole, Henry, ed. Calvin's Calvinism. Grand Rapids: Eerdmans, 1950. 350 Pp. The Westminster Theological Journal XIII (May 1951) 218, 219.

8. Dennett, Herbert. A Guide to Modern Versions of the New Testament. Chicago: Moody, 1966. xiv, 142 Pp. United Evangelical Action XXVI/4 (June 1967) 26.

9. Denzinger, H. and Roy J. DeFerrari. The Sources of Catholic Dogma. St. Louis: Herder, 1957. xxxiv, 653, 67 Pp. The Gordon Review III (1957) 119.

10. Eadie, John. Commentary on the Epistle to the Colossians. Grand Rapids: Zondervan, 1957. xlvi, 308 Pp. The Gordon Review IV (1958) 45.

11. Eadie, John. Commentary on the Epistle to the Ephesians. Grand Rapids: Zondervan, 1956. iv, 492 Pp. The Gordon Review IV (1951) 48.

12. Fairbairn, Patrick. Commentary on the Pastoral Epistles. Grand Rapids: Zondervan, 1956. xi, 451 Pp. The Gordon Review IV (1958) 45.

13. Geisler, Norman. Systematic Theology. 4 vols. Minneapolis: Bethany, 2000-2003. The Founders Journal.

14. Harris, Laird. The Inspiration and Canonicity of the Bible. Grand Rapids: Zondervan, 1957. 304 Pp. The Gordon Review III (1957) 171, 172.

15. Huby, Joseph S. J. Saint Paul. Epître aux Romains (Verbum Salutis 10) Paris: Beauchesne, 1957. viii, 643 Pp. The Westminster Theological Journal XXI (May 1959) 259, 260.

16. Kistemaker, Simon J. Revelation. William Hendriksen and Simon Kistemaker. The New Testament Commentary Vol 15. Grand Rapids: Baker, 2001. x, 635 Pp. The Founders Journal.

17. Morris, Leon. The Apostolic Preaching of the Cross. Grand Rapids: Eerdmans, 1955. 296 Pp. The Gordon Review II (1956) 154, 155. The Westminster Journal XIX (Nov 1956) 45-49.

18. Muller, Richard A. Post-Reformation Dogmatics. 4 vols. Grand Rapids: Baker, 2003. 2163 Pp. The Founders Journal 55 (Winter 2005) 28-31. See D80.

19. Murray, Iain. Evangelicalism Divided. Edinburgh: Banner of Truth, 2000. x, 342 Pp. The Founders Journal 42 (Fall 2000) 7-10. See D72.

20. Murray, John. Redemption – Accomplished and Applied. Grand Rapids: Eerdmans, 1955. 263 Pp. The Gordon Review II (1956) 155.

21. Picirilli, Robert E. Grace, Faith, Free Will – Contrasting Views of Salvation: Calvinism and Arminianism. Nashville: Random House, 2002. 245 Pp. The Founders Journal 52 (Sp 2003) 26-29. See D78.

22. Pink, Arthur W. <u>The Satisfaction of Christ</u>. Grand Rapids: Zondervan, 1955. 313 Pp. <u>The Gordon Review</u> II (1956) 155, 156.

23. Pinnock, Clark *et al.* <u>The Openness of God</u>. Downers's Grove, IL: Intervarsity, 1994. 202 Pp. <u>The Founders Journal</u> 22 (Fall 1995) 26-29. <u>The Westminster Theological Journal</u> LIV/2 (   ) 392-96. See D68 and *SF* 397-402.

24. Pinnock, Clark. <u>The Scripture Principle</u>. San Francisco: Harper, 1984. xx, 251 Pp. <u>Christianity Today</u>. 29/2 (Feb 2, 1985) 68-71.

25. Pinnock, Clark and Robert C. Brow. <u>Unbounded Love. A Good News Theology for the 21st Century</u>. Downer's Grove, IL: Intervarsity, 1994. 189 Pp. <u>The Founders Journal</u> 26 (Fall 1996) 8-12.

26. Ramm, Bernard. <u>The Pattern of Authority</u>. Grand Rapids: Eerdmans, 1957. 117 Pp. <u>The Gordon Review</u> III (1957) 82, 83.

27. Reyburn, Robert G. <u>What About Baptism?</u> St. Louis: Covenant College, 1957. 89 Pp. <u>Christian Life</u> xx/5 (Sept 1958) 64, 65.

28. Reid, J. K. S. <u>The Authority of Scripture</u>. New York: Harper, 1957. 286 Pp. <u>Christian Life</u> xx/5 (Sep 1958) 65.

29. Rogers, Jack B. and Donald K. McKim. <u>The Authority and Interpretation of the Bible</u>. New York: Harper, 1979. xxiv, 484 Pp. <u>The Christian Scholar's Review</u>. X/2 (1981) 161-165.

30. Van Stam, F. P. <u>The Controversy over the Theology of Saumur,1635-1650</u>. Amsterdam: APA – Holland, 1988. xiv, 497 Pp. <u>The Westminster Theological Journal</u>. LIV/2 (Fall 1992) 392-396.

31. Van Til, Cornelius. <u>The Case for Calvinism</u>. Philadelphia: Presbyterian and Reformed Publishing, 1964. xviii, 164 Pp. <u>United Evangelical Action</u> XXIII/8 (Oct 1964) 31, 32.

32. Vos, Geerhardus. <u>Biblical Theology: Old and New Testament</u>. Grand Rapids: Eerdmans, 1948. 453 Pp. <u>The Westminster Theological Journal</u> XII (Nov 1949) 101-103.

F.   Prefaces and Introductions

1. Buchanan, James. <u>The Doctrine of Justification</u>. Edinburgh: T & T Clark, 1857. Reprint. Grand Rapids : Baker, 1955. x, 514 Pp. "Preface." Pp. vi, vii.

2. Burroughs, Jeremiah. <u>Gospel Fear</u>. 1674. Reprint. Ligonier, PA: Soli Deo Gloria, 1991. xxiv, 166 Pp. "Introduction." Pp. i-xiii.

3. Goodwin, Thomas. <u>An Exposition of Ephesians 1-2:10</u>. Reprint. Ligonier, PA: Sovereign Grace Book Club, 1958. vi, 824 Pp. "Preface." P v.

4. Gundry, Stanley N. and Alan F. Johnson. <u>Tensions in Contemporary Theology</u>. Chicago: Moody, 1976. 366 Pp. "Foreword." Pp. 7, 8.

5. Hodge, A. A. and B. B. Warfield. "Inspiration." <u>The Presbyterian Review</u> II (1881) 225-260. Reprint. Grand Rapids: Baker, 1979. xiv, 5-108 Pp. "Introduction." Pp. vii-xiv. "Warfield on Scripture: Bibliography." Pp. 83-90.

"Charles Hodge's View of Inerrancy." Pp. 93-95. "The Westminster Confession and Inerrancy." Pp. 99-100. See A3 and B13.

6. Morey, Robert A. Death and the Afterlife. Minneapolis: Bethany, 1984. 315 Pp. "Preface." P 11.

7. Nichols, James A. Christian Doctrines. Nutley, NJ: Craig, 1970. xii, 322 Pp. "Foreword." Pp. vii, viii.

8. Nicole, Roger and J. Ramsay Michaels, eds. Inerrancy and Common Sense. Grand Rapids: Baker, 1980. 203 Pp. "Introduction." Pp. 11-13. See B15.

9. Sproul, R. C. Explaining Inerrancy. Oakland, CA: ICBI, 1980. 51 Pp. "Foreword." Pp. 3, 4.

10. Steele, David N. and Curtis C. Thomas. The Five Points of Calvinism. Philadelphia: Presbyterian and Reformed, 1963. 95 Pp. "Preface." P 7. 2nd enlarged ed. Phillipsburg, NJ: Presbyterian and Reformed, 2004. xxiv, 247 Pp. "Foreword." Pp. xiii-xv.

11. Stoutenburg, Dennis. Grammaire Grecque du Nouveau Testament.

12. Swete, Henry B. The Holy Spirit in the New Testament. London: Macmillan, 1909. viii, 417 Pp. Reprint. Grand Rapids: Baker, 1964. x, 417 Pp. "Introduction." Pp. i-iv.

G. Unpublished Writings

1. "Jesus and the Bible in Reference to the Doctrine of the Inspiration of the Scriptures." Unpublished B.D. thesis. Gordon Divinity School, 1939. v, 56 Pp. Summarized in Speaking the in Love, pp 38-52.

2. "A Study of the Old Testament Quotations in the New Testament with Reference to the Doctrine of the Inspiration of the Scriptures." Unpublished S.T.M. thesis. Gordon Divinity School, 1940. vi, 157 Pp. and 2 tables. Principles published in B3, B14, C5, D1 and in Speaking the Truth in Love, pp 53-59. The thesis contains an examination of all quotations in the New Testament.

3. "An Introduction to the Study of Certain Antinomies of the Christian Faith." Unpublished Th.D. thesis. Gordon Divinity School, 1943. xiii, 189 Pp. Briefly summarized in Speaking the Truth in Love, pp 60-63.

4. "Ordination paper covering: 1. Christian Experience; 2. Call to and Preparation for the Ministry; 3. Statement of Christian Beliefs." Worcester, MA, 1943. 8 Pp.

5. A Review of L. E. Froom, The Prophetic Faith of Our Fathers. Vol. I. Washington: Review and Herald, 1950. 1000 Pp. This was not published in The Journal of Religious Thought, but initiated a friendly correspondence with Dr. Froom.

6. "Personal Reactions to Dr. James Daane's recent series of articles appearing in The Reformed Journal (Oct 1964 – Feb 1965) and relating to atonement and grace. Mimeographed, 1965. 7 Pp.

7. "Moyse Amyraut (1596-1664) and the Controversy on Universal Grace. First phase (1634-1639)." Unpublished Ph.D. thesis. Harvard University, 1966. iv, 268 Pp. Summarized in C3 and in Speaking the Truth in Love, pp 100-106. The Bibliography, substantially enlarged, was published as A5.

8. "Report of Sabbatical Leave: Sep 1972 – June 1973." 10 Pp.

9. "The Theological Impact of the Dispensational System of Hermeneutics Versus Other Systems of Hermeneutics." A paper presented to the annual meeting of the Evangelical Theological Society, Dallas, 1974. 11 Pp.

10. "The Place of Theology in a Minister's Education." Address at the inauguration of the Andrew Mutch Chair of Theology and Roger Nicole's installation into it. Gordon-Conwell Theological Seminary, May 3, 1976. 7 Pp.

11. "A Brief Historical and Bibliographical Note on Definite Atonement." Prepared for a book never published, "Grace Unconditional," in response to Clark H. Pinnock, ed. Grace Unlimited (Minneapolis: Bethany, 1975). 22 Pp.

12. "The Westminster Confession of Faith and Catechisms, with Special Reference to the Decrees of God." A paper prepared for a volume on 17th century theology for which there was no place because of the page limitation of the book. Orlando, 1986. 9 Pp.

13. Correspondence with Dr. A. C. Clifford from Britain, concerning his pamphlet Calvinus (Norwich and Norfolk School of Theology, 1993. 21+13 Pp.) January and February 1994. 7+6+4+3 Pp. A fuller edition of Calvinus. Authentic Calvinism. A Clarification. Clarenton: Reformed Publishing, 1996. 94 Pp. (Pp 41-61 contain 90 texts from Calvin's Works quoted in support of universal atonement).

14. Dr. Pinnock and Inerrancy, 2003. 21 Pp. *An unpublished indictment of Dr. Clark Pinnock for the ETS annual meeting in Atlanta, Georgia.*

15. Dr. Sanders and Inerrancy, 2003. 21 Pp. *An unpublished indictment of Dr. John Sanders for the ETS annual meeting in Atlanta, Georgia.*

H. Tapes

Multiple tapes have been taken of sermons and lectures. This has been done regularly in the Philadelphia Conference on Reformed Theology. Tapes were taken of the ETS annual meeting and of the John Bunyan Fellowship. A whole set of 75 tapes was taken in classes at Gordon-Conwell Theological Seminary by John Sanders, South Hamilton, MA.

Index of Subjects

NEW "BURNING ISSUES" SERIES

Solid Ground has always been known for our *"uncovering buried treasure"* from the past and bringing them back before the church and the world. We are now introducing a new series of titles addressing the *Burning Issues* of our day from the hearts of those on fire for the Lord.

YEARNING TO BREATHE FREE? *Thoughts on Immigration, Islam & Freedom* by David Dykstra

"I have read David Dykstra's book with great interest. His description of the real nature of jihad and its continuing power today is valuable. What he has written is especially important since so many on the upper levels of government continue to claim that Islam is fundamentally a peaceful religion; it is not. Dykstra has made that very clear. I do hope that Dykstra's book is well accepted. Its main message is sorely needed."
- Dr. Joel Nederhood
Now available!

PULPIT CRIMES: *The Criminal Mishandling of God's Word* by James White

James White of Alpha-Omega Ministries is writing what may be his most provocative book yet. White sets out to examine numerous "crimes" being committed in pulpits throughout the land every week, as he seeks to leave no stone unturned. Based firmly upon the bedrock of Holy Scripture, one "crime" after another is laid bare for all to see. In his own words: "The pulpit is to be a place where God speaks from His Word: what has happened to this sacred duty in our day? Let pulpit crimes be exposed by the light of God's Word."
Now Available!

TWO MEN FROM MALTA by Joel Nederhood & Joe Serge

One of the men is the Apostle Paul, the other is Joe Serge, a Toronto newspaperman and columnist. In this book Serge describes his odyssey from Roman Catholicism to the faith of the Reformation. Serge invited Joel Nederhood, a theologian and long time radio and television teacher, to join him in examining primary Roman teaching such as "the Mass," "Mary," "the Papacy," and the essence of salvation itself. This is a warm invitation to Roman Catholics to examine their faith. Due Late Fall 2006.

COMMON FAITH, COMMON CULTURE by Joe Bianchi

"Joseph M. Bianchi has provided an inspiring aerial overview of Christianity's formative salt and light impact on world history. 'it is a culture that transforms societies by transforming people one by one.' Bianchi provides a tonic for believers disheartened by the contemporary darkness of encroaching postmodernism. Surely the gates of Hell will not prevail, for in Christ, we will triumph as more than conquerors. Well done!" -Rev. Mark Chanski, author of *Manly Dominion*

OTHER SGCB TITLES

We are delighted to offer several outstanding books from the past and present that open and apply the Holy Scriptures:

Opening Scripture: *Hermeneutical Manual* by Patrick Fairbairn

The Scripture Guide: *Introduction to Bible Study* by J.W. Alexander

The Poor Man's Old Testament Commentary by Robert Hawker

First Things: *Lessons Upon the First Lessons God Taught Man* by G. Spring

Heroes of Israel: *Abraham, Isaac, Jacob, Joseph & Moses* by W.G. Blaikie

Expository Lectures on the Book of Joshua by W.G. Blaikie

Expository Lectures on the Book of 1ˢᵗ Samuel by W.G. Blaikie

Expository Lectures on the Book of 2ⁿᵈ Samuel by W.G. Blaikie

Lectures upon the Book of Esther by Thomas M'Crie

Pathway into the Psalter by William Binnie

The Poor Man's New Testament Commentary by Robert Hawker

Sabbath Scripture Readings on the NT by Thomas Chalmers

Come Ye Apart: *Devotional Thoughts from the Gospels* by J.R. Miller

Lectures on the Book of Acts by John Dick

Paul the Preacher: *Studies on Discourses in Acts* by John Eadie

Notes on Galatians by J. Gresham Machen

Opening Up Ephesians by Peter Jeffery

A Commentary on the Greek Text of Galatians by John Eadie

A Commentary on the Greek Text of Ephesians by John Eadie

A Commentary on the Greek Text of Philippians by John Eadie

A Commentary on the Greek Text of Colossians by John Eadie

A Commentary on the Greek Text of Thessalonians by John Eadie

Short Explanation of the Epistle to the Hebrews by David Dickson

Exegetical & Expository Commentary on Hebrews by Wm Gouge

A Commentary upon the Epistle of Jude by William Jenkyn

Call us Toll Free at 1-877-666-9469
Send us an e-mail at sgcb@charter.net
Visit us on line at solid-ground-books.com

ABOUT THE AUTHOR

David W. Bailey is the founding pastor of Reformation Baptist Church in Eustis, Florida. He earned the B.A. in English from the University of Central Florida, and the M.Div. and Ph.D. degrees from New Orleans Baptist Theological Seminary. In addition to five other pastorates, he served for three years as Director and adjunct faculty member at the Orlando Center of New Orleans Baptist Theological Seminary (where he met Roger Nicole). His hobbies include fishing and target shooting. He and his wife Dawn have four children: Charissa, Claire-Elise, Catherine and Ethan.

Printed in the United States
88696LV00002B/112/A

9 781599 250939